WORSHIP AND CULTURE
IN DIALOGUE

REPORTS OF INTERNATIONAL CONSULTATIONS
CARTIGNY, SWITZERLAND, 1993
HONG KONG, 1994

Edited by S. Anita Stauffer

Department for Theology and Studies
The Lutheran World Federation
Geneva, 1994

© 1994 Lutheran World Federation, third printing 1997
Layout by Sally Long
Office for Communication Services
ISBN 3-906706-12-5

Published by   Lutheran World Federation
                  150 Route de Ferney
                  1211 Geneva 2, Switzerland
German version: "Gottesdienst und Kultur im Dialog"
French version: "Culte et culture en dialogue"
Spanish version: "Dialogo entre culto y cultura"

Printed by L'Imprimerie, Geneva

Printed in Switzerland

CONTENTS

III. CONTEMPORARY ISSUES

PREFACE

A hymn, very well known in my tradition, by the Danish poet N. F. S. Grundtvig (1837) begins with the following words,

Built on a rock the Church shall stand,
Even when steeples are falling;
Crumbled have spires in ev'ry land,
Bells still are chiming and calling....

These words portray the tension in which the Church lives. The Church has one foundation, but it gathers peoples from every nation, each one with its own particularities and specific cultures.

Surely in temples made with hands,
God the Most High, is not dwelling.
High above earth God's temple stands,
All earthly temples excelling;
Yet, God whom heav'ns cannot contain
Chose to abide on earth with us
Making our bodies his temple.

The font stands here before our eyes
telling us how God received us;
the altar recalls Christ's sacrifice
and what his table provides us;
the Scriptures teach us to proclaim
Christ yesterday, today the same
and to all ages of ages.

How are we to proclaim Christ in different cultures? The message must first embrace us, and speak not only to our brains and senses but also to our hearts. In order for this to happen it must be incarnated in the life of the people and their culture, just as it took root in one specific culture for the first time.

Thus the issue of how Gospel and culture relate always has been and always will be with us as we reflect on how to be God's Church. Being a perennial issue, it is one which calls for continued reflection.

This is what we are trying to do in our study on worship and culture. The Rev. S. Anita Stauffer has designed a comprehensive study process with the aim of promoting reflection on this issue in the member churches of the Federation. I do not think that there is a single other issue which is discussed more keenly among both clergy and laity than the question of how Gospel and culture relate to one another, especially with regard to worship.

This publication contains the major papers presented during the first phase of this study process. An excellent and dedicated group of people, profoundly engaged in worship life and in reflection on worship in the churches came together as a study team to explore the interactions between worship and culture. This book contains the results of their reflections and, its aim is twofold:

• To serve as a principle resource for the second phase of the study, which is carried out on the regional level; and

• To be a contribution to the ecumenical literature on this topic which today is of great interest worldwide.

The Department for Theology and Studies is especially grateful to the members of the study team who have contributed much of their time, energy and talent to this study. Without them this study would not have been possible, nor indeed without the generous support of the member churches and the related agencies.

May this book be an inspiration for our continued reflection on what is entailed when Grundtvig writes,

> We are God's house of living stones,
> Build for his habitation;
> God through baptismal grace us owns,
> Heirs of his wondrous salvation.

Viggo Mortensen
Director
Department for Theology and Studies

CHRISTIAN WORSHIP: TOWARD LOCALIZATION AND GLOBALIZATION

S. Anita Stauffer

From the four corners of the earth about 25 people from the Lutheran Communion, with observers from the Anglican Communion, the Roman Catholic Church, and the World Council of Churches, gathered in a quiet little Swiss town in October 1993 for a common purpose: to examine the roots of Christian worship, the common roots of what Christians do on Sunday morning as the baptized people of God. The group examined the Jewish matrix and the Hellenistic-Jewish heritage out of which Christian worship developed, and how the early Church contextualized its worship in Greco-Roman cultures.

The purpose was not to dig for these roots as an end in itself, but in order that branches might grow more richly in the cultures of each of the world's continents. The meeting was to begin a major study of Christian worship as that consequential activity which stands between Christ and culture, to help enable churches around the world to work toward both contextualization and transformation, both localization and globalization—that congregational worship might be both authentically Christian, and more culturally relevant. Thus, the group gathered a second time in March 1994, in Hong Kong, to consider contemporary issues related to the relationship between worship and culture. This volume contains the major papers from these two international consultations.

The topic is not new for the Lutheran World Federation. From 1976-1983, the LWF conducted a study on "Confessing Christ in Cultural Contexts," involving Lutheran churches in Indonesia and Germany,

Tanzania and Sweden, Japan and the United States.[1] In 1981 the LWF held a seminar in Tantur, Israel, for Third World pastors on the "Significance of the Jewish Heritage for the Task of Contextualization."[2] From 1978 through 1983 there was a series of LWF conferences, culminating in the Northfield Consultation.[3] Finally, the LWF sponsored the Latin American Lutheran Consultation on Liturgy in Caracas in 1986.[4]

Nor is the topic new for the wider Church. Roman Catholics especially have been addressing the issues for decades, and both the Anglican Communion and the World Council of Churches have also had the matter on their agendas. The relationship between culture and Christian worship is of ecumenical interest; the questions, the issues, the dynamics are shared across confessional lines. All Christians share "the same baptismal water of the same Spirit"[5] who creates the Church everywhere. Though there are a variety of cultures on the continents of this earth, there is one Baptism, one Gospel, one faith, one Lord. The core of Christian worship, its Jewish roots and its development in the early Church, is shared across our confessional and cultural lines. That core, those roots, constitute a common ecumenical foundation.

But there are different presuppositions, different perspectives, in examining these roots and addressing the matter of worship and culture. Personal histories and cultural backgrounds shape these perspectives. It is useful to set the specific topic of worship and culture

---

[1]   Yoshiro Ishida, "Introduction," in *Confessing Christ in Cultural Contexts*, ed. Maren Mattiesen (Geneva: Lutheran World Federation Department of Studies, 1981), 11-12.

[2]   See the resulting "Tantur Report on Worship, 1981," in *Worship Among Lutherans*, ed. Eugene L. Brand (Geneva: Lutheran World Federation Department of Studies, 1983), 15-23.

[3]   See the "Northfield Statement on Worship," in *Worship Among Lutherans*, 5-14 (especially sections C and E).

[4]   See the resulting *Declaración de Caracas sobre Liturgia* (Buenos Aires, 1986; and the English translation by Gerhard M. Cartford, *Caracas Statement on Liturgy* (Buenos Aires: Committee of Presidents of the Lutheran Churches in Latin America, and Lutheran World Federation Department of Studies, 1987).

[5]   J. M. R. Tillard, *L'Église d'Églises* (Paris: Cerf, 1987), 30; English translation in Joseph A. Komonchak, "The Local Church and the Church Catholic: the Contemporary Theological Problematic," *The Jurist*, 52:1 (1992), 443.

within its larger framework, which is the relationship between Christ and culture. One helpful model for considering this larger theological context is a typology developed by H. Richard Niebuhr. Niebuhr has laid out five possible relationships between Christ and culture:[6]

> Christ against culture
> Christ of culture
> Christ above culture
> Christ and culture in paradox
> Christ the transformer of culture

The first is **Christ *against* culture**. Culture is seen negatively, as something hostile to Christianity. In much of the early Church, and especially during the persecutions, it was natural that Christ and Christianity would be completely contrary to the culture. In recent decades in the Communist world, culture and Christ were once again set in mutual hostility. And in other societies of the world, where another religion (such as Hinduism) totally pervades the culture, perhaps this paradigm of Christ against culture is still operative in varying degrees.

The second is the **Christ *of* culture**. Culture is seen positively, as something consonant with Christianity. Christ is absorbed into the culture, and Christianity is seen as a "prop" for the culture. The problem is that this approach "risks reducing Christ to a culture-hero."[7] The culture and the Christian faith are identified with each other, and it is very difficult to critique the culture.

These first two paradigms are the two extremes. In between them, Niebuhr set three types of relationships.

The third paradigm, then, is **Christ *above* culture**. This is a synthesis: Christ is neither opposed to the culture nor absorbed into it. Rather, Christ is seen as coming to perfect the culture. Culture is

---

[6]   See his book *Christ and Culture* (New York: Harper and Row, 1951), as well as Geoffrey Wainwright's application of it to worship in his *Doxology* (London and New York: Oxford University Press, 1980; chapter XI).

[7]   Wainwright, 390.

seen as essentially good; it is preparation for the ultimate communion with God.[8] The danger here is that the culture becomes
absolutized, and its provisional character is forgotten.[9]

Niebuhr's fourth paradigm is **Christ and culture in *paradox***. This
is the dualist approach: Christ is the good, and human culture is
sinful and corrupt.

The final position is the most central one: **Christ the *transformer* of
culture**. This position is more hopeful about culture; culture is not
inherently evil, although it is the locus of disorder and sin. What is
needed is conversion or transformation of the culture, *a la* the death/
resurrection model of Baptism in Romans 6.

If these five positions were put onto a map, persons from various
cultures could place themselves in one of the positions, or a variation
of it. It is important to be conscious of one's own perspectives,
based on one's own background within one's own cultural context.

Interlocking Content

To consider the relationship between worship and culture is to be
concerned with three interlocking areas of content. Worship itself is
multifaceted; it includes not only texts but also actions, not only
music but also the space or place in which worship happens. The
topic is interdisciplinary. It involves not only liturgy, its texts and
actions, and church music in its many forms, but also church architecture and its furnishings and art. Christian worship is profoundly
shaped in one way or another by the space in which it happens. The
design and iconography and symbol-systems of church buildings
(particularly the worship space) are expressions of theology, just as
much as the liturgical texts which are spoken. Thus consideration of
the topic includes such things as what is beauty in various cultures.[10]

---

[8]   Niebuhr, 195.

[9]   Wainwright, 392.

[10]   See the chapter "Contemporary Questions on Architecture and Culture".

Overlaid on the three disciplines of liturgy, music, and architecture, are two questions which are crucial to worship. How, in a given culture, can worship be hospitable to those who come; how can the community or communal dimension be expressed? And how, in a given culture, can reverence be expressed in response to encountering the God who is holy and transcendent?

Tensions

The dynamics between worship and culture can be considered in the context of several tensions, or sets of axes. These are not tensions in the negative sense, but in the sense of several sets of values at opposite ends of a continuum or axis:

authentic - relevant

Lutheran - catholic

local - global

Christocentric - anthropocentric

The first tension is between **the authentic and the relevant**. This is the need for balance between worship being faithful to our common Judaeo-Christian roots, and being meaningful in each given culture. Our taproot is Jesus, and his death and resurrection, which itself is Jesus' new interpretation of the whole Passover event—this is the most central core of the Christian faith, and it provides a pattern for everything we do, including our worship, the pattern for Baptism and the pattern for Eucharist. The test of authenticity is the Gospel and the apostolic tradition, themselves patterned on Jesus the Christ.

For Christian worship there is no such thing as a *tabula rasa*, no blank slate. In matters of faith and liturgy we do not start from scratch. The starting point is already given in the death and resurrection of Christ, and in the Upper Room where the meaning of it all was made clear and the pattern for our own celebration of it was established. As Eugene Brand has said:

> Because of the historical and incarnational aspects of Christian faith, the Church's worship has remained anchored to the historical person of Jesus and the culture in which he lived. Since Jesus was a Jew, Christian worship has retained a Jewish character.... Adherence to liturgical forms rooted in the Judaism of Jesus' day is what marks Christian worship as authentic. The sharing of the loaf and the cup in the context of thanksgiving is the chief example.[11]

The balance to authenticity—the other end of the axis—is relevance. We might, again, think in terms of roots and branches—the roots as authenticity, and the branches as cultural relevance. How can worship be meaningful to people in a given culture? How can the common core of worship be "clothed" in such a way that it relates to people in a given culture? How can worship be "at home" in a given culture? How can the worship life of congregations be meaningful and inviting to people in the diverse cultures of the world, east and west, south and north? How can the taproot of the Christian faith—the death and resurrection of Jesus—itself take root in the world's cultures? How can liturgy and church music and church architecture and art be *both* truly Christian and truly Chinese, or truly Christian and truly East African, or truly Christian and truly Brazilian, and so on?

There are dangers at both extreme ends of this authenticity-relevance continuum. The danger on the authenticity end is that worship can become culturally irrelevant, out of touch, meaningless. On the other end, the relevance end, the danger is that worship can become captive to a given culture, isolated from the whole Church of Christ, and at the worst, syncretistic through becoming detached from Christian roots.

---

[11] Eugene L. Brand, "A Lutheran Agenda for Worship after Dar-es-Salaam," *A Lutheran Agenda for Worship* (Geneva: Lutheran World Federation Department of Studies, 1979), 25.

The second and third tensions could both be considered under a more general heading of the tension between universality and particularity, but it is worth looking at them separately.

The second tension is that between **Lutheran and catholic**, between the confessional and the ecumenical. Christian roots in faith and worship are shared with the whole Christian church, the church catholic. We are, each one of us, baptized into the Christian Church. There is no such thing as being "baptized Lutheran" or "baptized Roman Catholic," or anything else than "baptized Christian." There is one Baptism because there is one Lord. Likewise, there is no such thing as "Lutheran worship" or "Lutheran liturgy." There is worship as Lutherans do it, liturgy as Lutherans do it. But the liturgy does not belong to Lutherans, any more than it belongs to any other confessional communion. What is done in Word and Sacrament is shared at its core, at its roots, with the whole Church of every time and every place. To be sure, the manifestation of liturgical convergence is more apparent in some places in the world than in others. But the ecumenical reality exists—thanks be to God; it is only a matter of recognizing it and manifesting more and more.

The Lutheran Confessions express liturgical continuity with the wider Church. Article 24 of the Augsburg Confession says it clearly: "Our churches are falsely accused of abolishing the Mass. Actually, the Mass is retained among us and is celebrated with the greatest reverence." The Apology of the Augsburg Confession repeats and goes on: "We do not abolish the Mass but religiously keep and defend it. In our churches Mass is celebrated every Sunday and on other festivals.... We keep traditional liturgical forms, such as the order of the lessons, prayers, vestments, etc." (Article 24) For Lutherans there is no starting from scratch in matters of worship. We are not a sect; our worship is not idiosyncratic. The liturgical heritage we share with the wider Christian church is an inherent part of our identity as Lutherans. We are part of the whole *communio*, the whole communion of saints. As we strive toward the contextualization or inculturation of worship, we do it not only in the context of various world cultures, but also "within the context of the catholic and ecumenical Church."[12] That is why ecumenical cooperation in contextualization is vital, internationally and regionally.

The third tension is between **the local and the global**, between the contextual and the transcultural. Like the second tension, this is also a variation on the theme of the particular and the universal. On the one side is the local, the particular cultural context of a given people, a given group of congregations. How can cultural richness be reflected in worship? What are the thought patterns and linguistic styles that ought to shape how prayers and sermons and liturgical texts are written? What aspects of indigenous music ought to find their way into hymns and other music in the church? What aspects of the aesthetics, the artistic styles, the symbol-systems, the architectural prototypes in a given culture ought to be reflected in the rooms in which worship takes place? What gestures and postures from the culture can be meaningfully incorporated into Christian worship? What are the cultural manifestations of gathering into a community, of offering hospitality, of expressing reverence? All of this can be termed localization, or contextualization, or inculturation.

These efforts all need to be kept in balance with the other end of the spectrum, what could be called globalization. Worship needs not only to reflect the local, but also the wider Christian community. The God whom Christians worship is transcendent and transcultural, and there is no point to substituting one form of cultural captivity for another. No one cultural form can do justice to the God of the whole cosmos. One fruit of contextualization efforts is that worship resources from one cultural setting can be shared around the world. Not only, for example, might churches in Ethiopia and Papua New Guinea and in the Sami areas of the Nordic countries find ways to enable their worship to be more truly at home in their cultures, but also that some of the riches of those cultures can be shared with the wider church. Would such global sharing not enrich the life of the whole Church and strengthen the sense of *communio*? Such cross-cultural and ecumenical sharing, such global enrichment is the opposite of tribalization and apartheid and segregation and ethnic cleans-

---

[12] Eugene L. Brand, "Lutheran Worship in Cultural Context," *Lutheran Forum* (Reformation 1982), 17.

ing. Worship ought to be both contextual and transcultural, as a testament to the unity of the Church and to the God who is "far beyond our mind's grasp."[13]

A further facet of the localization-globalization balance is that the Church is called not only to inculturate, but also to be countercultural. Not everything in *any* given culture is worthy or appropriate of Christian worship. Everything human needs always to be critiqued by the light of the Gospel. Ultimately, Christ came to transform all things human, including our selves and our cultures. We are called not to conform to the world, in the final analysis, but to be transformed ourselves (Romans 12:2) and, in turn, to transform the world.

The final tension is that between **Christocentricity and anthropocentricity**, the balance between Christ-centeredness and human-centeredness. It is, on the one hand, vitally urgent that we strive to make worship at home in our variety of cultures. That requires considerable attention to our cultures—to ourselves, in a sense. But we must not forget that we worship Christ, the crucified and risen One, the Lord of the whole Church. We do not worship ourselves or our cultures.

Christian worship *must* be culturally relevant; it must be meaningful to those who worship in a given place. But at the same time, we must not lose Christ as the focus, or we will have cut off our roots and made dead branches.

---

[13]   First line of eucharistic hymn text by Filipino composer and writer Francisco F. Feliciano.
       See hymn 82 in *Sound the Bamboo*, a hymnal published in 1990 jointly by the Christian
       Conference of Asia and the Asian Institute for Liturgy and Music.

BAPTISM
IN THE NEW TESTAMENT
AND ITS CULTURAL SETTINGS

Gordon W. Lathrop

"Culture" is "the symbolic-expressive dimension of social life." So, at least one group of scholars has recently proposed.[1] Although there have been decades of reflection on the subject which have proposed hundreds of varying definitions of the term,[2] I will adopt this definition. I do so partly because of the importance of the definition for reflection on liturgy, an obvious case of socially significant symbolic expression. But this definition will be adopted here also because it helps to make clear how almost all of us in the contemporary world live in a variety of cultures. That is, we participate in many different systems of symbolic expression which are socially significant.

From one point of view, then, Christian liturgy can itself be regarded as an instance of "culture." Its ritual forms have been a "language" for the communication among Christians of meanings about themselves and about the surrounding world as seen before God. Its words, gestures and ceremonies— its hymns, preaching, sacraments, prayers, communally recited creeds—have been a means to pass on to newcomers and children and to reinforce among life-long believers the knowledge or wisdom the Christian community has concerning its understanding of God and the world. Its symbolic acts have been the basic units of a social communication, *i.e.* of *culture*.

---

[1]   Robert Wuthnow, James Davison Hunter, Albert Bergesen, Edith Kurzweil, *Cultural Analysis: The Work of Peter L. Berger, Mary Douglas, Michel Foucault, and Jürgen Habermas* (Boston: Routledge and Kegan Paul, 1984), 259; *cf.* 3: culture is "the symbolic-expressive aspect of human behavior," including verbal utterances, gestures, ceremonial behavior, ideologies, religions.

[2]   A. L. Kroeber and C. Kluckhohn proposed that there were 164 definitions in circulation!

But we also all live amidst many other complexes of symbolic communication which have their own ways of indicating world-meaning and shaping our identity. We speak diverse languages, tell different stories, know different seasons, eat different foods with diverse conceptions of hospitality, arrange community leadership differently. Because we are Christians, we believe these diversities are largely good, signs of the manifold riches of God's good earth.

Cultures exist as complexes of symbolic reinterpretation. The analysis of cultures must always involve "relating *specific* symbolic acts to the broader symbolic *environments* in which they occur."[3] In the case of Christianity, that means relating local liturgical particularities to such patterns as may be perceived to link the history of Christian worship or the geographical spread of Christian assemblies. But just as importantly, this linking of specific symbol and symbolic environment means that we must see the relationship between enacted Christian rituals and the many places—the regions of the world and the traditional and changing ways people live in them, the diverse languages, new social norms, diverse persons, new symbol-systems, new *cultures*—where the Christian assembly gathers to do the enacting. Christianity is a missionary religion on all of the continents, a *translation* religion, and there is nothing more traditional to its symbolizing life than the interior urge to relate its central symbols and its formative history—its own culture and its *faith*—to ever changing cultural situations.[4]

It is important for us to say at the outset that Christian worship has cultural characteristics, for the word "culture" is too frequently used in our day only as a kind of symbol for one's own ethnic or national identity, often sensed as threatened and therefore set over against all the others. By this construction, a study on "worship and culture" will be read as a kind of challenge: "how is your Christianity going to take my identity seriously?" On the other hand, there are threatened cultures in the world, and humanity would be generally impov

---

[3]   Wuthnow, *et al.*, 209, interpreting the work of Habermas.

[4]   See Anscar Chupungco, *The Cultural Adaptation of the Liturgy* (New York: Paulist Press, 1982).

erished by the loss of their specific wisdom. We need only to add that sometimes Christian liturgical/symbolical wisdom is among the threatened cultures of the present age.

Christian worship, then, itself has cultural characteristics. It has its own identity-giving and world-interpreting structures, and yet the meanings and identity it conveys belong to Christians who live within many other cultures. Thus Christianity is most frequently a culture among cultures, a symbol-system in contrast to or in cooperation with surrounding symbol-systems. This interaction of symbols is, in fact, acutely and poignantly experienced: the individual Christian, the baptized member of the local liturgical assembly, lives a life which is in touch with several cultures and struggles to sort out their meanings and their use in interpreting reality.

In this struggle, of course, Christians are not alone. Almost everyone in the world today lives within an actual situation of the confluence and conflict of cultures. The great double danger exists *universally* that, in the name of security, people will build rigid boundaries around local meanings, refusing anything strange or any exterior criticism and giving up on wider human meaning, or that, in the name of modernization and efficiency, local wisdom and local gifts will be lost to the pretended universal "culture" of consumerism or of a certain "westernism." For the Lutheran World Federation to engage now, at this moment in world history, in a study of worship and culture is for it to engage in an immensely important human undertaking against both of those dangers.

But the Christian interest in the discovery of *permeable boundaries* between cultures is not based only on the general hope for mutual respect and fruitful human exchange. The Christian interest in cultural interpenetration arises especially from the deep desire to speak the truth about the mercy of God so that this truth may be heard everywhere. And this interest is founded in the trust that in Christian worship there are certain specific central signs which, if they are allowed to speak largely and clearly, in "the fullness and integrity of the sign,"[5] are capable of universal human address, full of the truth of that mercy, capable of calling all people to the one faith. Christians believe that they bear a responsibility faithfully to conserve this Christian heritage of words and signs for God's mercy while at the same time plumbing the depths of that mercy as it comes to expression in ever new terms. When speaking of the astonishing grace of God, every cultural system is inadequate; every set of social symbols comes in for critique and radical re-ordering. Yet, Christians believe, God can transform our varying means of communication into bearers of saving grace; God can inhabit and dwell amidst our symbol-systems. And this is always happening locally. The universal liturgical patterns of Christians are always and only done *here*, in a particular local place, amid given particular people and their many cultures.

How does this happen? What are "the universal liturgical patterns of Christians?" What are those "central signs?" What is the *boundary* of Christian liturgical culture, and how is it *permeable*? What is "the heritage," and what is the responsibility to local patterns of meaning? How are our symbol-systems criticized and transformed?

The New Testament and the Central Signs

Christians have a wide—if not universal—agreement about the most central of their identity-creating signs. These are the washing or bathing which gathers a person into the Christian community, the reading and preaching of the Scriptures, and the thanksgiving meal which the community holds weekly as the memorial of Jesus. Lutherans call these signs "Word and Sacrament" and believe that they are set out in a participating community so that the "Gospel of Jesus Christ" may be heard by needy human beings.[6] Christians have taken the

---

[5]   Martin Luther, "Ein Sermon von dem hochwürdigen Sakrament des heiligen wahren Leichnams Christi und von den Bruderschaften," *WA* 2, 742: "umb der gentze und volkömenheyt willen des zeychens." *Cf.* 2:727 on immersion Baptism as "eyn rechts volkommens zeychen geben."

[6]   A nineteenth century bell in a Danish-American Lutheran parish in Luck, Wisconsin, USA, is inscribed: "Til badet og bordet, til bønnen og ordet, jeg kalder hvær søgende sjæl." (To the bath and the table, To the prayers and the Word, I call every seeking soul.) For an interpretation of the importance and meaning of these "central things," see Gordon Lathrop, *Holy Things: A Liturgical Theology* (Minneapolis: Fortress Press, 1993).

very accessibility and ordinariness of these central signs—water used for bathing and a new beginning, public speech in an understandable yet symbol-laden vernacular, a communal meal—as a gift of God enabling the universal mission of the Church and opening the door of dialogue with all cultures. Given the centrality of these ordinary things, that dialogue must at least begin with an inquiry into the local meanings of water, with the use of the symbolic powers of the local vernacular, and with an awareness of local meal-keeping practices.

But how does this dialogue take place? What help is there in the material of the New Testament and the earliest stages of the Lutheran Reformation?

The central signs themselves, the core actions of the Christian liturgy, can be found in the New Testament. To the extent that it is possible for us to see, all of the various communities behind the New Testament books presume Baptism, called *baptisma* (*passim*; the "dipping," the "immersion") or *loutron* (Ephesians 5:26; Titus 3:5; the "washing," the "bath"), though details of its ritual practice are harder to find. Scripture reading is suggested as a Christian liturgical practice by passages in Luke and Paul,[7] by the general sense of a liturgical setting for the Pauline letters (though here it is the writings of the *apostle* which are to be read in the assembly), and perhaps by the letters and the scroll in the Revelation.[8] Preaching is found everywhere.[9] And the Christian practice of the eucharistic meal is presumed by the "do this" of Luke (22:19) and Paul (1 Corinthians 11:24-25) and by such diverse reports as Acts 2:42, 1 Corinthians 10-11, and Jude 12. That the meal is held every Sunday is reported for the community in Troas (Acts 20:7 and perhaps thus assumed for the Lukan communities generally) and suggested by Luke 24:30-31 and perhaps John 20:20,27 and Revelation 1:10; 3:20.

---

[7]   Luke 24:27,32,45 (*cf.* 4:21); 1 Thessalonians 5:27; Colossians 4:16.

[8]   Revelation 2-3 and 5:1-10.

[9]   *E.g.*, the many sermons in Acts, or Romans 10:8,14-15, or 1 Corinthians 1:17; 2:1-5.

That the Risen Christ bids the community to baptize (Matthew 28:19; *cf*. Mark 16:16), that the crucified Risen One is known in Scripture and the meal (Luke 24:30-32; *cf*. John 20:20; Revelation 5:6-7), that preaching is filled with the powerful weakness of the cross of Christ (1 Corinthians 1:17)—these assertions of Christian faith only serve to underline the crucial significance of these central symbolic acts already among New Testament communities. These are acts, as Lutherans will later say specifically about Baptism and the Lord's Supper, "with a promise."

There are even passages which hold more than one of these central signs together. In Acts 2, after Baptism, the community is devoted "to the apostles' teaching and fellowship, the breaking of bread and the prayers" (2:42). At Troas, the community gathers on Sunday for preaching and the meal (and, as it happens, for a "raising" which might be seen as a type of Baptism; Acts 20:7-12), the same pattern which is found in the disciples' first-day meeting with the Risen One on the way to Emmaus (Luke 24:13-32). In Mark (10:38-39; *cf*. Matthew 20:22-23; Luke 12:50), Jesus uses together the cup and the Baptism, which the community knows, as metaphors for the martyr's death. Paul depends upon the community having Baptism and meal as central events in order to make his exhortation based on the crossing of the sea, the manna and the water from the rock (1 Corinthians 10:1-22) and, perhaps, in order to propose that Baptism and the eucharistic meal unite Christians in one body and one Spirit (1 Corinthians 12:13).

These texts suggest that the central signs of the ongoing Christian liturgy have a strong anchor in at least some of the New Testament-era communities. They do so the more when we realize that there are other suggestions of diverse local ritual practices among some of the New Testament communities —"Baptism on behalf of the dead," for example, or prophesying or the veiling of women or "manifestations of the Spirit" or, perhaps, footwashing[10]—which, while they have had some sporadic history among certain Christians, have not had the nearly universal acceptance accorded the central signs. But the

---

[10]   See Ephesians 4:11; Acts 19:6; 1 Corinthians 11:4-5; 12:7; 15:29; John 13:14-15; 1 Timothy 5:10.

New Testament does not give us anything other than hints about the actual ritual practice of these central things. It assumes the presence of Baptism, preaching and Lord's Supper. It does not describe them.

What the New Testament can do is provide us with remarkable suggestions as to how the basic Christian symbolic acts are set within their broader symbolic environment. Helped by such commentators as Paul and Luke—and, perhaps, John—we can see the meanings and the centrality of the things that have become the central symbolic acts of the Christian liturgy. But, at the same time, following up suggestions in many texts, we can reflect upon how these things are themselves critical reworkings of cultural/ symbolic materials from the environment of the origins of Christianity. The New Testament can thereby offer us a model for the ongoing relationship between the many cultures and the Christian assembly, a model for the permeable but focussed character of Christian liturgical culture.

The Origins of Christian Baptism

In order to explore the ways in which primitive Christian symbolization related to its cultural/symbolic environment, we need to have some awareness of that environment. We now know that "hellenistic" culture, the heritage of Greek expansionism under Alexander the Great, pervaded the lands of the eastern Mediterranean, including Palestine, the very lands of Christian origins. The hellenistic period in this area was marked by a widespread search for world-coherence evidenced in such phenomena as the unifying dominance of the Greek language, the priority given to Greek customs, the syncretistic flow and mixing of religious ideas, and the longing for the ideal empire.[11] This longing for coherence probably ought to be seen as a negative witness to the general experience of disorder and chaos. At the same time, significant resistance was offered to this vision of coherence by the survival of local cultures. In Palestine, this resistance took both linguistic and religious forms. Such forms, however, were never "pure," but always evinced the culture-conflict of the times. The popular use of Aramaic, for example, brought with itself a sense of

---

[11]   See Garth Fowden, *Empire to Commonwealth* (Princeton, NJ: Princeton University Press, 1993), 3-36.

local Semitic identity, but it also brought the memory of empire, now the older, pre-Greek empires for which Aramaic was the *lingua franca*. And such movements as those of the Sadducees, the Pharisees, the Zealots, and the Essenes were themselves marked in different ways by the very hellenism they were seeking counter. The early Christian movement arose within this tension and interpenetration of cultures.

It has been long and widely recognized that Christian Baptism was not created *ex nihilo*. All of the Gospels and Acts presume that the baptism of John preceded the Christian practice.[12] Indeed, the very fact that Baptism among Christians was to take place in the name of Jesus (Acts 2:38; 8:16; 10:48) or in the name of the Father and of the Son and of the Holy Spirit (Matthew 28:19) indicates that *this* particular Baptism was now taking place with a new content. But the bathing action itself and its potential for symbolic meaning were already known, at least among those who had encountered or heard of John. One might compare the sense that a pre-existent washing practice could now be "in" or "into" Christ with the way Paul could say that walking under the protection of the cloud and crossing the sea was being "baptized into Moses" (1 Corinthians 10:2).

But where did the "baptism of John" (Mark 11:30; *cf.* Acts 19:3) come from? According to the synoptic tradition, Jesus himself asks this question. The answer to his question is not simple. It was surely both "from heaven," in that according to Christian faith it came truly with God's own authority as the beginning of the Gospel, and, at the same time, from human cultural origin, in that there seems to have been an important symbolic use of water-washing before John. This is an answer very like the implied answer to the questions about Jesus' own origin in Mark 6:1-6. Indeed, that Mark (11:27-33, parr.) speaks of the "baptism *of John*" could be read as meaning that specific symbolic water-washing which John uses in the name of God, implying that there were others. The same implication is in fact present in Paul's question to the disciples in Ephesus: "Into what then were you baptized?" (Acts 19:3). There seem to be other answers avail-

---

[12]   Matthew 3:11; Mark 1:7-8; Luke 3:16; 7:18-30; John 1:25-26,31,33; 3:22,26; 4:1-2; Acts 1:22; 13:24; 19:4.

able to that question than the baptismal way of John or the Baptism in the name of Jesus. In fact, the Letter to the Hebrews (9:9-10) asserts that "the present time" has its "various baptisms" which function only "until the time comes to set things right." These may be various ritual washings required in the Torah[13] and still practiced in the "present time" of the author of Hebrews. But, called "baptisms," they are in any case full-body washings and may be some development of the Torah-washings in the then current religious culture.

Twentieth-century scholarship has sometimes been willing to identify a variety of baptizing/washing movements in the hellenistic cultural environment of the origins of Christianity.[14] In any case, one cannot ignore Josephus' report of his own teacher, Bannus (does the name mean "bather" from the Greek *balaneus* or the Latin root *baln-*?), who, in the middle of the first century, "lived in the desert, wore clothing supplied from trees ...and washed many times in cold water both day and night for purification" (*Life* 1:2:11),[15] nor his several reports of the repeated full-body washings of the Essenes.[16] Most modern scholars identify these Essenes with the community of Qumran and its ancient library.[17] We know from these Dead Sea scrolls that very similar washings are reflected in several of its texts,[18] only now the texts supply the eschatological significance of this repeated accent on purity, a significance Josephus would be almost certain to have suppressed.

---

[13]   *Cf.* Exodus 40:12; Leviticus 8:6; 14-15; Numbers 19:13.

[14]   See especially Joseph Thomas, *Le mouvement baptiste en Palestine et Syrie* (Gembloux: Duculot, 1935); Georg Kretschmar, "Die Geschichte des Taufgottesdienstes in der alten Kirche," *Leiturgia 5* (Kassel: Stauda, 1970), 9, 52; and Kurt Rudolph, *Antike Baptisten* (Berlin: Akademie-Verlag, 1981).

[15]   Greek text and translation available in Todd S. Beall, *Josephus' Description of the Essenes Illustrated by the Dead Sea Scrolls* (Cambridge: Cambridge University Press, 1988), 12-13.

[16]   Before the common meal, *Jewish War* 2:8:129; as part of the process of joining the community, 2:8:137-8; after defecation, 2:8:149; after contact with strangers or junior members, 2:8:150; and before or *instead of* offering sacrifices, *Antiquities* 18:1:19.

[17]   See the parallels listed in Beall, 123-127.

[18]   1QS 3:5-9; 4:18-23; 5:13-14; CD 10:10-13; 11:21-22; *cf.* CD 3:16-17; 1QH 8:4-22.

Thus the Manual of Discipline speaks of the *eschaton*, using the metaphor of the bath:

> In the mysteries of God's understanding and in his glorious wisdom, God has ordained an end for falsehood, and at the time of the visitation he will destroy it forever. Then truth, which has wallowed in the ways of wickedness[19] during the dominion of falsehood until the appointed time of judgement, shall arise in the world forever. God will then purify every deed of man with his truth; he will refine for himself the human frame by rooting out all the spirit of falsehood from the bounds of his flesh. He will cleanse him of all wicked deeds with the spirit of holiness; like purifying waters he will shed upon him the spirit of truth[20] to cleanse him of all abomination and falsehood. And he shall be plunged into the spirit of purification that he may instruct the upright in the knowledge of the Most High and teach the wisdom of the sons of heaven to the perfect of way. For God has chosen them for an everlasting covenant.... (1QS 4:18-22).[21]

But only shortly thereafter in the text, the metaphor has yielded to the reality of the community's bathing practice: the disobedient ones in the community

> shall not enter the water to partake of the pure meal of the saints, for they shall not be cleansed unless they turn from their wickedness (1QS 5:13-14).[22]

Indeed, given the washing practice reflected in the Dead Sea Scrolls, it is not surprising that the observant community, awaiting the day of God, should regard itself as planted by the "secret well," the wa

---

19   *Cf.* the remarkably similar image in 2 Peter 2:22.

20   Beall, 56: "He will cause the spirit of truth to gush forth upon him like lustral water."

21   Translation from G. Vermes, *The Dead Sea Scrolls in English* (Harmondsworth: Penguin, 1962), pp. 77-78.

22   Vermes, 79.

ters of life (1QH 8), near a cistern "rich in water" (CD 3:16). "The cistern," says the Damascus document, "is the Law" (CD 6:4).

In addition to these witnesses, ancient Jewish and Christian sources of at least the second century list a variety of groups who seem to be identified by their accent on repeated and central washings: the daily baptizers, the Masbotheans, the Sabaeans, the Banaim, the morning bathers.[23] Two ancient texts, recently identified as most likely Jewish first-century writings, give central importance to full-body washing in a river.[24] And some scholars believe the root baptizing traditions of the much later Mandeans of Mesopotamia must be traced to the Transjordan during the time of the origins of Christianity.[25] While what is called "proselyte baptism" is probably a much later phenomenon,[26] New Testament texts do point to washing traditions among the Pharisees (Mark 7:3-4) and Jewish purification rites requiring a large amount of water in stone jars (120-180 gallons; John 2:6). What is more, archeological evidence also points toward a considerable interest in bathing at about this time. Cisterns with stairways

---

[23]   See Thomas, 34-45; and Rudolph, 8-10.

[24]   *Sybilline Oracles* 4:65 and the *Life of Adam and Eve* 6-11; in the latter the rivers are the Tigris for Eve and the Jordan for Adam.

[25]   See Kurt Rudolph, "Mandean Sources," in Werner Foerster, *Gnosis* 2 (Oxford: Clarendon, 1974), 132, 140-143; and "Die Religion der Mandäer," in Hartmut Gese *et al., Die Religionen Altsyriens, Altarabiens und der Mandäer* (*Die Religionen der Menschheit* 10,2; Stuttgart: Kohlhammer, 1970), 445-452.

[26]   The oldest clear reference is in the Babylonian Talmud. No convincing evidence can be found for the first century. See Adela Yarbro Collins, "The Origin of Christian Baptism," *Studia Liturgica* (19,1: 1989), 32-35. If *Asenath* is indeed a Jewish text and is to be dated between 100 BCE and 115 CE, as C. Burchard, "Joseph and Asenath," *The Old Testament Pseudepigrapha* 2 (New York: Doubleday, 1985), 187-188, proposes, then a flood of light would be cast on the origin of Christian Baptism, so many of the practices of later, especially Syrian-Christian initiation being present there: the use of Sunday or the Eighth Day, the importance of virginity, the bridal imagery, the initiator as a syzygy of the Lord, preparatory fasting and almsgiving, washing in living water, revelation of mysteries, the kiss, the meal, and, especially, this whole process as initiation. Since we lack exterior means of dating the text, however, and precisely because of these parallels as well as the presence of other imagery and language until now found only in Christian sources, it seems much wiser to regard *Asenath* as a romance of Christian provenance, close in community of origin to the community of the *Didache* and close in spirit to the later *Acts of Judas Thomas*, also a romance. If this proposal is correct, however, *Asenath* remains a text which should be studied for its importance to the second- and third-century development of Christian Baptism. Note that in *Asenath* 14 the protagonist washes only her face. This should be compared to *Didache* 7:2-3 and *Acts of Thomas* 132 and contrasted with bYoma 87a.

that seem to be designed for full-body bathing and that utilize, at least in part, an unbroken access to fresh rainwater, are found in considerable numbers at Jerusalem, Jericho, Herodium, Masada, and at Qumran itself as well as elsewhere.[27]

These various "baptisms" cannot be used easily to construct a genealogy of Christian Baptism. There have probably been rather too many naive attempts to say that John's baptism (and with it the subsequent Christian practice) derive directly from one or the other of these sources. On the other hand, the presence of these practices in the cultural environment of Christianity can also not be ignored. There may have also been rather too many "protestant" assertions[28] that such ritual practices have nothing to do with the origins of Christianity. The sense alive in the second-century Church that Christian Baptism was situated amid many other washings seems instead to be the case. Thus Clement of Alexandria asserts that the Lord has, "by means of the one Baptism, taken over [*perilabon*, gathered up, supplanted] the many baptisms of Moses" (*Stromateis* 3:82:6). And both Justin (*1 Apology* 62) and Tertullian (*De baptismo* 5) see in a variety of hellenistic-era washings an empty shadow of Baptism into Christ. We are today simply able to be a little more precise about the character of these hellenistic/Mosaic washings in the cultural surroundings of the origins of Christianity.[29]

But only a *little* more. It is not that we are able clearly to identify "baptizing sects." Even the history and the shape of the "Qumran community" are debated issues: the Dead Sea *library* may have been exactly that, a library, not the careful description of contemporary communal practice. But we are able to say that washing for purifi

---

[27]   John Peter Oleson, "Water Works," *Anchor Bible Dictionary* 6 (New York: Doubleday, 1992), 887. See also Eric M. Meyers and A. Thomas Kraabel, "Archaeology, Iconography and Nonliterary Written Remains," in Robert A. Kraft and George W. E. Nickelsburg, *Early Judaism and its Modern Interpreters* (Philadelphia: Fortress Press, 1986), 181; and Beall, 56-57.

[28]   For a critical appraisal of "catholic" and "protestant" presuppositions in research on Christian origins see Jonathan Z. Smith, *Drudgery Divine: On the Comparison of Early Christianities and the Religions of Late Antiquity* (Chicago: University of Chicago Press, 1990).

[29]   Kretschmar, 9.

cation and, at least sometimes, washing for purification in view of the expected day of God were ideas and practices that were in the air, were *available cultural symbols*. The availability of this symbolism may have been due to many things: the influx of Iranian water-devotion; the development and use of Roman bath-technology in Palestine; the importance of water-narratives (the creation, the Flood, the Exodus, the entry into the land, the lustrations given in the Torah) and of eschatological water imagery[30] in the Hebrew Scriptures; the longing (seen in the movement of the Pharisees but also at Qumran) to generalize—laicize—the priestly purity and, thus, the priestly access to God; and, probably most importantly, the experienced disorder of the Palestinian world. The imposed order of the Roman occupation and the interior sense that the "times were evil" could have led many people to wash and wash, seeking order in purity and in the coming judgement of God. In any case, we ought to bring some cultural sympathy to imagining the reasons for the multiplication of baths.

What we know of some of these baths includes these characteristics: They were full-body washings[31] in cold, flowing or rain-originating, stone-held water. They were repeated, even exaggeratedly multiplied.[32] They probably *did not* involve oil.[33] They could involve white or "pure" clothing,[34] sometimes kept on during the bath. They preceded communal eating.[35] They could be part of the process of entering a community,[36] but then only as yet another purification or as an entering on the way of purification. They set off the bathed from strangers or juniors, from the "impure,"[37] the bath being a symbol of the law[38] and only appropriately used by the ethically pure and observant.

---

[30]   Isaiah 4:2-6; 35:6-7; 44:3; Ezekiel 16:1-14; 36:24-28; 47:1-12.

[31]   *JW* 2:8:129; CD 10:10-13; *Sybilline Oracles* 4:165; *Life of Adam and Eve* 6-11.

[32]   Thus Bannus and the daily baptizers.

[33]   *JW* 2:8:123; *cf.* CD 12:15-17; *Life of Adam and Eve* 41-42.

[34]   *JW* 2:8:123,129, 131, 137; *cf.* Bannus.

[35]   *JW* 2:8:129 and 1QS 5:13.

[36]   *JW* 2:8:137-8; *cf.* 1QS 6:13-23.

[37]   *JW* 2:8:150; 1QS 5:13; Mark 7; *cf.* 1QH 8.

[38]   CD 6:4.

Indeed, ethical behavior was to follow from the bath — or no amount of water, not even oceans, would be able to cleanse.[39] In such evidence as we have, these intensified baths seem to involve only men (with the exception of the *Life of Adam and Eve*—and even then, Eve does not complete the washing and is tempted away from it!). And they are done by the bather himself;[40] there is no evidence for a "baptizer." Finally, these repeated baths seem best understood as an enacting ahead of time of the bathing that God is coming to do, when truth and the Spirit are poured out[41] amidst all the falseness and disorder of the times, as a preparation to be part of the pure remnant on that day, perhaps even, by a kind of sympathetic magic, as a prayer for and urging of that day.

If even some of these characteristics were generally understood, then the way that John the Baptist makes use of this cultural/symbolic "language" is stunning. The baptism of John has much in common with these intensified hellenistic Jewish baths: full body washing in flowing water, ethical implications, the evocation of "the day," even his own simplified manner of life. We do not know if his bathing included women, though Luke speaks of "crowds" coming to him and of the "people" being baptized (3:7,10,15,18,21). Nor do we know if he intended to form a group of disciples, a community, though the latter seems to exist in New Testament witness and in some subsequent tradition.

The invitation to this bath, however, is public, not withdrawn and communal. And now this bathing is not just in any stone cistern; it is at the *Jordan*,[42] as if for the people to come through that water again were for them to be formed into Israel coming into God's land.[43]

---

[39]   1QS 3:4-5.

[40]   Bannus; CD 10:10-13.

[41]   1QS 4:18-23.

[42]   Although, once John is reported as baptizing at Aenon (Aramaic: "springs"), which may or may not have been near the Jordan; John 3:23.

[43]   That "Jordan" could function in such a symbolic way in the times of John is clear from a painful story recounted in Josephus. The *Antiquities* (20:5:1; *cf.* Acts 5:36-37) tells of a certain Theudas who, probably in the mid-first century, gathered people at the Jordan, with the promise of crossing it in what was to be manifestly a new "conquest," a new parting of the waters to claim the land for God. The Roman cavalry killed and imprisoned the people who gathered with him and carried Theudas' head to Jerusalem.

The very location— as well as the *washing*—appeals to the sense of disorder which has been proposed here as a possible social setting for the multiplication of baths. But John's baptism does not seem to be multiple. In any case, he does it; he is the baptizer. In the Hebrew Scriptures, those occasions in which someone is passively bathed include the priest-making of Aaron and his successors (Exodus 40:12-15; Leviticus 8:6-13), the preparation of Jerusalem as the bride of God (Ezekiel 16:1-14), and the promised eschatological washing of the people (Isaiah 4:2-6; Ezekiel 36:24-28), *not* the ordinary bathings of ritual purity. While the former two may have figured in John's meaning, it is probably the latter which is signified by his acting to bathe.

By a kind of prophetic sign then,[44] John indicates and anticipates *God's* coming to wash the people. Both the location and the practice of having people be baptized point to the imminence and centrality of God's action rather than private human action for the sake of ritual purity. John calls for repentance, for "turning around" in the water to see the coming God. John's practice receives the current interest in baths and radically reinterprets it by the juxtaposition of profound biblical imagery.

But, for Christians, the chain of reinterpretation goes on. According to the entire Gospel tradition, Jesus comes to Baptism. Simply that coming, whereby he becomes the pattern and the content of all Christian Baptism, is what the Christian tradition has meant by the "institution of the sacrament." Christians do not believe that Jesus invents Baptism, but rather that Baptism is even more radically reinterpreted in him than the many baths were reinterpreted in John's singular prophetic practice.

Jesus is baptized, thus all three of the synoptics witness (Matthew 3:13-16; Mark 1:9-10; Luke 3:21). By that action, Jesus also stands with all the people amid the current oppression and disorder, in need of the eschatological coming of God. He stands there as surely as he was later crucified, crying out to God, according to Mark (15:34-35), in a cry that was also a cry for the eschaton. He is baptized and,

---

[44] So Collins, 35

according to these same synoptics, this washed one is made unclean, both by his associations and by his utterly unclean death.[45] He is baptized, with the sign of the coming day of God, yet his obvious inheritance is not that glorious day but the same fate as John the Baptist (Mark 6:17-29; 9:11-13). By these means, the synoptics indicate that the Jesus-tradition as they know it has received both the baptism of John and the situation of disorder and pain which made it urgent.

The same assertion is made in a different way in the Fourth Gospel: Jesus baptizes (John 3:22,26; 4:1-2). The Baptism which Jesus enacts—or, rather, in what comes down to the same thing—the Baptism which the disciples of Jesus enact in his name is simply John's baptism continued.

But this Baptism of the Christian community is also John's baptism utterly changed. The assertions of both the synoptics and of John are, of course, already interpretations, *theologoumena*, but they do make clear the universal tradition that Christian Baptism is made out of John's baptism. They also make clear the deep-going reinterpretation that the washing tradition now undergoes. We cannot say with certainty whether or not the historical John actually preached, "I have baptized you with water; but he will baptize you with the Holy Spirit" (Mark 1:8), or some variant thereof. He could have done so, of course, meaning *God* as the coming Mighty One.[46] Other of the contemporary users of the bath also expected the coming God to pour out the Spirit like water (1QS 4; see above) or like fire. Such language was simply another image for the expected day. But in Christian use, the meaning is clear. Jesus is the coming Mighty One; his Baptism transforms Baptism itself, making it the very presence of God (the voice and the dove); and henceforth Baptism into him is the outpouring of the Spirit, the dawning of the day of God. Such is the inevitable meaning of the account of Jesus coming to John's Baptism when it is told in the midst of Christian communities still doing Baptisms as central, identity-giving events.

---

[45]   Mark 2:15-17; 7:1-5; 15:27; *cf.* Matthew 11:19; Luke 7:34.

[46]   *Cf.* Collins, 30.

The Christian Content and Meaning of Baptism

But the meaning is more radical yet. In Mark's Gospel, for example, the day that dawns at the Baptism of Jesus and is again glimpsed at the transfiguration (9:2-10), comes at the cross. Here, the one who is known in secret as the Son (1:10-11; 9:7) is proclaimed openly (15:39). Elijah—and thus the day of God—has come in a way unexpected (9:11-13; 15:36), in John the Baptist and in the cross. Jesus does drink the new cup of the dominion of God (14:25), and it is sour wine (15:36). No wonder the unwashed (7:2) and the impure (2:15) are welcome into him. No wonder one who appears like a candidate for a washing appears before and after his death (15:51-52; 16:5).[47] Jesus and his cross *are* their Baptism. At Qumran, old baptizers could say, "The cistern is the Law" (CD 6:4). In the Markan tradition, the washing is Jesus' death (9:38-39). The grace which John the Baptist proclaimed has been continued and radically deepened.

Something very like this radical interpretation is also present in the Fourth Gospel. Here, John the Baptist himself sees the descent of the Spirit on Jesus and hears the voice (John 1:32-34). Here, a woman—from among the unclean Samaritans—and a sick man unable to get to the washing-pool and a cast-out blind man are welcome to the water which is from Jesus (4:1-42; 5:2-18; 9:1-41), indeed, which *is* Jesus (9:7; *cf.* 17:3). But, finally, what replaces the tradition of washing, giving more than the purity and order for which it reached, is the new wine of Cana (2:1-11), a "sign" which points forward to Jesus' death and resurrection. For the water which flows from Jesus' heart (7:37; *cf.* Ezekiel 47:1-12), the very presence of the outpoured Spirit, flows from the crucified one (19:30-35) who is risen (20:20-22). Indeed, the slave-service of the crucified is all the washing one needs (13:1-11), the full meaning of both Baptism (13:10) and of the Lord's Supper (13:2-4).

These texts of Mark and John may be seen as *interpretations of Baptism.* Indeed, they come alive when they are seen against the background of the cultural washings in the environment of earliest

---

[47]   See the discussion of the "secret gospel of Mark" in Thomas J. Talley, *The Origins of the Liturgical Year* (New York: Pueblo, 1986), 207-209.

Christianity. One could read them, however, not simply as reinterpretations but as refusals of the washing rite. Cana and the footwashing story in John and the cross- as-Baptism in Mark might suggest one needs no actual washing-rite at all. But that would be to misread what is a much more interesting proposal. In Mark, Jesus *is baptized*, paradigm for all subsequent Baptisms. The added conclusion of Mark therefore rightly includes Baptism in the instructions of the risen one (16:16), while rightly placing it only on the side of promise, never of requirement and threat. And in John, Jesus himself *baptizes* and invites to the water.[48] The rite is not set aside. Rather, the meaning of the footwashing—of the cross—is exactly what must always be added to the bath (13:10), thus utterly transfiguring the bath. Culturally significant material, including the "language" of washing rites, has been received in these accounts of the tradition of Jesus, has been criticized and even destroyed, and yet has been re-used for the purposes of a Christian speaking of eschatology, grace and the presence of God's all-washing mercy in Jesus. The cultural symbol of washing for the day of God has been "broken."[49] Its power to evoke hope for God in the midst of disorder and death has been used, but its conceptions of purity and "insiderhood," indeed its deep-rooted anxiety, have been rejected.

There are many other interpretations of Christian Baptism in the New Testament. It is not necessary here to set them all out nor to arrange them in a pattern of chronological occurrence. It can be asserted, however, that the current interest in diversity ought not lead us too quickly to assume that different language implied different practice or even different root-understanding. Most of the varying conceptions can be traced to varying ways to assert that the eschaton is occurring in Jesus Christ and is encountered in the Baptism which

---

[48]   John 3:5 might also be considered. Although "water" here could mean ordinary birth from the womb, it might also mean that water which is full of the Spirit, that water which, with the Spirit, flows from the crucified risen one. The ambiguity could be intentional.

[49]   See Paul Tillich, *Dynamics of Faith* (New York: Harper, 1957), 52-54. For Tillich, in a "broken myth" the terms of the myth and its power to evoke our experience of the world remain, but the coherent language of the myth is seen as insufficient and its power to hold and create as equivocal. The myth is both true and at the same time wrong, capable of truth only by reference to a new thing, beyond its own terms. For an application of this idea to the symbols of the liturgy, see Lathrop, *Holy Things*, 27-31.

is into him. Thus Baptism is preparing the community for marrying God (Ephesians 5:26; *cf.* Ezekiel 16:1-14). Baptism is the making of a new people of priests (1 Peter 1:22-2:10). Baptism was prefigured by the Flood and is a standing with the Resurrection of Christ in appeal to God (1 Peter 3:21). Baptism is the coming of the eschatological promise and the forgiveness of sins (Acts 2:38-41). Baptism is rescue from the darkness and transfer to the dominion of Christ, in whom is forgiveness of sins (Colossians 1:13-14). Baptism is rebirth and renewal through the outpoured Holy Spirit (Titus 3:5-6). It is enlightenment, tasting the heavenly gift and sharing in the Spirit (Hebrews 6:2-4). It is entering through Jesus into the new sanctuary, bodies washed with pure water (Hebrews 10:22). Baptism is all people, men and women, Jew and Gentile, being clothed in Christ (Galatians 3:27-28). Baptism is being plunged into Jesus' death; it is being buried with Christ in order to be raised with him in newness of life (Romans 6:1-11; Colossians 2:12). It can easily be seen how especially this latter Pauline conception powerfully corresponds to the eschatology and the theology of the cross which are present in both Mark and John.[50]

None of these accounts gives us clear information about the actual ritual practice of Baptism in the New Testament communities. It should not surprise us, however, if so rich a field of meaning depends upon the strong signs of an evocative ritual practice. In any case, if Christian Baptism is a critical re-use of available cultural "language," then the ritual practice we have seen among the self-baptizers and with John the Baptist will also hover behind the Christian use. Thus, Christian Baptism will also ordinarily have been a full-body washing in flowing, cold water. Paul's burial metaphor requires some such usual practice as does also the death-metaphor of the synoptic Jesus (Mark 10:38-39; Luke 12:50). Christian Bap-

---

[50] Being washed in the blood of Christ, Hebrews 9:14, or having one's robe washed in the blood of the Lamb, Revelation 7:14, may be other ways to speak the same meaning: the ritual washing has its fulfillment in the death of Christ. Some similar meaning, related to John 19:30-35, may be behind the mysterious assertion of the three witnesses—the Spirit, the water and the blood—in 1 John 5:8. In any case, the Pauline sources are not the only New Testament texts which link Baptism and the death of Christ. Oscar Cullman, *Le baptême des enfants* (Neuchatel: Delachaux et Niestlé, 1948), 15-16, was right: the death of Jesus can be called the "general Baptism."

tism may have sometimes involved new, clean clothing.[51] It also led to the community meal.[52] It bore within itself ethical consequences.[53]

But, at their best, these were now the ethics of love and mercy, not the ethics of separation. And the Baptism which led to them was also utterly different from the available cultural language, with a difference corresponding to Christian faith in Jesus Christ and Christian eschatology. It was now not the Jordan River which was the appropriate place of Baptism, but wherever there was water (Acts 8:36), for the eschatological reality is Christ, not the recovered land. Ultimately, the amount or temperature of the water used was also not to be rigidly measured, though "living water" remained the ideal (*Didache* 7:2-3). For exactly the same eschatological reason, there was now *one* Baptism, not multiple washings (Ephesians 4:5; *cf.* Hebrews 9:9-12). This one Baptism together with the continuation of John the Baptist's practice of having people passively washed (Acts 8:38; 1 Corinthians 1:14) were intended to speak clearly of the final grace of God coming now upon people in Christ, constituting them as community. In fact, entrance into the community of the last day in Christ (Acts 2:41-42) now became the specifically Christian use of the washing rite. This bath was for all people: women and men, Gentile and Jew, slave and free, at least as its implications were finally understood in the Gentile mission.[54] From a Markan or a Johannine point of view, it would now be the *rejection* of women or the outsiders or the ritually unclean which would, paradoxically, be "unclean." And since the point of this Baptism was now faith in the crucified and risen Christ, not ritual purity, it was accompanied by teaching and preaching (Acts 1:14-22; Matthew 28:19-20).

There may have been, already, in some of the communities of the New Testament, specifically new and Christian use of signs to accompany this washing. The use of fire or light (Hebrews 6:4), of the

---

[51]   *Cf.* Galatians 3:27; Colossians 3:9-10; Ephesians 4:22-24; Revelation 7:13-17; 22:14; Mark 14:51-52; 16:5.

[52]   1 Corinthians 10:2-3; Acts 2:41-42; *cf.* 1 Corinthians 12:13; Revelation 22:14; Hebrews 6:4-5; 1 Peter 1:22-2:3.

[53]   Romans 6:4; Hebrews 6:4-8.

[54]   *Cf.* Galatians 3:27-28; John 4:1-42; 1 Corinthians 12:13; Colossians 3:11.

laying on of hands (Hebrews 6:2; Acts 19:6), perhaps even of oil (1 John 2:20,27; 2 Corinthians 1:21) or of signing with the cross (Revelation 7:3-4; *cf.* 2 Corinthians 1:22; Ephesians 1:13; 4:30) could be inferred as standing behind some of the references of the New Testament. But we do not know. Anointing with oil at Baptism might easily have followed from the name "Christ," from the explicit rejection of the old purity rules and from the sense that Baptism into Christ was the new form of that old passive washing whereby priests were made (Exodus 40:12-15; Leviticus 8:6-13) or that old prophetic metaphor in which Jerusalem was prepared to be married to God (Ephesians 5:26; *cf.* Ezekiel 16:1-14). The actual ritual beginnings of anointing among Christians, however, remain unclear.

When noting such as may be said about baptismal liturgy from the texts of the New Testament, it is important to indicate that "Baptism in the name" (Matthew 28:19 and Acts 2:38, *etc.*) probably does not mean that an explicit formula of words was recited by the baptizer during the bath. Paul uses the same terminology in 1 Corinthians 1:12-17 and it is unlikely that anyone would have imagined a formula which runs, "I baptize you in the name of Paul." Paul rather means that were *he* to have baptized, those baptisms could have been regarded as in the presence and power of Paul and through his agency, *i.e.*, "in the name of Paul." He wishes instead to make clear that all true Baptism is in the presence, power, and agency of Jesus Christ. This eschatological meaning of the washing is what "Baptism in the name of Jesus Christ" is intended to express. In the same way, Baptism "in the name of the Father and of the Son and of the Holy Spirit" was not Baptism with a certain formula but that same Baptism in which the Spirit descends and the Voice speaks and the Son is revealed, which occurs at the beginning of Matthew's Gospel (3:16-17). In other words, this washing is Baptism as the Christian community does it, with the old washing rituals now broken open to speak God's grace in Christ.

The old washing rituals did not always stay broken. Suppressed or transformed materials from the cultural environment could reassert themselves much as the later basilica could reassert its original meanings to the detriment of its transformation by the Christian assembly. So, the idea of purity and obedience could appear again (2 Peter 2:20-22), as could conceptions of purity and insiderhood (2

Corinthians 6:14-7:1). So also, much later, could the practice of self-washing[55] or the perceived need for multiple washings.[56] And the Christian conviction that this washing in Christ is full of the outpoured Holy Spirit could be turned into a new ritual *requirement*, if we read the layings-on-of-hands in Acts (8:17; 19:6) as a liturgical description rather than a literary feature associating earlier washings with the apostolic church.

Conclusion

For our purposes, however, there are two major insights which these New Testament texts suggest:

1. Insofar as the liturgical practice and meaning of the earliest Christian communities can be reconstructed, those communities made use of the *strong* but *broken* symbol of washing, now as entrance to the community and as one of their central and identifying practices. The cultural washing symbolism was thus received and turned to the purpose of proclaiming God's grace in Christ. Christians today, who similarly practice Baptism as central, do well to ask whether their practice is similarly both strong and broken, marked by a full use of water and its attendant signs and a full panoply of interpretive images, but always turned to the speaking of grace, resisting the use of the water-rite to create separation and "works righteousness" and ideas of cultic purity.

2. This very use of cultural/symbolic material from the environment of the origins of Christianity proposes to us a model for the ongoing cultural dialogue with Christian worship. Anything brought into the worshiping assembly can be received with the same sympathy to its meanings, but also with the same powerful critique as seems present in the Christian use of the ancient washing practice.

---

[55]   In Syria, if *Asenath* is a Christian document; see above, note 26.

[56]   Among those Christians influenced by the Parthian Jewish prophet Elchasai; cf. 2 Corinthians 7:1. See Rudolph, *Antike Baptisten*, 13-17. See also G. P. Luttikhuizen, *The Revelation of Elchasai* (Groningen dissertation, 1984).

BAPTISM
IN THE EARLY CHURCH
AND ITS CULTURAL SETTINGS[1]

Anscar J. Chupungco

One of the remarkable traits of the Greco-Roman period of the Church, especially during the third and fourth centuries, was the rapid development of the shape of liturgical worship. Stepping out of the Jewish world, the young missionary Church entered into contact with the culture and cultic practices of pagan Greece and Rome. Considering the staunch monotheism inherited by the Church from Judaism, contact with the pagan world entailed a considerable effort to adapt to the new situation without detriment to her basic tenets. This is not to say that the Church had had no previous experience in this matter. The dream of Peter in the city of Joppa (Acts 11:4-18), the council of the Apostles in Jerusalem (Acts 15:4-29), and the entire apostolic activity of St. Paul to the Gentile world bear witness to the early Church's struggle with problems arising from contact with paganism or with cultures outside Judaism.

Yet the experience of the Church in the third and fourth centuries had a different tenor from the apostolic period. It was not a question merely of admitting the Gentiles into the Church and exempting them from some of the mosaic laws that still bound Christians; rather it was a question of investing the Christian rites of worship with elements from the culture and traditions of the Gentiles. It was an altogether different process to which we give the name of inculturation. We may say that inculturation at this early stage of liturgical development became a distinct liturgical concern of the young missionary Church.

---

[1]   An elaborated form of this chapter appears in the author's book, *Tradition and Progress*, copyright Pastoral Press, 1994.

What led the Church to inculturate its form of worship, and how did she do it? She could have continued to celebrate Baptism in the utter New Testament simplicity of "washing in water with the word," using perhaps the language of Palestine. But she did not, nor did she settle with merely delivering catechetical instruction to converts, as did the missionaries in China in the 17th century. In their antagonism to native Chinese words and rites, the missionaries foisted Latin words like *Deus* and *gratia* on their converts for whom such words meant absolutely nothing. Furthermore, they forbade them to perform the rite of ancestral veneration, a rite which was and continues to be the mainstay of Chinese civilization. China was lost to the Church, because at that moment in history the Church did not know how to bend to the inevitable. The history of inculturation certainly signals the danger of eclecticism and even syncretism. But it also warns us that when we ignore the relationship worship should have with culture, we might also come to ignore the dynamics of evangelization.

The early Church, on the other hand, not only catechized; she also made necessary adjustments in her liturgical rites. If the liturgy must communicate the Church's faith to people, that faith had to be expressed with words, rites, and symbols that were familiar to them. It had to become recognizably incarnate, that is, as having taken flesh in the cultural milieu of the worshipers. Furthermore, it must allow itself to be claimed and owned by them as a part of their existence as a Christian people. It does not mean that inculturation reduces the liturgy to becoming a component of culture. The core of the liturgy is a supracultural reality which the Church received through apostolic preaching and preserves intact in every time and place. What inculturation means is that worship assimilates the people's language, ritual, and symbolic patterns. In this way the people are able to claim and own the liturgical core they received through the apostolic preaching. Today we have come to regard both the process of incarnation and the claiming of the Christian message by the people as an imperative to evangelization.

The question is how the early Church inculturated worship. What method did she employ, so that inculturation did not become an occasion for eclecticism? We know what eclecticism is about: it is a random, indiscriminate, and undigested borrowing of alien doctrines and practices regardless of whether or not they accord with the faith received from the Apostles. What eclecticism tries to accomplish is to present to the faithful a kind of a multiple choice whereby each one may select those elements that one finds suitable or convenient. Christianity detests every form of eclecticism. It is by nature partial to the assimilation in liturgical worship of those cultural elements and patterns which can be reintepreted in the light of God's revelation. This process of reinterpreting or re-reading culture in the light of the Christian mystery is a method of inculturation which the early Church employed. In other words, inculturation does not lead to a juxtaposition of unrelated elements. Rather, it allows the liturgy to develop its shape in the cultural milieu of worshipers, without danger to its original meaning.

Because Christianity detests eclecticism, it views culture with a critical eye. Today we speak of this as being countercultural. In the area of the liturgy, the Church not only welcomes culture; it also critiques culture. The Church realizes that while every culture possesses beauty and nobility, not everything cultural can be assimilated into liturgical worship. In this connection being countercultural can mean one of three things. The Church can ignore what she considers unsuitable or, to put it more strongly, unredeemable. Silent reproach is one way of being countercultural. Thus the slaughtering of sacrifical animals in some mystery rites as part of an initiation process was neither assimilated by nor spoken of in the early rite of Christian Baptism. The second way of being countercultural is by denunciation or protest. Early patristic writings, as we shall have occasion to see, did not spare such pagan initiation rites as lustrations, pomps, and meals. These were ineffective, costly, or even devilish. The third way of being countercultural is by the reinterpretation of cultural elements, including religious rites, in the light of God's revelation. This method, which requires a critique of the value and suitablility of cultural components previous to their assimilation, affirms that culture and traditions can serve as vehicles of the Christian mystery. We may say that they enter the realm of Christ's redemption through the liturgy.

Baptismal Elements in the First Two Centuries

The cultural setting of the first two centuries has left an indelible impression on the shape of baptismal liturgy. To appreciate this point it is helpful to recall that in the New Testament the celebration of Baptism centered on the bare essentials. Ephesians 5:26 mentions only the "washing of water with the word." On the other hand, the references in Romans 6:4 ("when we were baptized we went into the tomb with him") and Acts 8:38 ("Philip and the eunuch went down into the water") seem to imply the mode of immersion. At any rate, washing or bathing and the Word or some ritual formula would appear to have made up the core or nucleus of the New Testament baptismal rite. Throughout the centuries the Church has maintained that the Baptism of Jesus consisted basically of the act of washing in natural water accompanied by an invocation of the name of the Blessed Trinity, as Matthew 28:19 indicates. In fact, in cases of emergency all that is required by the Church is the washing with water and the recitation of the Trinitarian formula, or in other words, the bare essentials of the New Testament baptismal liturgy.

Around the year 90 A.D. the author of *Didache* informs us that Baptism was administered "in the name of the Father, and of the Son, and of the Holy Spirit."[2] Whether this was the actual formula or was meant to define the trinitarian character of Baptism as presented by Matthew 28:19 is difficult to determine. All that we are allowed to conclude is that the three-part Name was invoked at Baptism. Later patristic writings mention the use of the more elaborate creedal formula. Thus, in the third-century *Apostolic Tradition* attributed to Hippolytus of Rome, the formula is in the form of question and answer before each of the threefold immersions: "Do you believe in God, the Father almighty? I believe. Do you believe in Jesus Christ, the Son of God, who was born by the Holy Spirit and the Virgin Mary, was crucified under Pontius Pilate, died, was buried, and on the third day rose from the dead, ascended to heaven, sits at the right hand of the Father, and will come to judge both the living and the dead? I believe. Do you believe in the Holy Spirit, the holy Church, and the resurrection of the body? I believe."[3]

---

[2]   *Didaché*, ed. W. Rordorf and A. Tuilier, *Sources Chrétiennes* 248 (1978) 7, 170-71. W. Rordorf, "Le baptême selon Didaché," *Mélanges liturgiques offerts à Dom Botte* (Louvain, 1972), 499-510.

[3]   *La Tradition Apostolique de Saint Hippolyte*, ed. B. Botte (Münster, 1989), no. 21, pp. 48-50. M. Metzger, "Enquêtes autour de la prétendue Tradition Apostolique," *Ecclesia Orans* IX (1992/1), 7-36.

As regards the baptismal water, *Didache* mentions living, that is, the running water of springs and rivers, or if this is not available, also such bodies of water as pools and reservoirs where water does not flow. Are we to perceive here an early preoccupation for the symbolism of baptismal water as life-giving water? Is it evident that the mode of washing was immersion, or was it submersion? The practice of Baptism by immersion is confirmed by a later interpolation to the text which directs the baptizer to "pour water three times on the head," in case water was scarce in the region. Thus infusion would appear to have been rather exceptional. We have here an example of ritual adjustment that laid aside the original meaning of *baptein* or *baptizein* as immersion-bath in view of a concrete situation.

Didache enjoins both the baptizer and the baptizand to fast for a day or two before the rite of Baptism.[4] Fasting before initiation was an element of the ancient nature rites that developed in the third century as mystery rites. It was a form of ascetical preparation for the initiation rites and may be considered a component of the religious cultural milieu of the early centuries. Although no less than the New Testament itself praised the practice of fasting (Matthew 6:17; 17:20; Luke 2:37), there is no indication that fasting was observed in connection with Baptism. Hence it would appear that the practice of fasting prior to Baptism was borrowed from the religious cultural setting of the time. Since *Didache* is a first-century document, its point of reference would seem to be the ancient nature rites before they developed into mystery rites.

We must presume that some catechesis was given to the candidates.[5] Baptisms in Acts were normally preceded by instruction on the faith. We need only think of the grand Baptisms on Pentecost, the Baptism of the eunuch, and the Baptism of the jailer at Philippi. These were preceded by instruction on Christian faith, which surely included moral or ethical norms, similar to what other religions would require an initiate to know. We may presume that the candidates were required also to learn sacred formulas by heart. One likely example is

---

4   *Didaché* 7, 172. Prebaptismal fasting is clearly distinguished from the ascetical fasting enjoined on Christians every Wednesday and Friday by the author.

5   Possibly the first six chapters of *Didache* on the two ways are what chapter 7 refers to: "After the foregoing instructions, baptize...." See note 3 of the editors.

the Lord's Prayer, which is recorded for the first time outside the New Testament by *Didache*. Since *Didache* requires that the Lord's Prayer be recited three times a day, we may conclude that those initiated into faith had to memorize it. Learning sacred formulas was a standard preparation for initiation.

Thus until the end of the first Christian century, the rite of Baptism was confined to the essentials, namely, immersion in water accompanied by the recitation of the Trinitarian formula. In *Didache* the core of the baptismal liturgy retained the original simplicity of the apostolic rite, yet marginal elements borrowed from the cultural setting of the period began to accrue. In *Didache* these are catechesis, which was normally required by the sacrament, and fasting. Today we call such accrued elements introductory, explanatory, or concluding rites.

The influence of the pagan mystery rites can be felt more strongly in the writing of Justin Martyr. Justin wrote his *First Apology*, whose Chapter 61 describes Baptism, between the years 148 and 161.[6] Of particular interest to the historical development of the baptismal rite is the mention of the Trinitarian formula: "There is invoked over the one who wishes to be reborn and who has repented of one's sins, the name of God, the Father and Master of all... Furthermore, the one being illuminated is washed also in the name of Jesus Christ, who was crucified under Pontius Pilate, and in the name of the Holy Spirit who predicted through the prophets everything concerning Jesus."[7] These words ring a familiar bell: they are quite similar to the Trinitarian components of the Christian creed. Can we say that in the second century the baptismal formula was already as elaborate as the creed or at least contained a number of creedal elements?

Justin, who studied philosophy under the Stoics and later the Platonists, was also conversant with mystery rites. It might be useful to note in passing that mystery rites seem to have originated from nature rites which formerly were performed to renew the fertility of

---

[6]   Ed. by L. Pautigny (Paris, 1904); partial English translation by W. Jurgens, *The Faith of the Early Fathers* (Collegeville: Liturgical Press, 1970), 50-56.

[7]   *First Apology* 61; Jurgens, p. 54.

mother earth. Although mystery rites always alluded to one or another natural element like water, fire, and wind, they also included initiation into the community of believers. Until the fourth century, when these rites began to wane, the more common examples were: the Eleusinian rites which honored the bereavement and reunion of the corn-goddess Demeter with her daughter Persephone; the Egyptian cult of Osiris and Isis, featuring the water of the Nile; the Phrygian fertility rites in honor of mother earth and Attis; the Assyrian rites for Juno which centered on the element of air; and the initiation rites which featured the Persian god Mithras and the sun-god.[8]

Justin's description of Baptism is evocative of the pagan mystery rites of initiation. He mentions a type of scrutinies, whereby the candidates pledged to live according to "what we say and teach." He informs us that candidates "are taught in prayer and fasting to ask God to forgive their past sins, while we all pray and fast with them." He refers to Baptism as *photismos*, or enlightenment, and the baptized as the enlightened ones. It is called so, "because it enlightens the intelligence of those who learn these things."[9] Although the baptismal hymn in Ephesians 5:14 speaks of Christ as one who shines on those who are awakened from sleep, we cannot exclude the possibility that Justin borrowed the word *photismos* directly from the mystery rites. Here we have a remarkable example of how the anthropological axiom "water illumines, while fire washes" is put to work in Baptism. The water of Baptism not only washes, it also enlightens. Likewise, words like consecration and rebirth, which Justin employs to describe the effects of Baptism, were also in use among the different mystery rites.

Initiation meals were part of many mystery rites. Justin could have regarded the first Eucharist of the neophytes as the Christian counterpart of such meals. In Chapter 65 of his book the eucharistic celebration appears as the conclusion of the initiatory rite of Baptism. It begins with intercessions which follow Baptism. Justin's reference

---

[8] Edward Yarnold, "Baptism and the Pagan Mysteries in the Fourth Century," *Heythrop Journal*, XIII (1972), 247-67.

[9] *First Apology* 61; Jurgens, 54.

to the Mithraic meal reveals the connection he makes between the initiatory rite and the meal. He notes that the Mithraic initiation rite also includes a meal with water and bread, but he claims with typical early Christian disdain that this is a falsification of the Eucharist fabricated by the devil, surely in order to cause confusion among Christian believers.[10]

Since Baptism was regarded as an initiatory rite, it was to be expected that both the language and the symbols of the prevalent mystery rites, which were initiatory by nature, would eventually creep into the Christian rite. Thus at an early stage the shape of Baptism was influenced by this type of religious culture. For the sake of historical accuracy it is necessary to add here that while the Church during these first two centuries welcomed elements of mystery rites, she absolutely condemned idol-worship and refrained from the use of anything related to it: temples, use of incense and candles, and *pompae* or the ornate carriages of idols. Descending from the monotheistic tradition of Judaism, the Church had a physical aversion for such things; she regarded them as devil worship. Not so those elements of pagan initiation rites which could shed light on the meaning of Baptism and clearly indicate it to people as the Christian counterpart of pagan initiation rites.

Baptismal Elements in the Third and Fourth Centuries

In the third century more cultural elements found their way into the rite of Christian Baptism. Unlike in the preceding centuries, the process of baptismal inculturation in this period was characterized by a broader cultural base. The Church began to admit into the liturgy of Baptism not only suitable initiatory elements from the pagan mystery rites, but also socio-cultural rites that were not strictly connected with idol-worship. Her "liturgists" then did this at random, with no overall planning, and with enviable creative spirit. They had,

---

[10]   According to Yarnold, "apart from common terminology, there are other striking points of resemblance between the Christian and pagan ceremonies themselves: scrutinies, catechesis, the learning of sacred formulas, fasting, stripping, anointing, immersion, the putting on of a white robe, consignation (even with a permanently visible sign in the form of a tattoo or brand), a meal of initiation (a honeyed drink forms part of both the Eleusinian rites and the neophyte's first communion) all feature in both Christian and pagan rites." *Ibid.*, 135.

one might say, the fantasy and vigor of youth. Many of the things they did would quite simply be unthinkable today. Yet we cannot reproach them for lacking sense of responsibility. They took time to explain to the people the meaning of what the Church was doing. What were some of these cultural elements and how were they explained?

1. Baptismal Anointing: The first time mention of the practice in the Western Church of anointing the neophytes is in Tertullian's book *On Baptism* which he wrote toward the year 200.[11] We note in passing that also for the first time we receive information regarding the epicletic blessing of the baptismal water, the mention of the Church in the baptismal formula, and the preference for the festivals of Easter and Pentecost as days for conferring Baptism.

As regards anointing, Tertullian records that after Baptism the neophytes are anointed, it would seem, on the crown of their head, "as Moses anointed Aaron unto priesthood."[12] He describes the rite as a generous pouring of oil. "The oil," he writes, flows down our bodies." Tertullian explains the meaning of anointing in the context of the anointing performed by Moses on Aaron, namely unto priesthood. Perhaps he was thinking of this when he wrote in his *Exhortation to Chastity*, "are we of the laity not also priests?"[13]

A point of interest here is the origin of this rite. Baptismal anointing is nowhere to be found in the New Testament. In fact, it is not mentioned even by patristic literature prior to Tertullian.[14] We know that certain mystery rites observed the practice, and so it is possible that Christians borrowed it from them. But what makes the practice Christian is the meaning that was attached to it: the priesthood of the baptized. To bring this out, Tertullian employs a biblical type, the

---

[11]   *De Baptismo*, in *Corpus Christianorum* I/1 (1954), 277-95. B. Botte, "Le symbolisme de l'huile et de l'onction," *Questions liturgiques* 62 (1981), 196-208.

[12]   *De Baptismo* 7, 282.

[13]   *De Exhortatione Castitatis* in *Corpus Christianorum* I/1 (1954) 7, 1024.

[14]   Botte thinks that the following statement of Tertullian in *De Corona* (chapter 3) refers to baptismal anointing: *Hanc si nulla scriptura determinavit, certa consuetudo corroboravit, quae sine dubio de traditione manavit.* The text seems, however, to refer to *linea serra.*

anointing of Aaron. Later authors, like Ambrose of Milan and Cyril of Jerusalem, explained the meaning of this postbaptismal anointing in the same way as Tertullian. For instance, Ambrose in his work *The Mysteries* tells the neophytes: "You were anointed that you may become a chosen race, priestly, precious; for we are all anointed unto the kingdom of God and unto priesthood with spiritual grace."[15]

Biblical typology, both from the Old and the New Testaments, was a favorite method among the Fathers for reorienting cultural elements to the Christian mystery. Tertullian applies this method also to the baptismal water, when in connection with it he recalls the water of creation, the great deluge, the Red Sea, and the Jordan River. Biblical typology was probably the best method at hand to insert culture into the stream of salvation history and thus make it a bearers of the Christian mystery.

In addition to the postbaptismal anointing, there existed another anointing which was made before the baptismal bath. The third-century author of *Apostolic Tradition* distinguishes two kinds of baptismal oil blessed by the bishop: one he calls "oil of thanksgiving" (which we today call chrism), the other, "oil of exorcism." After the rite of renunciation the author directs the presbyter to anoint the candidate with the oil of exorcism, as he prays, "Let all [evil] spirits depart from you." He gives no further explanation of this rite, although the formula clearly points to exorcism.[16] A century later Ambrose of Milan in his mystagogical catechesis *The Sacraments* delivers the following instruction to neophytes regarding the prebaptismal anointing: "You were anointed as an athlete of Christ, as one who will fight the battle of this world."[17] It is difficult to miss the allusion to 1 Corinthians 9:24-27, which describes Christian life in the context of athletes in the arena, though it is unlikely that the rite was introduced with this biblical passage in mind. Yet does not this allusion to athletes allow us to detect the entry of a secular ritual

---

[15]   *De Sacramentis/De Mysteriis*, ed. B. Botte, in *Sources Chrétiennes* 25bis (1961) 6, 117.

[16]   *La Tradition Apostolique de Saint Hippolyte*, no. 21, p. 46. R. Cabié, "L'initiation chez Hippolyte," *Mens Concordet Voci* (Paris, 1983), 544-58.

[17]   *De Sacramentis* I,4, 55.

into the rite of Christian Baptism? Is it not possible that baptismal anointing, whether it was done before or after the sacramental bath, was in some way influenced by the practice of athletic anointing, that is, massaging the body of athletes with oil before the combat? This could sound trite and banal. However, in the context of early cultures where there was no neat distinction between the sacred and the profane, where the daily preoccupations of life intertwined with the supranatural reality, where mortal combats in the arena were invested with divine purpose, could the "anointing" of athletes be considered trite and banal? And in a situation where neophyte Christians found themselves surrounded by the lures of paganism or were subjected to hostility and persecution, what could have been more meaningful for them than anointing?[18]

2. Toward the West and the East: Some Oriental versions of *Apostolic Tradition*, namely the Sahidic, Arabic, and Ethiopic, direct those who are being baptized to face the West as they renounce Satan. The symbolism is rather obvious. The West is the region where the sun sets, where there is darkness, and hence where Satan ruled. This ritual detail was observed by some churches as far as Milan in the time of Ambrose, but not by the Roman Church (which probably did not consider it appropriate).[19] After the rite of renunciation the catechumens faced the East, saying: "Father, Son, and Holy Spirit, I believe in you, I bow before you and place myself at your service."[20] Again the symbolism is obvious. For the early Christians, Christ was the *Sol Salutis*, and they believed that as he had ascended toward the East, he would return on the last day also from the East. Yet we should not disregard the influence of the cult of the sun which was introduced by Emperor Aurelian when he made the *Sol Invictus* the god of the Roman empire. At any rate, the practice of facing the East at the baptismal rite would have received a friendly welcome from the new converts, especially along the Mediterranean where the sun cult was firmly established. As late as the seventh century, the Church of Rome still observed the tradition of facing the East at some parts of the mass like the *Gloria* and the collect.

---

18 G. Winkler, "The Original Meaning of the Prebaptismal Anointing and its Implications," *Worship* 52 (1978), 24-25.

19 *De Mysteriis* 2, 109.

20 *La Tradition Apostolique*, note, 46.

3. Cup of Milk and Honey: A charming baptismal rite, which did not survive the test of time, is mentioned in *Apostolic Tradition*: a cup of milk mixed with honey offered to neophytes between the reception of the consecrated bread and wine.[21] The positioning of this rite leaves a sharp impression of recklessness. There was doctrinally much at stake regarding the possible popular interpretation of the cup. But the author takes the necessary precautions. He urges the bishop to explain diligently to the neophytes the meaning of the cup.[22] According to him, the mixed drink symbolizes the "fulfillment of God's promise to our ancestors that he would lead them to a land flowing with milk and honey." The symbol fits perfectly the meaning of Baptism as *pascha* or the passage of God's people through the sacramental water of Baptism to the Church. Having crossed the new Jordan, they enter the new promised land flowing with the eucharistic milk and honey. Ritually the place of the mixed cup in the order of Communion seems to strengthen the meaning of the Eucharist as the fulfillment of God's promise.

One might be tempted to conclude that since the author uses biblical typology to explain the mixed drink, he must have derived the practice directly from the Old Testament. But this would seem unlikely. Outside the core of apostolic tradition, liturgical forms (especially the explanatory rites) seem have developed not by the process of incorporating biblical elements to the liturgy, but by admitting into them suitable elements of contemporary culture and investing them with biblical meaning. It would be rather amusing to picture the early liturgists reading through the pages of Scripture in search of ritual elements which they could possibly use as introductory or explanatory rites of the liturgy. They were pastors and catechists who had a keen perception of how their people lived their lives in the cultural milieu of the time. They were profoundly cognizant of people's rituals, their needs, and their aspirations. These they introduced into the liturgy, so that the liturgy would not be divorced from the reality of human life. They were great liturgists, because they were pastors. Tertullian alludes to the same practice of offering to the neophytes

---

[21]   *Lac et melle mixta simul ad plenitudinem promissionis quae ad patres fuit, quam dixit terram fluentem lac et mel. 21, 56.*

[22]   *De universis vero his rationem reddat episcopus eis qui percipiunt. Ibid.*

the cup of milk and honey. In his work, *The Crown*, he writes, "After we have been welcomed [by the bishop], we taste the cup of milk and honey which signifies concord."[23] The word "welcome" roughly translates the Latin *susceptio* or *munus susceptionis* which was the Roman legal term for a father's official claim that the new-born infant was his.[24]

Can we trace the source for the cup of milk and honey in the Roman cultural milieu? The ancient Romans had the custom of giving milk mixed with honey to new-born infants. The drink was expected to strengthen them against sickness and the influence of evil spirits. It was thus considered to possess an apotropaic quality. But together with the *susceptio* it could also have signified the act of welcoming the infant to the family. Tertullian had this probably in mind, when he described the mixed cup as *lactis et mellis concordiam*. But the early Church might possibly have been inspired by 1 Peter 2:2's baptismal discourse: "Like the new-born infants you are, you must crave for pure milk." One difficulty with this is the unlikeliness of direct borrowing from scriptural passages. It is not difficult to imagine that the Roman custom had its share in the introduction of the cup into Christian rite of initiation. Nor should we lightly dismiss the possible influence of the Eleusinian mystery rite which included the offering of a cup of honeyed drink to the initiates.

4. White Garment and Lighted Candle: Ambrose of Milan, Gregory of Nyssa, and Cyril of Jerusalem mention the white garment and the lighted candle which were given to neophytes. The white garment was explained as symbol of Christian dignity or of the Church's baptismal innocence. In *The Mysteries* Ambrose writes: "You received the white garment as sign that you had put off the covering of sins, and had put on the chaste robes of innocence."[25] Again we can ask where and how the rite originated. It could have

---

[23]   *De Corona* in *Corpus Christianorum* II/2 (1954), 1042-43: *Inde suscepti lactis et mellis concordiam praegustamus.* Note the temporal relationship between *suscepti* and *praegustamus.*

[24]   *Susceptio* in this legal context is echoed by the Rule of St. Benedict, c. 58, which carries the title *De Disciplina Suscipiendorum Fratrum* (Collegeville, 1981), 266.

[25]   *De Mysteriis* 7, 118.

been inspired by the *toga candida* of the Roman citizens, hence symbolizing the admission of the neophytes into the "heavenly city." There was also the white *toga virilis* worn by Roman boys at the end of their fourteenth year of age, but its similarity to the baptismal garment is not immediately clear. A more likely source is the initiatory white garment used in the Mithraic mystery rite. On the other hand, the use of candles, which Christians until the fourth century did not have because of association with pagan worship, was introduced into the baptismal rite, most probably to illustrate the meaning of baptism as *photismos* or enlightenment.

5. The Washing of Feet: The washing of the feet of neophytes as they ascend from the baptismal pool is attested to by Ambrose of Milan in his work *The Sacraments*.[26] Ambrose defends this Milanese practice against Roman critics who felt that it was too secular an act to be incorporated into the sacred celebration of Baptism. He notes that the Church of Rome itself used to observe it in the past, but "perhaps on account of the multitude [of neophytes] the practice declined." Considering the famous Roman sense for practicality, Ambrose's guess might not be far from the truth. Ambrose concludes the debate with these lapidary words: "In all things I desire to follow the Church in Rome, yet we too have our common sense. Others elsewhere have the right to keep their practices; we also have as much right to keep ours."

In defense of his local church's practice, Ambrose searched for a biblical basis which he quite easily found in John 13's washing of feet at the Last Supper. But was this also its direct inspiration and source, or did it serve merely as a biblical type? For one thing, this New Testament type is not convincing, especially since it was inserted in the context of a meal, not of Baptism. But it was his way of giving scriptural force to a local tradition. We may note in passing that Chapter 53 of the sixth-century Rule of Benedict directs the abbot and the entire community to wash the feet of guests who come to the monastery. At a time when most people travelled on foot, nothing could have been more soothing than water for one's tired and

---

[26]   *De Sacramentis* III,1, 72-74.

dusty feet. Washing the feet of guests was a sign of welcome and hospitality. Could this have been the original meaning of this Milanese baptismal footwashing (*pedilavium*)? It would seem that the washing of feet upon coming up from a pool of water has little sense outside this cultural setting.

6. Baptismal Terminology: The influence of the pagan mystery rites upon Christian Baptism was not confined to ritual gestures. *Photismos* or enlightenment, *loutron* or bath, *mystagogia* or the initiatory instruction, *mystes* or the instructor, and *myomenos* or the initiate, were words which the pagans shared with Christians. These were words whose meaning an average Christian would have easily grasped and probably used with a certain awareness that pagans had entered them even earlier in their religious lexicon.

But the influence did not come only from mystery rites. In the writings of Tertullian dealing with Baptism, there are words which possessed a legal character. Tertullian, it will be remembered, was a jurist. In his book *The Crown*, he calls the rite of baptismal renunciation *eiuratio*. This legal term was used to indicate cessation of contractual service. Applied to Baptism, it implies that the Christian has disclaimed all further obligation to serve the devil. In another book, *The Spectacles*, Tertullian speaks of the baptismal profession of faith as *sacramenti testatio* and *signaculum fidei*.[27] These terms had likewise a legal force. They were used in reference to the oath of allegiance soldiers swore to the Roman emperor. Used for Baptism, they reminded the Christians that they had solemnly vowed to serve Christ alone and with absolute loyalty. By employing such legal terms, Tertullian impressed a certain juridical character on the neophytes' act of renunciation and profession of faith. He seems to tell them that these were serious things that should not be taken lightly.

Summary

From this historical review of the rite of Baptism in the early Church we gather the following information.

---

[27] *De Spectaculis* in *Corpus Christianorum* I/1 (1954) 24, 248.

1. The core of the New Testament tradition on Baptism, which consists of washing in water with the Trinitarian formula, was the axis around which the ritual shape of Baptism in the early Church developed. It is not easy to determine the role which culture played in the ritual elaboration of the baptismal bath and the wording of the formula. From an early period immersion seems to have been the normal way of washing, though infusion (pouring) must, on occasion, have also been admitted. Likewise preference was expressed for running or living water, probably to stress symbolism. At least by the third century the baptismal water was already being blessed in an epicletic manner and explained in the light of biblical typology. The baptismal formula itself, as early as the second century, seems to have been already elaborated in a creedal form. In the third century it developed fully into the form of the Creed and would stay so until the ninth century, when the short declarative form was introduced in the Western Church.

2. The pagan mystery rites have imprinted unmistakable marks on Christian Baptism. Both the ritual and verbal elements of these rites found their way into the baptismal celebration. Several words like *mystagogia* and *mystes* have become part of standard Christian vocabulary. On the other hand, some symbols which could have been derived from mystery rites like the giving of white garment and the lighted candle are now part of the baptismal practice. The Church's program of incorporating elements from pagan initiatory rites, provided these did not obscure Christian faith, can be explained by the nature of Baptism as a rite of initiation.

3. Other cultural elements, which did not necessarily come from the mystery rites, also exerted influence on the baptismal liturgy. Examples are prebaptismal anointing, washing of feet, the cup of milk and honey, and the legal terms used by Tertullian when he spoke of baptismal renunciation and commitment. It seems that at a certain point in history the moral implication of Baptism, such as absolute loyalty to Christ and the Church's faith, especially in times of persecution, led Tertullian to adopt legal terms that would emphasize the moral aspect of Baptism.

4. Underlying all this was an attempt to bring the Christian liturgy closer to the experience of people. Concretely this meant admitting into the baptismal liturgy those suitable elements from religious and other cultural traditions that were able to illustrate the meaning of the sacrament. In several instances these elements became part of the introductory or the explanatory rites of the baptismal liturgy. Thus while the apostolic core of Baptism remained basically the washing in water with the Trinitarian formula, new elements were introduced to elaborate the ritual shape of Baptism. This process is what is known today as inculturation. It aims ultimately to render the baptismal rite culturally accessible to people, because it is expressed in words, actions, and symbols with which they are familiar.

5. The early Church used a method which is called biblical typology. After considering whether a particular religious or cultural element was suitable for the baptismal liturgy, the early liturgists searched in Scriptures for a corresponding or appropriate type (or foreshadow). This was part of the process of critiquing culture, of being countercultural. The idea was to reorient the meaning of the cultural element, so that it could enrich the people's understanding of the sacrament. It was a matter of reinterpreting culture in the light or context of the Christian mystery. Sometimes though the biblical types have only a vague or distant similarity with the cultural element, or they might even ignore its original meaning. This was part of being countercultural. From the cultural standpoint anthropologists might regard this as a negative aspect of biblical typology. The mixed cup of milk and honey, for example, fits the paschal dimension of Baptism, but its original cultural meaning is not at all evoked by the Exodus typology. In other words, we should also consider the question of cultural evocation, when we introduce cultural elements into the liturgy. James 5:14, which deals with the anointing of the sick, is a fine example of cultural evocation: oil was normally used to soothe the pain of the sick. Nonetheless, biblical typology has the distinction of allowing culture to participate in salvation history as it unfolds in sacramental celebrations.

6. In conclusion, we may note with envy and admiration how the early liturgists were filled with creative and venturesome spirit. For example, the cup of milk and honey offered to neophytes at their first Communion was surely at the fringes of what was acceptable be-

cause of the real risk of misinterpretation. Today such a practice would simply be unthinkable. But alas times have changed. Yet something of the youthful boldness and creativity of the early liturgists is always needed by the Church. And this is what inculturation is able to bring about within the confines of what liturgical tradition allows.

CULTURAL SETTINGS OF ARCHITECTURE FOR BAPTISM IN THE EARLY CHURCH

S. Anita Stauffer

Baptism is by water and the Spirit (John 3:5). While the Holy Spirit can be anywhere and everywhere, water needs a container, a place to be. In nature, of course, water's containers are oceans and seas, lakes and ponds, streams and rivers. It was in those large natural water "vessels" that Christian Baptisms first occurred. The spatial context of Baptism was the natural world created by God.

Jesus was baptized in the River Jordan, but most other New Testament accounts of Baptisms do not indicate where they took place. For example, there was the Baptism of the Ethiopian eunuch by Philip, which happened simply when they "came to some water," and the two "went down into the water," where Philip baptized him (Acts 8:36, 38). The closest we come to having a location mentioned is in Acts 16:13-15, in which Lydia and her family were baptized in a river outside a gate to Philippi.

Just as the writers of the New Testament seem to have assumed that Baptisms would be done in natural bodies of water and thus did not exert much effort in describing the places, so too in post-apostolic times. In the first two or three centuries of Christianity, the usual sites for Baptism were also natural bodies of water: streams, rivers, lakes, and the sea.

The *Didache*, a church manual probably from Syria sometime between the mid-first and mid-second century, said that Baptism in the Triune Name is to happen "in running water," but added that if there is no running water, "other water" could be used. In Rome in the mid-second century, the First Apology of Justin Martyr indicated simply that Baptism occurred "where there is water."[1] In approximately A.D. 215, in Rome, the *Apostolic Tradition* of Hippolytus said that the water should be "pure and flowing."[2] The presbyter stood "at the water," as the deacon and candidate went "down...into the water."[3] It is not known whether this was in a natural body of water or perhaps a pool in a building. In Carthage, North Africa, sometime in the late-second or early-third century, Tertullian wrote that it "makes no difference" whether Baptism happens "in a sea or a pool, a stream or a [fountain], a lake or a trough...."[4] Here, then, is an acknowledgment that both natural bodies of water and constructed pools were being used for Baptism.[5]

As early as the second century, while there were persecutions of Christians, sometimes Baptism probably occurred in the baths and courtyard fountains of private homes and perhaps in small public baths. Domestic baths as well as monumental public baths were all over the ancient Roman world; bathing was a prominent part of the culture in which early Christians found themselves.

In the early and middle third century, private houses began to be renovated to become Christian house churches. The oldest one which has been found by archaeologists is in Dura-Europos, in what is now Syria. Typical of middle-class homes of that area and time, it was built in peristyle form, around a central courtyard. (House churches varied considerably by area. In Rome they were more likely to have been in apartments, but in Syria and North Africa the peristyle plan around a courtyard was typical.) Two rooms were combined to serve as the eucharistic space, and another room was transformed into the baptistery. The mid-third-century font—the earliest font which has

---

[1]   English text in E. C. Whitaker, *Documents of the Baptismal Liturgy* (2nd rev. ed.; London: SPCK, 1977), 2.

[2]   XXI:2; Whitaker, 5.

[3]   XXI:11; Whitaker, 5.

[4]   *On Baptism* 4; text in Alexander Roberts and James Donaldson, eds., *The Ante-Nicene Fathers*, III (New York: Charles Scribner's Sons, 1918), 670-671.

[5]   For an illustrated history of early Christian fonts and their theology, see S. Anita Stauffer, *On Baptismal Fonts* (Nottingham, England: Alcuin/Grove Joint Liturgical Studies, 1994), and the videotape *Re-Examining Baptismal Fonts* (Collegeville, Minnesota: Liturgical Press, 1991).

ever been discovered—is a rectangle, which seems to have been the normal shape of the most ancient fonts. The rectangle, of course, is the shape of a coffin or sarcophagus. What is interesting is that this font with its niche resembled Roman and Syrian tombs.[6] However, the way this font was constructed matched "that of the basins found in the Roman baths at Dura."[7] Thus, in this earliest font, there are architectural connections with both bathing and burial. These connections are important culturally as well as theologically and liturgically.

The earliest fonts seemed always to be rectangular, as at Dura-Europos. The first font in Aquileia, northeastern Italy, dated to the mid-fourth century, and was also rectangular. Originally it may have been the bathtub of the first-century Roman house on which the church was built. It was not uncommon for baptisteries to be built over baths in the Roman world, because the water source and drain would already be in place. It is interesting to recall the understanding in First Corinthians (6:1) of Baptism as bath, as being washed in the name of Jesus, being cleansed from sin and purified by the Holy Spirit. But the main point is that an architectural form from the Roman culture was adapted for Christian liturgical use.

In the fourth century, particularly after the Roman Emperor Constantine ended the persecutions in A.D. 313, special places for Baptism were constructed or adapted. During that period, generally, adult Baptism was the norm, and it usually occurred during the Easter Vigil. To accommodate all of the candidates for Baptism, and to provide privacy, since they were baptized naked, the baptisteries in the West were usually detached from or only loosely attached to the church buildings. These early baptisteries—that is, the buildings in which the fonts were located—have at least two architectural antecedents, two cultural references to the Roman Empire.

---

[6]   See C. Hopkins, *Christian Church at Dura-Europos*, Preliminary Report of Fifth Season of Work 1931-1932 (New Haven, CT: Yale University Press, 1932), 249ff.

[7]   Carl H. Kraeling, *The Christian Building*, in C. Bradford Wells, ed., *The Excavations at Dura-Europos*, Final Report VIII, Part II (New Haven, CT: Dura-Europos Publications, 1967), 26.

One architectural antecedent of early baptisteries in the West was the Roman bath. The earliest important baptistery in the West, the Lateran in Rome, was modeled after a bath. The history of the Lateran baptistery is exceedingly complicated, but in brief it was built on the site of a first-century mansion in Rome, over which a bath had been constructed. The circular room of the frigidarium (or cold bath) was adapted into a baptistery in the mid-fourth century. In plan the original Lateran font or pool was very similar to two frigidaria in Pompeii. What is not known, however, is why some baptisteries were based on plans for Roman baths. Was it because of the understanding of Baptism as bathing, or was it simply because the baths suggested a practical way to construct a facility for that much water? It does seem that Roman public bathing practices influenced to some degree early Christian baptismal practices, so it is not surprising that this culture would also have influenced baptismal architecture in Rome.

While the Lateran baptistery in Rome was influenced by bath architecture, the other most important ancient baptistery, that of Milan, was influenced instead by burial places, specifically by imperial mausolea—buildings for the burial of members of the imperial family.

The fourth-century baptistery of St. Ambrose, in Milan (where Ambrose baptized Augustine in A.D. 387), was modeled after a third-century imperial mausoleum in Milan.[8] Both the baptistery and the mausoleum are octagonal buildings with alternating rectangular and semicircular niches. The baptistery was probably built about A.D. 380, and it was approximately 19 meters in diameter. But again, what is not known is *why* the baptistery was built on the octagonal plan of the mausoleum. Some scholars have been quick to say that it was to give architectural expression to the paschal understanding of Baptism in Romans 6—that Baptism is being buried and raised with Christ—and that therefore using the plan of a burial edifice was only natural. But others wonder if it might simply have been convenient, in planning the centralized baptismal space, to use the plan of another centralized space which was nearby, namely the mausoleum of

---

[8]   For details on both the baptistery and the mausoleum, see Mario Mirabella Roberti and Angelo Paredi, *Il Battistero Ambrosiano di San Giovanni alle Fonti* (Milano: Veneranda Fabrica del duomo, n.d.); and Mario Mirabella Roberti, *Milano Romana* (Milano: Rusconi Immagini, 1984).

Maximian. We may never know which theory is correct—but what is important is that a mausoleum structure from the imperial culture was the architectural prototype for an extremely important early Christian baptistery.

The font or pool in the Ambrosian baptistery in Milan was octagonal, rather than circular like the Lateran font in Rome. The archaeological remains of the font show that it was large—about 6 meters across. It had two steps on seven of the sides. On the eighth side, where Bishop Ambrose stood to preside at Baptism, there were no steps. Presumably the candidate descended the steps on one side, was immersed,[9] and came up the steps on the opposite side of the font. It seems clear from an inscription in the baptistery as well as in Ambrose's writings,[10] that the symbolism of the number eight was very important.[11] The inscription connects the number eight with Christ's resurrection, and hence with the octagonal font, the eight sides symbolizing the Eighth Day, the day of Christ's Resurrection, the eschatological dawning of the new age which we enter in Baptism. Ambrose himself, no doubt basing his theology on Romans 6, wrote that Baptism "is a death, not in the reality of bodily death, but in likeness. When you are immersed you receive the likeness of death and burial, you receive the sacrament of his cross."[12]

Ambrose also spoke of the font as "a kind of grave."[13] For whatever reason the Ambrosian baptistery and font are octagonal, Christians in late fourth-century Milan could easily have made a visual connection with the octagonal imperial mausoleum—and thus the paschal understanding of Baptism would have been natural. The connection

---

[9]   Ambrose, *De Sacramentis* II:19, 20, 23.

[10]   See F. J. Dölger, "Zur Symbolik des altchristlichen Taufhauses," in *Antike und Christentum*, 4 (1933-34); and Richard Krautheimer, *Studies in Early Christian, Medieval, and Renaissance Art* (New York: New York University Press, 1969), 115-141, especially 138.

[11]   Krautheimer points out, however, that "symbolical significance is something which merely accompanied" rather than determined particular shapes; *Studies*, 122.

[12]   *De sacramentis* II:23; translation in Edward Yarnold, *The Awe - Inspiring Rites of Initiation: Baptismal Homilies of the Fourth Century* (Slough, England: St. Paul Publications, 1971).

[13]   *De sacramentis* II:19; Yarnold, 117.

between burial and Baptism was easy to grasp in the fourth-century culture of Milan. The church had adapted a secular architectural form and given it a new, although related, meaning.

In addition to baths and mausolea, there are least two other architectural influences on baptisteries from Roman culture. The first is the peristyle, or colonnaded courtyard, which was frequent in houses in ancient Tunisia, North Africa. Often there was a pool or a basin within the peristyle. The sixth-century baptistery of Dermech I in Carthage, Tunisia, also had such a peristyle. Unlike the domestic peristyles, however, the baptistery was undoubtedly covered by a roof. But once again, the church took a common architectural form from Roman culture, and adapted it for liturgical use.

Considerably more radical than copying an architectural feature of a Roman house was transforming pagan temples into churches, which happened at least several times in fifth- and sixth-century Tunisia. In Thuburbo Majus, a pre-existing pagan temple was transformed into a Christian church. The temple's *cella*, where the statue of the divinity was placed, was used for the baptistery. The room was left essentially the same, but the statue of the pagan god was removed, and a font was installed in the center of the room. The font was cruciform, or cross-shaped, making a very clear statement that Baptism is participation in the death and resurrection of Christ; the old pagan self is crucified and buried in the waters of the font. Another site in ancient Tunisia where the *cella* of a pagan temple was transformed into a baptistery is Jbel Oust. Again, the statue of the pagan god was removed, and an in-ground font was placed in the center.

Baptismal fonts as well as baptisteries have architectural antecedents in Roman culture. Some basins from Roman houses in Tunisia were of the quatrilobe form (that is, with four rounded lobes). This form was also used frequently, by the sixth century, for Christian baptismal fonts. Examples of quatrilobe fonts remain in Henchir el-Faouar, Carthage, and Kelibia. The very elaborate font from sixth-century Kelibia, now in the Bardo Museum in Tunis, is 1.4 meters deep, and about 1.7 meters across. The entire surface is decorated with mosaic. Here again is an influence from Roman culture in North Africa. It was very common for pools and basins in Roman houses and baths in second-and third-century North Africa to be decorated with mosaics, and quite often fish were depicted. It is natural that in a place like Tunisia, on the Mediterranean Sea, fish would be shown frequently in fountains and basins in mosaics in the Roman period. Sometimes they were used simply for their decorative value, and perhaps sometimes also because fish were thought to have a magical value in "increasing or preserving" prosperity, or for good luck.[14]

Since baptismal fonts are essentially pools, it is not surprising that fish would also be used in their decoration, though with a transformed meaning. In Christian mosaics of the fourth- to sixth-centuries in North Africa, often "The faithful were likened to fish, born from the water of Baptism."[15]   On one lobe of the Kelibia font, a dolphin is in the center, surmounted by a monogrammatic cross. The dolphin often symbolized the resurrected Christ. All in all, to understand the meaning of the symbolism of this font, we think of Tertullian from nearby Carthage, who wrote in his sermon on Baptism: "We, being little fishes, as Jesus Christ is our great Fish, begin our life in the water, and only while we abide in the water are we safe and sound."[16] We can conclude that in this time and place—the late sixth century on the Cap Bon peninsula of North Africa—those who designed the font for the Kelibia congregation took the fish motif from common Roman mosaics, and used it for the font. However, the meaning of the fish was transformed, reinterpreted to be a visual image of the meaning of Baptism. Thus, here is an iconographic convergence between pagan culture and Christianity, but one which is external. That is, the fish design was used, but its meaning was changed. In the Kelibia font, a pagan artistic pattern was used, but it was infused with Christian meaning. Clearly by this time, Christians in Kelibia had overcome some of their suspicion of all things pagan, a suspicion held by Tertullian several centuries earlier. By the late sixth century, there was some level of interaction between Roman culture and Christian baptismal fonts. (It is perhaps also

---

[14]   Katherine Dunbabin, *The Mosaics of Roman North Africa* (Oxford: Oxford University Press, 1978), 126.

[15]   Margaret A. Alexander, "The Symbolism of Christianity," *Archaeology* (1950), 244.

[16]   *De Baptismo* I; translation by Ernest Evans, *Tertullian's Homily on Baptism* (London: SPCK, 1964).

true of baptismal liturgies in ancient Tunisia, but all of the texts were destroyed in the Arab invasion at the end of the seventh century, so the only remaining evidence of liturgical life are the archaeological monuments—the remains of churches, baptisteries, and fonts.)

Similar iconographic assimilation is evident much further south in Tunisia, on the font at the church of Vitalis in Sbeitla. The mosaic design on the top surface of the rim is a laurel garland, a common motif in Roman mosaics of the area. In Roman iconography, laurel was understood as a symbol of eternity. Used on a baptismal font, the meaning was transformed to refer to the eternal life which is entered in Baptism. The interior of the Vitalis font is 2.3 meters long and 1.2 meters deep. Compared with fonts of the same period in, for example, northern Italy, it is amazingly deep. Perhaps the extraordinary depth of many of the fifth- and sixth-century North African fonts was also influenced by the surrounding Roman culture.

 In the land that is now Tunisia, the people in the Roman and early Christian period obviously loved water. Every city had large and small bath complexes, and some of them are absolutely monumental. One of the most striking things about visiting Tunisia today is seeing all of the ancient public baths, domestic baths, aqueducts, springs, cisterns, and other water devices that abound everywhere in the arid climate. The peristyles and other courtyards of private homes almost always had one or more basins or pools for water.

The people of the fourth and fifth centuries in Tunisia clearly valued water for bathing, for drinking, and very much for pleasure. For example, there is a very striking water cascade and basin in a house in Utica. Water, spouting up from pipes, poured over the mosaics making the fish look as if they were alive. The lower pool probably dates to the second century, and the slanting cascade to the fourth or fifth century. Water was not just a necessity of life for these people; it was also clearly a source of great delight. Indeed, there is abundant archaeological evidence in Tunisia of bathtubs in private homes as early as the Punic period—five centuries before Christ![17]

---

[17]   See Mhamed Hassine Fantar, *Kerkouane: Une cite punique au Cap-Bon* (Tunis: Institut National d'Archeologie et d'Art), 1987.

In addition, every city was built near a water source and boasted large public bath complexes. In what has always been a very dry land, baths public and private, as well as decorative and recreational pools were obviously very important in the Roman era. Perhaps the depths of many of the ancient Tunisian fonts reflects the influence of the importance of water in the surrounding Roman culture.[18]

Thus far we have considered possible influences of culture on baptismal fonts. There is also a possible countercultural connection—that is, the possibility that the design of some early Christian fonts in ancient Tunisia was intentionally antithetical to the surrounding culture. There were many cruciform fonts in North Africa in the sixth century. Unlike some other shapes of fonts, the cross shape did not occur in public or private baths in Roman culture of ancient North Africa. Even while adapting some Roman mosaic iconography, it might be that designing fonts in the shape of an instrument of torture and crucifixion was a statement that to be Christian is to reject at least certain things in the surrounding culture. Perhaps the cruciform font is even a reference to the periodic persecutions of Christians in North Africa.

In this sense, some ancient North African fonts might provide an icon or an image for the complex relationship between worship and culture. Christian worship stands in a complex juxtaposition to the cultures of the world. Without a doubt, it is vital that Christian liturgies and church buildings be hospitable to people in their particular cultures around the world. But also without a doubt, it is vital, too, that Christian worship and its spaces transcend all cultures. Christ, the Word made flesh, seeks ultimately to transform all human culture. The entire relationship between Christianity and culture is multifaceted and very complicated. It is vital to seek to discern when it is theologically appropriate to contextualize Christian worship, and when it is theologically necessary to be countercultural and transcultural. Both dynamics seem to have occurred in the form and iconography of early Christian baptisteries and fonts in North Africa.

---

[18] Regarding water, see David Soren, Aicha Ben Abed Ben Khader, and Hedi Slim, *Carthage* (New York: Simon and Schuster, 1990), especially chapters IX and X.

EUCHARIST
IN THE NEW TESTAMENT
AND ITS CULTURAL SETTING

Gordon W. Lathrop

The New Testament itself evidences an awareness that the cultural treasures of the nations are to be both welcomed and criticized in the life of the Church. Thus, the Fourth Gospel makes use of themes and symbols drawn from current Jewish Tabernacles observance[1] or current Greek Dionysian myth.[2] But it also critically requires both sets of cultural material to yield to Christ, the true water-source, the true revolution in religion. It is "water" from Christ's heart, from his death, which will water the whole earth, not the repeated libations in the Temple at the feast of Tabernacles (John 7:38-39; 19:34-35). It is the "wine" of Christ's "glorification," of his cross, which will both gladden and cleanse us, assuaging all thirst, not either Dionysian drunkenness or continued Jewish purification rites (John 2:4-11; 13:1; 19:28-30). Baptism and Eucharist can be seen as celebrating these assertions of Christian faith. In Christian worship as well as in John's Gospel, both Jewish and pagan cultural symbols are freely used *and* strongly criticized.

If the Church can be understood as, in some sense, like the city of God which the Revelation of John sees as "coming down out of heaven" (21:2), then the entrance of the nations into that Church can be explicitly described as both welcome and critique (21:24-27). Into God's city—and, by extension, into the Church—the nations come, the kings with their "glory" and the people with their "honor." This weighted burden brought by rulers and people, this carried treasure,

---

[1]   John 7:37-39. On the custom of pouring out water in the Temple during the feast of the Tabernacles, perhaps as a rain-making prayer or as an eschatological symbol, see C. K. Barrett, *The Gospel According to St. John* (London: S.P.C.K., 1962), 270-271. *Cf.* Ezekiel 47:1-12; Zechariah 14:8.

[2]   John 2:1-11. On the incognito wine-maker as Dionysus, whose ecstasies were intended to overthrow established religion, see Barrett, 157-8.

can be interpreted as the "cultures" of the nations. The apocalyptic image is, of course, an elaboration of the old prophetic hope that the nations would at last come to Jerusalem as to the center of the earth, bringing their wealth for the building and sustenance of the city (*cf.* Isaiah 60). But the bringing of "the cypress, the plane, and the pine, to beautify the place of my sanctuary" (Isaiah 60:13) also implies the coming of the craftspeople—and therefore the coming of the *culture*—of the nations (*cf.* 1 Kings 7:13-14). Their "skill, intelligence, and knowledge" is to enter into the city in praise of God and God's light-giving mercy. In the Christian vision of Revelation, that Light is to be seen in the "Lamb" in the midst of the city; the nations bring their "glory" not to the Temple but to Jesus Christ who is at the center of the praise of God's new city.

But, in the Revelation text, the vision of the open gates and the welcomed treasures of the peoples are immediately paired with an evocation of powerful critique. Not only must the royalty and the wealth of the nations, their cultures, be reoriented to an utterly new center—the central presence of God and the Lamb—but "nothing unclean will enter" the city (Revelation 21:27). The "treasures" are both reoriented and sifted; not *every* cultural phenomenon is welcome, certainly not those which serve "abomination or falsehood," not those incapable of serving God and Christ at the center.

Except for the centrality of the Lamb, the Revelation text does not give us clear criteria for the critique of cultural gifts, for what is "abomination." But it does give us an *image* for what much of the rest of the New Testament *actually does* in reorienting and sifting cultural materials. The interesting thing is that the Revelation image is one of welcome and critique in the context of *worship*: the nations come streaming toward that which, in the Christian vision, replaces the Temple—toward God and the Lamb at the center of the open-gated city. Similarly, in John's Gospel, the Tabernacles libations, the "six stone water jars for the Jewish rites of purification," and the Dionysian practices all are *ritual* matters. They are all re-used verbally in the Gospel to proclaim the meaning of Jesus, and they can at least suggest some meanings surrounding the actual use of water-washing and wine-drinking in the Church.

But, as we have seen in considering the critique and reorientation of those water-washings which became Christian Baptism,[3] much of the New Testament does have an idea of what constitutes the "unclean" which may not enter. It is exactly the opposite of what usually constitutes ritual uncleanness. For Mark or Paul or John, for example, that is "unclean" which excludes the unclean, the outsiders, the women or the crucified. That is "unclean" which limits the free Gospel and which thus cannot be ordered to the centrality of the Lamb. Not every cultural phenomenon is welcome in the city of God. Insofar as the Church and its worship mirror that city, this critical sorting must occur in Christian liturgy as well.

Meal Practice and Culture

Among the treasures of the nations are their meal practices. Meals create and express a human group. Meals are complex symbols, not just functional edibles. They are a primary form of culture, passing on the primary values of the group. To know what a people eats, who eats it, in what order and when, is to know a great deal about a society.[4] To know what stories are told at a community's meals and what symbols function there, passing on what values, is to know the heart of a culture.[5] Meals *are*, concretely, communities and their survival. Meals are far more than simply enough food to get through the next hours. They symbolize and participate in social relationships, hierarchies, inclusion and exclusion, the boundaries around a group and the transactions across those boundaries.

It comes as no surprise, then, that the story of Israel, the narrative of Israel's identity, can be told in the terms of a series of symbolically important meals: Abraham and the angels at Mamre,[6] the Passover and the manna,[7] the meal of Moses and the elders before God on

---

[3] See "Baptism in the New Testament and its Cultural Setting."

[4] See Gillian Feeley-Harnik, *The Lord's Table* (Philadelphia: University of Pennsylvania Press, 1981), 11: "In establishing precisely who eats what with whom, commensality is one of the most powerful ways of defining and differentiating social groups."

[5] See Feeley-Harnik, 6-18

[6] Genesis 18:1-15.

[7] Exodus 12; 16.

Sinai, prototypical of all the meals of sacrifice in Israel,[8] and the promised great meal on the mountain,[9] to name only the most important. Such stories, of course, do not establish a clear pattern for the actual celebration of a meal. But they do determine a tradition of meaning: this community's national identity is reconfirmed and celebrated in common meals.[10]

Hellenistic Judaism seems to have recalled such stories while using an essentially Greek pattern for the actual manner of communal eating. The characteristics of the *deipnon* and the *symposium*, the general Mediterranean way of eating, were mixed with a memory of the sense that eating was always before God, as a people.

Ancient classical sources allow us to make some generalizations about this Mediterranean pattern for a meal.[11] Houses included a dining room, often as the most important of rooms and usually arranged for reclining at the meal. A banquet, which may be taken as the paradigmatic example for all meal practice, involved a host and invitations: the meal was for a select group, often only free men.[12] Arrangement at the table indicated rank. The meal was preceded by washing, of the feet, by a servant, and of the hands: "water over the hand, tables brought in" says one ancient synecdoche for what modern English would express with the phrase "we dined."[13] The actual eating, the "tables," seems to have followed this order: sometimes an appetizer course, with conversation; then the *deipnon*, the meal itself; then the removal of the tables, the bringing of the mixed wine-cup, the ritual libation to the gods, and the *symposion* or common drinking and entertainment (or, among the philosophically inclined, drinking and

---

[8]   Exodus 24:9-11.

[9]   *Cf.* Isaiah 25:6.

[10]   For an interesting history of Judaism conceived as a history of its *meals*, see Jacob Neusner, *A Short History of Judaism: Three Meals, Three Epochs* (Minneapolis: Fortress Press, 1992).

[11]   For the following, see Dennis E. Smith, "Greco-Roman Meal Customs," in *The Anchor Bible Dictionary* (New York: Doubleday, 1992), 4:650-653; and Dennis E. Smith and Hal E. Taussig, *Many Tables* (Philadelphia: Trinity Press International, 1990), 23-28.

[12]   *Cf.* Plato, *Symposium*, 176e.

[13]   Athenaeus, *Deipnosophists* 14.641d, in Smith and Taussig, 25.

conversation). Of this order of the meal, Plato reports: "Socrates took his place on the couch; and when the meal was ended, and the libations offered, and after a hymn had been sung to the god, and there had been the usual ceremonies,...they were about to commence drinking."[14]

Many of these very characteristics recur in the shape of Jewish meal practice as it can be reconstructed for the time of Christian origins from the New Testament and other ancient sources. Also among the Jews, common features of meals included dining rooms,[15] invitations[16] and the closed male group,[17] washing,[18] reclining,[19] rank at table,[20] and the two-staged banquet, with the mixed cup "after supper."[21] At meals, Hellenistic Judaism was culturally *Greek*. Indeed, even the daily sacrifice in the Temple could be described in the Greek pattern: a meal for God (Sirach 50:12-13), a libation for God (50:14-15) and an "entertainment" (50:16-19)!

Only now, this cultural material had undergone a transformation to serve the purposes of primary Jewish values. There was to be no idolatry here, so the libation after the *deipnon* and before the *symposion* became the blessing of God over the mixed cup. The Greek ceremonial moment at the end of the *deipnon*, over time, became the great place for the Jewish *Birkat ha-Mazon*,[22] the lengthy prayer of

---

[14] *Symposium* 176a, translated in B. Jowett, *The Republic and Other Works by Plato* (Garden City, N.Y.: Anchor, 1973, 1973), 323.

[15] Josephus, *The Jewish War* 2:8:129; Mark 14:14.

[16] Luke 14:12-14.

[17] 1QS 5:13; 6:20:22; Josephus, *JW* 2:8:129; Mark 14:17-18; 16:14.

[18] Josephus, *JW* 2:8:129; 1QS 5:13; Mark 7:1-21; Luke 7:44; John 13:5.

[19] Matthew 9:10; Mark 14:3,18 par.; *Mishnah Berakoth* 6:6.

[20] 1QS 6:4; Matthew 23:6; Luke 14:7-11.

[21] Luke 22:20; 1 Corinthians 11:25.

[22] See already Jubilees 22:6-9, where Abraham eats and drinks and then blesses God in a three-fold prayer, praising God for creation, thanking God for salvation and protection, and beseeching God for the future. This is the very pattern found in the much later *Birkat ha-Mazon*, in the prayer of Polycarp over his own death as over a libation-cup at the end of a meal in the *Martyrdom* 14, and, with an inversion of the first two parts, in the prayer after the meal in *Didache* 10. Note also that the pattern of Sirach 50 is meal, libation, hymns and prayers.

thanksgiving and supplication which many scholars see as the proto-type of Christian *eucharistia* at table.[23]   Indeed, all food was to be taken with thanksgiving, and this fact yielded the sense that the meal is taken before God. Furthermore, the principal ceremonial food was now not only wine but also bread—recalling the bread of Abraham's and Gideon's meals with God, of the Passover, of the Exodus, and of the Temple. So, not only the *symposion* but also the *deipnon* was now begun with ceremony; the meal was always inaugurated with a blessing over bread, as a kind of perpetual first-fruit ritual.[24]   The meal was thus a reconstitution of the people as God's people and a reinsertion in the faith of Israel, the faith that God has made the world and redeemed the people. The washing had, thus, become a religious ritual, an enactment of the purity necessary to be part of the people.[25]   At Qumran "the purity of the holy men" came to be a standard term for the communal meal,[26] and such a term would have been widely understandable. Furthermore, the Greek philosophical *symposium*, the conversation over wine after the *deipnon*, in certain circles was to become a discussion of *torah*, a teaching of the "phi-losophy" of Israel.[27]

The meals of the context of Christian origins, then, were already complex cultural symbols. Determined in pattern by the dominant Greek culture, these meals were also events in which Jewish identity was reconstituted by bread, by prayer, by ritual purity, and by teach-ing and narrative memory. The very fact that the meal prayers came to be addressed—perhaps already in the first century—to God as *melech ha-olam*, "king of the universe," and to pray for the reign of

---

[23]   Thomas J. Talley, "From Berakah to Eucharistia: a Reopening Question," *Worship* 50 (1976), 115-137.

[24]   Josephus, *JW* 2:8:130-131: "the baker serves the loaves in order...the priest prays before the meal...both when they begin and when they end, they honor God as the supplier of life." Translation in Todd S. Beall, *Josephus' Description of the Essenes Illustrated by the Dead Sea Scrolls* (Cambridge: Cambridge University Press, 1988), 17. Cf. 1QS 6:4-5; 10:14-15; 1QSa 2:17-21. Note also the priority of the blessing over bread in *Mishnah Berakoth* 6:5.

[25]   Josephus, *JW* 2:8:129: "themselves now pure, they go into the dining-room, even as into some holy shrine." Translation in Beall, 17.

[26]   See Beall, 56.

[27]   Sirach 9:15-16; 32:3-6; John 13-17; Acts 20:7.11; *cf.* 1QS 6:2-3.

God gives evidence of the depth of this complexity. These meals took place in a distressed social situation, full of military oppression and apocalyptic longing. The prayers at meals could be seen as an interior, religious response — even as a protest — to the horrors of that other *melech*, the one who ruled the Roman empire.

The Origins of the Eucharist

From a Christian point of view, this Hellenistic-Jewish meal practice, this concrete cultural pattern, was a treasure which was "brought into the city." Indeed, it came to the center of the life of the churches. And the sorting occurred. Exactly as with Baptism and its relationship to the cultural washing symbolism, in the Eucharist the New Testament communities both continued and critically re-formed Hellenistic-Jewish meal practice. Both a *yes* and a *no* were spoken to the complex cultural meal symbolism we have here briefly explored.

The Eucharist of the Church is rooted in the fact that the churches were meal-keeping communities[28] which remembered the meal-keeping of Jesus and which believed that they encountered the risen Christ "in the breaking of the bread."[29] These meals, of course, would have been in the general cultural mold of Mediterranean/Greek practice. They were held in dining rooms or, at least, in houses, perhaps using the largest available room or the enclosed and partially covered courtyard of the house. In any case, "the church in the house of so-and-so"[30] should probably be understood as another indication of the meal-fellowship which met at a certain house. There would have been hosts at these meals—perhaps the householder, originally— responsible for the arrangements and the rituals of the meal. The meals themselves involved a use of wine after the *deipnon*[31] and, perhaps, a continuing conversation.[32]

---

[28]   Acts 2:42,46; 20:7,11; 1 Corinthians 10:16-21; 11:17-34; Didache 9:1; 14:1; *Martyrdom of Polycarp* 7:1; Pliny the Younger, Letter 10.

[29]   Luke 24:13-35.

[30]   *Cf.* Romans 16:5; 1 Corinthians 16:19; Philemon 2; Colossians 4:15.

[31]   See above, note 21.

[32]   See Acts 20:7,11.

But these meals of the Church were also marked by particular Jewish transformations of the Greek *deipnon* practice. Also in the Christian community there was prayer over bread at the outset of the meal.[33] Also among Christians the ritual of the libation and its hymnody had become the thanksgiving and petition after supper.[34] Here, too, the sense may well have prevailed that a meal was taken before God, that a meal involved a reinsertion into the faith that God made the world. It is these meals, meals which came to be held especially on Sunday,[35] meals which were probably marked by much diversity in actual practice, which were the primitive form of Eucharist. In the earliest period of the Church, we cannot make any easy distinction between *agape* meals and Eucharist;[36] there is only the *deipnon/symposion* of the Church.

But why was the Church a meal fellowship? One might answer, exteriorly, that the Christian movement was a society, a club, and the most obvious means available to such a society in Greek culture was the shared meal. Surely a deeper answer, however, one closer to the meaning of these meals for Christians, is that Christians remembered the meal practice of Jesus. At the center of that memory, as at the center of concentric circles of meaning, they came to remember the association of Jesus' death and resurrection with meals and, most especially, his own words of promise and gift at a meal.

It was these words—and their association with the principal ceremonial foods and ceremonial acts of the Hellenistic-Jewish *deipnon/symposion*, the blessing over bread at the beginning and the lengthy thanksgiving over the cup at the end of the meal—which enabled the Christian Eucharist to survive the banning of supper clubs imposed upon the Christians in the persecutions. The bread-blessing of the beginning and the wine-prayer of the end of the meal, accentuated by Jesus' words, could be simply moved to the morning, away from

---

[33] Mark 6:41 par.; 8:6 par.; Luke 22:19; 24:30; 1 Corinthians 11:23-24; Didache 9:3.

[34] See above, notes 22 and 23. *Cf.* the prayer of Polycarp after supper in *Martyrdom* 7:3-8:1.

[35] Acts 20:7; Didache 14:1; Pliny the Younger, Letter 10. *Cf.* Luke 24:13-35, 36-43; Revelation 1:10; 3:20.

[36] See the work of Bernd Kollmann, *Ursprung und Gestalten der frühchristlichen Mahlfeier* (Göttingen: Vandenhoeck und Ruprecht, 1990).

supper, away from the *symposium*, away from the insider club, away from the looming, Greek-cultural possibility of drunkenness.[37] The food of the meal, the actual food the church was accustomed to take together, could then be given away.[38] The Eucharist was finally more than a Hellenistic supper and *symposium*, even one with Jewish over-tones. It was the meal-gift of Jesus Christ alive in the Church.

We cannot say much with certainty about the historical Jesus. How-ever, the widespread attestation, in many different sources, of the striking character of his meal practice makes that practice one of the more likely things than can be said of him. As in all Hellenistic-Jewish practice, he prayed over bread at the beginning of the meal.[39] Also for Jesus, then, the meal was an event of the people before God. Indeed, the meals of Jesus seem to bear a special witness to the tor-tured situation of this Jewish cultural symbol for faith in the God of creation and covenant. Echoing the Jewish meal prayers which speak of the "kingdom of God," the meals of Jesus enacted a prophetic sign of the profoundly needed nearness of the reign of the *melech ha-olam*. Thus in Mark 2:18-20, Jesus and his company do not fast but rather feast, in celebration of the presence of the "bridegroom," an old prophetic image for the presence of God in Israel. And the peti-tion in Jesus' prayer for "daily bread" may well be a way in which he sees the hoped-for "day of God" already imaged in the shared meals of his company.

But Jesus welcomed "the many" to participation in these signs. He ate and drank with sinners. "Forgive us as we forgive," he also taught his disciples to pray. If meals were indeed signs of God's coming day, Jesus then welcomed sinners to life-giving participation in that day. He rejected the rules of purity, intended to accentuate the iden-tity of the very people the meal was meant to constitute. There are women at his meals. While the Gospels show him visiting dining

---

[37]   1 Corinthians 11:21-22,34; 2 Peter 2:13; Jude 12.

[38]   Thus, when we first find clear evidence for the Christian Eucharist no longer being a full meal but a bread-and-wine rite after a Word service, we also find, in the same description of the Eucharist, reference to a collection for the poor: Justin Martyr, *1 Apology* 67. See Gor-don Lathrop, *Holy Things: A Liturgical Theology* (Minneapolis: Fortress Press, 1993), 44.

[39]   *Cf.* Mark 8:6; Luke 24:30.

rooms on invitation, he is also shown in the dining rooms of sinners or welcoming the outsiders into other dining rooms, or using no dining room at all. The great "feeding" stories have him outside, with no walls to limit the approach of the thousands. A dining room will hardly be sufficient to hold the people of the highways and byways, the lame, maimed, blind, who figure in his meal parable.

The churches seem to have continued these meals of Jesus. Sometimes the invited, closed group of the Greek *deipnon* or the group-constituting concern for purity found at Qumran could emerge as a central ecclesial meal practice as well: witness the factions of Corinth (1 Corinthians 11:21-22) and the fierce critique of meal-participants in Jude and 2 Peter (2 Peter 2:4-13; Jude 8-12). For the most part, however, the old sense that eating with Jesus enables outsiders and sinners to participate in God's day, and that Jesus' invitation is wide, did maintain its crucial centrality in the great writers of the New Testament tradition. Only now it is the crucified and risen one with whom the Church eats. It is the blood of Christ which is for "the many;" his cross is their participation in the meal of God's kingdom (Mark 14:24-25).

Paul's criticism of the Corinthian meal-practice is a criticism of factionalism, of the socio-economic exclusiveness of those who actually eat and drink (1 Corinthians 11:17-34). This critique is so strong that it leads Paul to propose that full-scale food consumption take place away from the Christian gathering, while the bread and cup which bind "the many" into one body (10:16-17) remain. If the Corinthian community was also following the practice, which we can detect elsewhere, of keeping this communal meal on Sunday, it is fascinating that we find the same Paul who urges the elimination of banquet and drinking also urging the Corinthians to set aside gifts for the poor on the first day of the week (16:2; cf. 2 Corinthians 8-9).[40] But the center of this critique is Paul's assurance that the shared bread and cup are participation in the body and blood of Christ, are the proclamation of the death of the Lord until he comes. The bread of the beginning of the Jewish *deipnon* and the blessing-cup of the

---

[40]   See above, note 38.

Jewish *symposion*, now associated with Christ's presence and gift, are enough to stand for the whole meal, enough to unite "the many" into one body.

In Mark's Gospel one finds repeated reference to Jesus' meals,[41] doubtless as a challenge to the Church, not unlike Paul's challenge to Corinth, to find the center of the meaning of its meal practice in the crucified Christ. The whole of Mark's Gospel seems to ask, "Are you able to drink the cup that I drink?" (Mark 10:38), while giving away the bread to sinners and outsiders (7:28). In Mark, of course, the new cup of the kingdom of God is none other than the cup of Christ's death (14:25,36; 15:36); it is finally in and because of this death that the outsiders and sinners are welcome to God's meal.

Indeed, if the practice of the Church was a regular *deipnon* and *symposion*, it is important to note that it is at a reclining meal that a woman proclaims Jesus' forthcoming death (14:8). This woman *signs* in love what is *done* in hatred and lust, shame and abuse, by and to the daughter of Herodias, the anti-type of the unnamed woman at Bethany. This girl, providing the entertainment at Herod's *symposion*, obtains the death of John the Baptist in the midst of the meal (6:17-29). This grisly foreshadowing of the Last Supper helps us to see the more clearly that the final meal of Jesus has no *symposion*; the bread and cup and their meaning are given in the midst of the supper, and the meal ends with a hymn instead of the mixed cup and conversation or entertainment. Here, the *symposion* cup is the cup of the garden (14:36) and the surprising, spoiled-wine drink of the cross (15:36) which *is* the arrival of the kingdom of God.

These three banquets—at Herod's birthday, at Bethany, and at Passover—are reported in Mark's Gospel not to establish a rubrical pattern of Christian celebration, but to propose the deepest meaning of the Church's meal-practice. At Passover, the bread and cup are set out in the middle of the meal, rather than framing it, and the *symposion*

---

[41] Mark 2:15-28; 3:20; 5:43; 6:31,34-44; 7:1-23,27-28; 8:1-9,14-21; 10:38-39; 11:12-13; 12:39; 14:3-9,12-26,36; 15:36. It is also of interest that the two great parables which frame the ministry of Jesus in Mark, that of the sower (4:1-20) and that of the vineyard (12:1-12), use the imagery of the production of *bread* and the production of *wine*; see Bas van Iersel, *Reading Mark* (Edinburgh: T. and T. Clark, 1989), 155-156.

is moved to the garden, in order for us to understand, in a manner appropriate to Mark, that the cross welcomes all—"the many," the sinners, the women—to God's table. In Mark, in a way much like Paul, an exclusive *symposium* of invited, powerful or "pure" men is strongly criticized. It is very likely that Mark's church continued to keep their meal-*cum-symposium*; these Christians too would have had the cup "after supper." Such was the available meal-practice. But they could only have understood that practice more profoundly after reading Mark.

The critical transformation of the meal is also to be found in John. Here, what is in the midst of the meal, giving meaning to the meal, is Jesus' washing of feet (John 13:1-5). This washing is the more noticeable since it is not where it belongs in Hellenistic meal-practice—at the beginning, at the welcome of the guests—and since it is done by the host. This slave-service is, in John, a sign of the cross. Just as in Mark, this literary device should not be understood as ecclesial rubrics but as an indication of critical meaning: the Church's *deipnon* is nothing if it is not focused on the cross. The very first action of the arrival of Jesus' "hour," that time toward which the whole Gospel has been leaning in pre-figuration, is the meal made into footwashing. So, Jesus' cross-service *is* the presence of the water made into new wine (2:4); it *is* the pouring out of the Spirit like water (7:39). In John, the *deipnon* becomes the footwashing, an image the more powerful because the Johannine Jesus has already said that he gives his flesh and blood to eat and drink (6:53-58). And, in John, the *symposion* becomes the "farewell discourse" and "high-priestly prayer" (13:31—17:26), a discourse marked by talk of going away and coming again, of Jesus' death and resurrection, and centered in the image of the vine (15:1-11), as is fitting to this wine-accompanied meal tradition. Again, the Fourth Gospel is not proposing a pattern for liturgy nor rejecting the practice of the Church's meal. It is breaking the cultural symbolism of the meal,[42] requiring it to speak the meaning of Jesus Christ's cross and resurrection. Henceforth, in the Johannine community, the *deipnon* and the *symposion* are to be seen in new depth.

---

[42] See "Baptism in the New Testament and the Cultural Setting."

This growing awareness of the gift of Jesus, this finding of the center of the concentric circles of eucharistic meaning, yielded the Eucharist in the Church. The Eucharist did not have two sources, an *agape* and a cross-cult meal.[43] It had many sources—the many meal-keeping Christian communities, with their own versions of Greek/Mediterranean meal practice—and, yet, a single source—the gift and presence of Jesus Christ. Its origin was in a "breaking" of Hellenistic meal meanings to the purposes of the Gospel, a breaking found already in the meal practices of Jesus, and received and understood and believed in the texts of Paul, Mark and John.

The Lukan texts[44] provide a relatively clear idea of what may have been the actual meal practice of the Church. Here, the Hellenistic-Jewish bread before the meal (sometimes with the *kiddush* cup of the festival, as well; Luke 22:17)[45] and wine "after supper," together with their associated prayers, come to recognizable expression. It is also true that Luke helps us see the growing association of the meal with the Word: perhaps as a *symposium* conversation in Luke 22:21-38 and Acts 20:11, but also as something that looks much like a Word-service, the reading of texts and preaching, in Luke 24:13-27 and Acts 20:7. It is this latter pattern which prevails in the Church's ongoing worship life. But it does so, at least in part, because Mark and John and Paul have seen the gift of the bread and cup as something larger and more important than the closed-room, invited-guest, stomach-filling event of a supper club. Indeed, the Word-service conjoined with the bread and cup rite, found in the second-century Church, is a faithful development of the meals of Jesus with which the Church began.

The Eucharist as Broken Symbol

For central texts of the New Testament, then, the Eucharist is one of the *broken symbols* of the Christian faith. It is made out of received

---

[43]   *Pace* the influential classic study of Hans Lietzmann, *Messe und Herrenmahl* (Bonn: A. Marcus and E. Weber, 1926). For a more recent two-meal theory, see Xavier Léon-Dufour, *Sharing the Eucharistic Bread* (New York: Paulist Press. 1987).

[44]   Luke 22:14-20; 24-30-31; Acts 20:7-11.

[45]   *Cf.* Didache 9:2.

cultural material, still full of the power to hold the human experience of the world into such meaning as that culture conceives—but that material is also criticized, reoriented, sifted, seen as insufficient and equivocal.

Faithful Christian meal practice *received* current cultural symbolism. The Hellenistic meal enacted a community, ordered that community in rank and meaning, ritualized some contact with the gods, used wine to establish relaxation and, in some circles, conversation about values. The Hellenistic-Jewish meal transformed that symbolic/cultural tradition to serve biblical faith. The community was seen to be Israel before God, and this sense came to expression in meal prayers. The washing before the meal was thus a rite of ritual purification before entering a holy place. Bread came to ritual importance. Idolatry was resisted. Thus, the libation to the god became the thanksgiving and beseeching addressed to Israel's God over the cup after the meal. The whole meal practice proposed eschatological meaning in a troubled time. Christians, too, used the *deipnon* and the *symposion*, found this gathering to be a regular center of order and meaning, used bread and wine and ran the risk of rather too much wine, prayed at table, resisted idolatry, and, with the Jews, believed that their meals had something to do with the last day of God.

But faithful Christian meal practice also *resisted* the cultural power of the banquet, in both its Greek and its Hellenistic Jewish forms. At their best, at least according to the counsel of Paul and Mark, Christian meals sought to enact openness and grace and to resist cultic concepts of purity.[46] Early Christians did this, if in nothing else, by becoming a community of men and women at table and by taking a collection for the hungry and by understanding that the cup was "for the forgiveness of sins" (Matthew 26:28). They did this even though the evangelical ideal of the open-air meal and the streaming thousands was not possible, and the unity of rich and poor at table may not have been frequently realized. They nonetheless built a critique of the closed meal-society into their tradition: the bread and cup were for "the many." They accentuated the bread and wine while giving the rest of the food away. If they used a dining room, to begin with,

---

[46]   In addition to texts considered above, see Acts 10:9-16 and Galatians 2:11-21.

for their meals, this dining room needed an open door, like the modern Jewish Passover. Faithful use of the meal, finally, "exploded" out of the dining room into the courtyard and then into the basilica. They did all this by proposing that the eschaton is Jesus Christ crucified. Thus, they filled their meal prayers with reference to him, through whom alone they could stand before Israel's God. Because of this Christocentric meaning, the Eucharist came to be juxtaposed to the Scriptures read of the crucified and risen Christ, and to be linked especially to Sunday.

So then, "blessed is anyone who eats bread in the kingdom of God" (Luke 14:15), one might say of primitive Christian meal practice. But also, "the kingdom of God is not food and drink but righteousness and peace and joy in the Holy Spirit" (Romans 14:17; *cf.* Colossians 2:16). Both texts are true.

Conclusion

Besides meal practice, many more cultural symbols were similarly drawn from the Hellenistic-Jewish matrix of primitive Christianity in the formation of Christian patterns of worship: observance of the week and of *pascha*, the shape and postures of prayer, the very idea of assembly, Scripture reading and preaching, roles in leadership, and music, to name some. But our concern here has been to trace the way in which the New Testament gives evidence of the cultural setting of the Eucharist and the Christian use of that setting.

When we approach the New Testament, inquiring how its material Eucharist is seated within then-current culture, we are given several critical principles for the on-going Christian relationship of worship and culture:

1. Jesus Christ judges and saves all things.

2. The central signs of the Christian assembly are made up of ancient cultural symbols which have been required to serve the purpose of the Gospel.

3. The ongoing history of the liturgy, the manner in which these central things were unfolded and enacted in new cultural situations, should

be evaluated according to the same principle: both welcome and critique. Christians today do well to receive this whole history of cultural interactions, this palimpsest of cultures, as a gift and as a pattern for further work.

4. Word, Baptism, and Eucharist in Jesus' name are not dispensable in new situations. They do need to be done in new ways. In the case of the eucharistic meal, however, fidelity in practice will include the general use of the pattern already found in Luke-Acts: thanksgiving prayers centered in Jesus Christ, the connection to Sunday, openness and the accent on grace, the critique of purity and insiderhood, the use of staple food and festive drink, and the connection to concern for the poor. New cultural material brought to this communal action will also undergo welcome and critique for the sake of the Gospel.

5. The city of God has a center and permeable boundaries, the Lamb and the open gates.

EUCHARIST
IN THE EARLY CHURCH
AND ITS CULTURAL SETTINGS[1]

Anscar J. Chupungco

A number of elements of the eucharistic liturgy show how the early Church developed the shape of the celebration in the cultural setting and context of a home. Of particular interest are such components of the celebration as the place, language, rites, and vessels. These are examined in the light of the domestic character of the Eucharist. The question of music is treated in another chapter.

The Place for Celebration

The Acts of the Apostles, 2:46, depicts an idealized portrait of the Christian community which gathered "day by day attending the temple together and breaking bread in their homes, partaking of food with glad and generous hearts." Acts 20:7-12 records the Sunday breaking of bread presided over by Paul "in the upper chamber" of a house in Troas.

The Eucharist, the specific and characteristic celebration of Christians, was held at home. It is evident that from the earliest times the Eucharist was regarded as a domestic liturgy. The disciples of Jesus attended the temple and synagogue services, but they did not, or more precisely could not, break bread in those places. For neither the temple nor the synagogue was ever meant to be a place for a fellowship meal. The temple was for sacrifices and the synagogue for the proclamation of the Word and community prayers. Fellowship meals, such as the Eucharist, were held at home.

This was the tradition which the Church brought with her when she moved out of Palestine. Before the year 165, Justin Martyr wrote

---

[1]   An elaborated form of this chapter appears in the author's book, *Tradition and Progress*, copyright Pastoral Press, 1994.

that the Christians of Rome, "whether they live in the city or the countryside, gather together in one place" to celebrate the Eucharist.[2] Justin prudently does not specify the "place," for in time of persecution this would be revealing to the Roman emperor the place where Christians gathered. Of course, there is no reason to believe that the place was not the home of one of them. In A.D. 304 the lector (reader) Emeritus bravely admitted to the proconsul of Carthage (North Africa) that "it is in my house that we hold the *dominicum*," that is, the Lord's meal.[3] Acta Saturnini, Datii....., PL VIII, col. 710-11. F Converts offered the use of their homes which, in the Roman tradition, were usually a four-sided structure built around an open courtyard with a well of water at the center. The *triclinium* or dining room, especially if the house belonged to a wealthy family, could easily be rearranged for the celebration of the Eucharist.[4] Rome claims several such houses which can still be visited under the churches of John and Paul, Cecilia, Clement, and Pudentiana. But such houses, even if they were large, might not easily accommodate large assemblies. As the community grew in number, a larger space was needed for the assembly of worshipers.

Since persecutions were sporadic occurrences, in time of peace Christians acquired ordinary houses and adapted them permanently to the requirements of the liturgy. The story is told of Emperor Alexander Severus (+235) who preferred to sell to Christians a house that was in the public domain, "for it would be better that a god, of whatever sort, be adored there rather than to use the building for the sale of drinks."[5] The houses owned or bought by the Christian community for their worship came to be known as *domus ecclesiae*, the house of the community. In the course of time this name was shortened to *ecclesia*, the church building. From here is derived the theology of the house church as the image of the Church community. A famous example of such houses of the Church was the third-century house at Dura-Europos on the Euphrates (in Syria). It had a function room of

---

[2]   *First Apology* 67, ed. L. Pautigny (Paris, 1904). Partial English translation by W. Jurgens, *The Faith of the Early Fathers* (Collegeville, MN: Liturgical Press, 1970), 57.

[3]   *Acta Saturnini, Datii....*, PL VIII, col. 710-11.

[4]   Gregory Dix, *The Shape of the Liturgy* (London, 1982), 19-35.

[5]   English text in R. Cabié, *History of the Mass* (Washington, D.C.: Pastoral Press, 1992), 22.

about 16 feet by 43 feet [4.9 meters by 13.1 meters], which served
for the eucharistic assembly, and a smaller room probably for the
baptistery, as the fresco of Christ walking on the water suggests.[6]

After the conversion of Emperor Constantine there came a dramatic
shift from the simplicity of homes to the splendor of imperial basilicas. The domestic dining room gave way to the large public halls,
where formerly the emperor, seated on the throne, had held court and
given audiences. Yet for all its imposing majesty, what was the basilica but basically one of the function rooms of a Roman house?
There was, of course, more space: a larger nave for the assembly and
ample room in the sanctuary for the table, ambo, presidential chair,
and seats for the presbyters and ministers. Even in the basilica the
Eucharist retained the essential traits of a domestic liturgy, though
on a larger scale. When Constantine decreed in A.D. 321 the observance of Sunday rest in the empire, the celebration of the Eucharist
acquired a more solemn character. Surely the atmosphere and ambience of the imperial hall would, at any rate, have demanded a corresponding liturgical splendor. Prayer formularies took on a more solemn, hieratic, and rhetorical form; gestures imitated the imperial court
ceremonials; and the music became more elaborate requiring trained
performers.[7]

The first Christian basilica was the Lateran palace in Rome, which
Constantine gave as a gift to Pope Sylvester. The emperor ordered
the construction of new basilicas for Christian use: on the Vatican
hill where the Apostle Peter was buried, at Via Ostiense where the
Apostle Paul suffered martyrdom, at Campo Verano where the deacon Lawrence was buried, and in several other places in Italy. His
mother Helena, on her part, had the basilicas in Bethlehem, Nazareth,
and Jerusalem built to commemorate the events of Christ's life. These
roofed structures were rectangular in shape and divided into three or
five naves marked by rows of columns. At the far-end of the apse

---

[6]   J. Boguniowski, *Domus Ecclesiae. Der Ort der Eucharistiefeier in den ersten
      Jahrhunderten* (Rome 1986). N. Duval, "L'espace liturgique dans les églises
      paléochrétiennes," *La Maison-Dieu* 193 (1993), 7-29.

[7]   R. Cabié, "The Eucharist," *The Church at Prayer* II (Collegeville, MN: Liturgical Press,
      1986), 7-123.

was the *cathedra* or chair of the bishop, surrounded by benches for the presbyters and ministers.[8]

Architecture, which is one of the finer expressions of a people's culture, has immensely influenced the development of the shape of the Eucharist from the intimacy of a home gathering to an awesome imperial convocation. The influence of the basilica, as we shall have occasion to see, was felt in both the rites and the language of the celebration. Through the centuries the architectural and artistic design of the *domus ecclesiae* has continued to undergo remarkable modifications from the Romanesque to the Gothic, from the Renaissance to the Baroque, from the neoclassic to the modern and postmodern.[9] But beneath such variations one can perceive the original core: the Eucharist is a meal, regardless of how the cultural setting determines the architecture.

The earliest Christians, whether for theological or practical reasons, chose not to celebrate in temples, whose *cellae* would have been too dark and small and whose open colonnades would have been most unsuitable for a meal. Nor did they gather for the Eucharist in the tiny, dark underground rooms of the Roman catacombs, which being public burial places would have been the worst place for gathering in time of persecutions, not to mention the prospect of celebrating the Lord's Supper amidst entombed bodies. The early Church celebrated in one of their homes or in a house the community had acquired. For the Eucharist is a meal: it is the Supper of the Lord. Attempts to pattern new churches after the temples of other religions, like pagodas and mosques, miss altogether the point about the Lord's Supper as a domestic liturgy. They also miss the point which Cabié has expressed with profound insight. The house of the Church, rather than the temple, signifies the welcome and hospitality the eucharistic community shows to strangers and the poor with whom it shares the same faith in Christ. It "challenges the divisions that run through

---

[8]   Louis Bouyer, *Liturgy and Architecture* (Notre Dame, IN: University of Notre Dame Press, 1967), 39-60.

[9]   Walter Huffman and S. Anita Stauffer, *Where We Worship* (Minneapolis, MN: Augsburg Fortress, 1987); James White and Susan White, *Church Architecture* (Nashville, TN: Abingdon Press, 1989); and S. Anita Stauffer, "Inculturation and Church Architecture," *Studia Liturgica* 20/1 (1990), 70-80.

human society." Cabié presses the point to its limits, when he writes: "a special welcome is to be given to the poor, even if the bishop has to surrender his chair and sit on the floor".[10]

Origen fittingly sums up the domestic ambient of the Eucharist. In his *Homily on Jeremiah* he writes: "Those who celebrate the pasch as Jesus wants will not stay on the lower floor of the house; rather those who celebrate the feast with Jesus go up to the great hall, to the lighted hall, to the adorned hall which is prepared for the feast. If you go up with him to celebrate the pasch, he gives you the cup of the new covenant; he also gives you the bread of blessing: he gives you the gift of his own body and blood".[11] Though the text, coming as it does from Origen, is allegorical, it allows us to catch a glimpse of how the Church in the third century readied the "upper chamber" of their house for the celebration of the Eucharist. The "upper chamber," he explains, signifies hospitality, which the widow showed to Elisha when she readied for the man of God the upper room of her house (2 Kings 4:10). The feast to which Jesus invites us is held in the great hall on the upper floor; it is lighted and adorned, as befits the Lord's Supper. The domestic quality of the Eucharist does not subtract from its festive character. It does not lead to banality and improvisation. Domesticity, to rephrase a proverb, does not breed contempt.

The Influence of Latin on Eucharistic Formularies

An element of the eucharistic celebration, and of the liturgy as a whole, that has been strongly conditioned by culture is the corpus of the early liturgical formularies. The use of living or current language in public worship necessarily involves inculturation in the deepest sense of the word. Language is not merely a compendium of words and phrases; it is above all the mirror of a people's pattern of thought and values. It expresses their cultural traits and identity.[12] That is why the option of the early Church in the West to use Greek and Latin, that is, the living languages of her converts, opened the door

---

[10]   Cabié, "The Eucharist," 39.

[11]   *Homily on Jeremiah* XIX, 13, *Sources Chrétiennes* 238 (1977), 228-30.

[12]   Paul De Clerck, "Le langage liturgique: sa nécessité et ses traits spécifiques," *Questions liturgiques* 73 (1992/1-2), 15-34.

wide to inculturation. What this means is that she formulated the Gospel she preached using the cultural patterns, indeed the philosophical systems of thought, of the Greeks and the Romans. For the liturgy this meant that Greek and Latin became its languages. But this was not all. Greek and Latin were not merely vehicles of communication. Because languages contain and mirror the culture of the people, Greek and Latin impressed on liturgical formularies the thought and value patterns of Greeks and Romans. Thus we may say that the liturgy not only spoke Greek and Latin; in effect it became Greek and Latin.

To appreciate the role of language in the development of liturgical texts, it is helpful to recall briefly the history of the liturgical language in the first four centuries.[13]

Outside Palestine and Syria, Greek *koiné* was the lingua franca of most people in both the eastern and the western regions of the Roman empire. *Koiné* differed from classical and literary Greek in that it was of a popular type. By A.D. 40 and certainly 64, when the Church in Rome was established, the prevalent language in the City was *koiné*. It had become the language of the empire, and the Roman citizens themselves spoke it. It is interesting to note that during the first two centuries, ten out of the 14 bishops of Rome were Greek-speaking. It was to be expected that the Roman Church would use the *koiné* in the liturgy and official documents.

The process of the latinization of the liturgy began, not in Rome, but in North Africa, thanks to the efforts of Tertullian, Cyprian, Arnobius, Lactantius, and Augustine. From these writers we inherited the use in the liturgy of such words as *plebs* or assembly, *sacramentum*, *ordo*, and *institutio*. These words did not originate in a religious milieu, but by force of usage they acquired a distinct liturgical meaning. When Tertullian, for instance, spoke of the baptismal promises as *sacramenti testatio*, he was imposing a Christian meaning on a legal phrase.[14] From North Africa these and similar words found

---

[13] Cyrille Vogel, *Medieval Liturgy: Introduction to the Sources*, (Washington, D.C.: Pastoral Press, 1986), 294-97; Theodor Klauser, *A Short History of the Western Liturgy* (Oxford: Oxford University Press, 1979), 18-24; 37-44.

[14] *De Spectaculis* in *Corpus Christianorum* I/1 (1954) 24, 248.

their way into the eucharistic formularies of the Roman Church. Likewise the first authorized Latin translation of Scripture for use in the Eucharist appeared, not in Rome, but in Africa about the year 250.

The first attempt to introduce Latin into the liturgy of Rome came from Pope Victor I, an African by birth, who died in 203. His success was partial. The language of the Roman liturgy, until the fourth century, remained in a state of transition. It was bilingual, although by the third century Rome was speaking Latin again. It was never an easy matter for the Roman Church to abandon her traditions. Compromise was a preferred solution. Thus the prayer formularies continued to be in Greek, but the Scripture readings were now in Latin. Not until the papacy of Damasus I, who died in 384, did a definitive transition from Greek to Latin take place in the eucharistic celebration of the city. It happened a century too late, but it was nonetheless a courageous enterprise for a Church known for venerating her traditions. We should not regard this as being romantic, but was it not rather difficult to abandon the language used in apostolic times and the age of martyrs in favor of the current?

From the fourth to the late sixth century, the Roman Church developed the Latin liturgical language.[15] Even the Roman liturgy was not built in one day. Those were centuries of an intense creativity that produced several classic prayers for eucharistic use, such as collects, prayers over the gifts, prayers after communion, and prayers over the assembly. These texts have come down to us in sacramentaries or, as these books came to be known from the Middle Ages, missals. A good number of these compositions are preserved in the *Roman Missal of Paul VI*. The chief authors of the early Roman texts were none other than the bishops of Rome: Damasus, Innocent I, Leo the Great, Gelasius, Vigilius, and Gregory the Great. The literary style of the formularies indicates that their authors received their education from the Roman schools of rhetorics, arts, and classical studies. The style of their composition and the product itself pertained more to the segment of the Roman elite than to the ordinary people.

It is not possible to deal here in detail with the different literary forms employed by the authors of the Latin formularies. For the sake of

---

[15]   C. Mohrmann, *Liturgical Latin: Its Origin and Character* (Washington, D.C., 1957).

completeness, however, it might be useful to mention typical examples, such as binary succession, antithesis, *cursus*, and *concinnitas* or symmetry.[16] One of the remarkable rhetorical traits of the early Latin formularies is the *cursus*, which was perfected by Pope Leo the Great.[17] It consists of the rhythmic arrangement of the last word of a line for the sake of cadence and sometimes also to suggest such sentiments as joy and wonder. The vowel length and the accents, both principal and secondary, given to such words constitute what are known to specialists as the *cursus planus*, *tardus*, and *velox*. By their arrangement and composition they are able to produce the desired cadence and sentiments. This is a type of rhetorical device that must have immensely pleased the listeners, provided they belonged to the class of the elites.

A classic example is the Christmas collect composed by Leo the Great, found in the *Sacramentary of Verona*: *Deus, qui humanae substantiae dignitatem et mirabiliter condidisti et mirabilius reformasti....*"[18] The verbs *condidisti* and *reformasti* are both in the *cursus velox*, and they express the sentiments of admiration, joy, and gratitude for God's work of creation and salvation in Christ. One quality of the *cursus* is its ability to imply such sentiments in the way the words are arranged, without the need to employ explicitly the verbs and substantives of admiration, joy, and gratitude. It is not necessary to say, "we admire and thank you for creating humankind;" the *cursus* takes care of that. It is possible to imagine that on any cold Christmas night a good number of the assembly would not have caught the theology behind Pope Leo's dense formulary, but they would have delighted in listening to its rhythmic cadences, symmetrical arrangement of phrases, antithetical construction, and play of words.

---

[16] M. Haessly, *Rhetorics in the Sunday Collects of the Roman Missal* (Cleveland, 1938); M. Augé, "Principi di interpretazione dei testi liturgici," *Anamnesis* 1 (Casale Monferrato, 1979), 159-71.

[17] W. Halliwell, *The Style of Pope Leo the Great* (Washington, D.C., 1939); A. Echiegu, *Translating the Collects of the "Sollemnitates Domini" of the "Missale Romanum" of Paul VI in the Language of the African* (Münster, 1984).

[18] *Sacramentarium Veronense*, ed. L. Mohlberg (Rome, 1978) 1239, 157.

Besides the rhetorical quality of Latin there was another cultural factor that influenced the early eucharistic texts. It is the proverbial Roman sobriety, which the great scholar E. Bishop has called "the genius of the Roman rite."[19] There is agreement among historians today that what used to be regarded as the "sensuousness" of the Roman liturgy was actually not of Roman origin but of Franco-Germanic making. Sensuousness in this use referred to those medieval symbols and formularies which stirred religious sentiments or encouraged some undefinable experience of awe and wonder in the presence of God's mystery. The Romans were a sober and practical people whose language was equally sober and direct. Thus the Roman prayers for the Eucharist which date around the fifth century avoid words that are colorful and picturesque or that tend to arouse human emotions.

A cursory examination of the collects in the early sacramentaries reveals a language addressed to the intellect rather than to the heart of the listeners. Today only a few would probably link the following collect of Gregorian Sacramentary to the Christmas feast: *Deus, qui hanc sacratissimam noctem veri luminis fecisti inlustratione clarescere; da, quaesumus, ut cuius lucis mysteria in terra cognovimus, eius quoque gaudiis in caelo perfruamur.*[20] Translated literally, the text reads: "God, you made this most holy night resplendent with the clarity of the true light. Grant, we pray, that we may experience in heaven the joy of him, whose mystery of light we have come to know on earth." This text, composed for the winter solstice or victory of light over the darkness of winter, understandably focuses on the element of light. But it requires special catechesis to show the association of the feast of Christmas to the winter solstice.

Roman sobriety is even more striking in the prayers after communion. While medieval prayers often spoke of the sacramental bread and wine quite simply and directly as the body and blood of Christ, the Roman prayers, in keeping with the *romana sobrietas*, rarely

---

[19]   E. Bishop, "The Genius of the Roman Rite," *Liturgica Historica* (Oxford 1918), 1-19.

[20]   *Le Sacramentaire grégorien*, ed. J. Deshusses (Fribourg, 1971) 36, 99.

mentioned them. Rather they tend to confine their language to such expressions as "sacraments," heavenly bread," "food and drink," and "heavenly gifts." Not that the early Church in Rome did not believe in the Real Presence, but it was not part of her cultural pattern to depict the mystery with vivid imagery. We have grown used to being told at communion "the body of Christ" and "the blood of Christ." But the Romans of the classical period would have been rather uncomfortable hearing these words as they received the consecrated bread in their hand.

The Roman Canon, which is quoted in part by Ambrose of Milan, is thoroughly imbued with the culture of classical Rome. Its language portrays the Roman taste for a certain gravity in speech as well as simultaneous redundance and brevity. Such phrases at the start of a sentence as *te igitur*, *hanc igitur*, and *unde et memores*, are elegant, hieratic, and solemn. They are difficult to capture in translations. The use of the title *Clementissime Pater* gives to the Roman Canon an imperial tone, and so does the phrase *supplices te rogamus ac petimus*. True to its sacrificial orientation, the Roman Canon uses pre-Christian sacrificial expressions like *accepta habeas*. It incorporated also a pagan funeral inscription, namely *refrigerium lucis et pacis*. The legalistic Roman mentality resonates in the threefold declarations *haec dona, haec munera, haec sancta sacrificia inlibata* and *hostiam puram, hostiam sanctam, hostiam immaculatam*. Lastly, the Roman Canon observes balance in its structure. Balance, which is akin to equanimity, was highly prized by the Romans. This is especially evident in the mementoes of the living and the dead and the double commemoration of saints before and after the narration of the Last Supper.[21]

This rather brief review of the Latin liturgical language reveals how the Roman culture profoundly influenced the texts for the eucharistic liturgy of the early Church. The liturgy was not only in Latin; it was expressed in a highly cultivated Latin, in a kind of *Kulturlatein* demanded by the solemn ambit of the Roman basilica but not necessarily by the familiar setting of a home. Thus, it was accessible al-

---

[21] For bibliography and treatment of the Roman Canon see A. Nocent, "La preghiera eucaristica del canone romano", *Anamnesia* 3/2 (Casale Monferrato, 1983), 229-45; see also E. Mazza, *The Eucharistic Prayers of the Roman Rite* (New York: Pueblo, 1986).

most exclusively to the educated segment of the Roman Church. The majority spoke the *Volkslatein*. In this sense the language of the liturgy itself became rather exclusive; it failed to welcome the masses. It was not congenial for expressing the supreme value of the eucharistic liturgy, namely, hospitality to all regardless of one's station and attainment in life.

The Influence of the Imperial Court Ceremonial

Justin Martyr in his *First Apology* gives us information on the shape of the Sunday Eucharist as it was celebrated in the second century, presumably in a Roman house church.[22] The format of the celebration consisted basically of what are known today as liturgy of the Word and liturgy of the Eucharist. The liturgy of the Word began with readings, by a lector, from both the "memoirs of the Apostles" and the "writings of the prophets," that is, from the New and Old Testament books. This was followed by an explanation of the readings or homily by the *proëstós*, the presider, and concluded with prayers of intercession. The kiss of peace was given at this point, at least when Baptism preceded the Eucharist. The liturgy of the Eucharist began with the presentation (we may presume by the assembly) of bread and wine mixed with water, followed by a "long prayer" recited by the presider. At the end of the prayer the assembly answered "Amen." The second part ended with the distribution of the eucharistic bread and wine by deacons. After the celebration, offerings were made for the poor, widows, and transients of the community. As early as the second century the format of the Eucharist, which no longer included the *agape* of the apostolic period, though it was still a home celebration, was already sufficiently defined to become the type and exemplar of the Roman eucharistic celebration.

The information of Justin, however, gives no clue as to how, if at all, the Greco-Roman culture influenced the celebration of the Eucharist. We presume that the language used was the *koiné*, that the bread and wine were those found in the region, and that the place of gathering was the home of one of the converts. Other than these the cul-

---

[22]   Chapter 67; Jurgens, 57.

tural setting of the Eucharist can only be guessed. While the baptismal liturgy had, as early as the second century, already assimilated traits of the pagan mystery rites, the Eucharist did not seem to have been affected by the communion rites of pagan initiations. On the contrary, the liturgy of the Word appears to have been a direct descendant of the synagogal service, while the liturgy of the Eucharist seems to have been patterned after the Last Supper narrative or at least focused on it.

It was after the fourth century that the ritual shape of the Eucharist began to be increasingly bound up with the culture of the period, thanks largely to the conversion of Emperor Constantine and the Edict of Milan in A.D. 313. For Rome and the other metropolitan cities, especially in the East, culture meant, concretely, the culture of the imperial court. Under the patronage of the emperor himself the Church quite understandably assimilated into her liturgy some of the ceremonials of the "ruling class." Unfortunately, our chief document, the *Roman Ordo I*, dates from the seventh century or the end of the sixth at the earliest, and hence is a rather late record of what transpired between the fourth and the seventh century.[23] However, historical studies supply us with helpful information regarding this time gap.[24] We may reckon that what the *Roman Ordo* describes originated in the time of Constantine or at least during the Constantinian era.

The so-called *Donatio Constantini*, which is quoted by the *Liber Pontificalis*,[25] reports that Constantine gave to Pope Sylvester the Lateran palace as a gift and authorized him to use the imperial insignia, including the throne, and the privilege to have his portrait hung in public halls. We know that in the year 318 Constantine conferred on the bishops, for good or ill—often ill—the power of jurisdiction in civil proceedings. In the process they received titles, insignia, and privileges which belonged to the office of state dignitaries. It was a kind of marriage that produced unwanted offspring. On the other

---

[23] *Les Ordines Romani du haut moyen âge* II, ed. M. Andrieu, (Louvain 1971), 67-108.

[24] A. Chavasse, *La liturgie de la ville de Rome du Ve au VIIIe siècle* (Rome, 1993).

[25] L. Duchesne, *Le Liber Pontificalis: Texte, Introduction et Commentaire* (Paris, 1955), 170-202.

hand, the *Constitutio Constantini*, forged about A.D. 750 under Pope Stephen II, tried to establish the legal basis for the papacy's temporal claims against Byzantium. The document concludes with these menacing words: "Whoever shall transgress these provisions which hold good for all time shall burn in hell with the devil and all the ungodly".[26]

The eucharistic liturgy described by *Roman Ordo I* was the solemn papal mass celebrated at the Basilica of St. Mary Major on the Esquiline hill in Rome on Easter Sunday morning before the year 700. It is not possible nor is it necessary to describe here the entire procedure, which was long and quite complicated. Our interest is in several of its elements which are strikingly imperial in character. The historian Theodor Klauser has identified them for us.[27] The pope rode on horseback from the Lateran palace to the stational basilica. He was accompanied by the mayor and other dignitaries of the city. He wore the *cappa magna*, a cloak that reached to the feet of the horse. This was a garb worn by the emperor for solemn processions. As the pope walked to the sacristy, two deacons supported him ritually on either side. This was a court ceremonial known as *sustentatio*. In the sacristy his ministers surrounded him, as demanded by the Byzantine court ceremonial, in order to assist him as he vested for the liturgy. He put on an insignia called a *pallium* over the chasuble. The *pallium* is a white woolen band with pendants in front and at the back. This was originally another imperial insignia of authority. Although the *Roman Ordo* does not mention the ring, the special shoes, and the *camelaucum*, which later developed into the miter, we may presume that he wore these imperial insignia as well.[28]

As the pope processed to the sanctuary, he was preceded by acolytes bearing seven lighted torches or candles and a censer, while the *schola cantorum* of men and boys sang the introit or entrance song. We note that candles and incense were used in solemn processions to honor

---

[26]   *Constitutio Constantini*, ed. C. Mirbt, *Quellen zur Geschichte des Papstums und des römischen Katholizismus* (Tübingen, 1924) no. 228, 107-12.

[27]   *A Short History of the Western Liturgy*, 59-72.

[28]   R. Berger, "Liturgische Gewänder und Insignien", *Gottesdienst der Kirche* 3 (Regensburg, 1987), 309-406; *A Short History of the Western Liturgy*, 32-37.

the emperor, and that he was greeted by a choir of singers when he entered an assembly hall for public audiences. Before proclaiming the Gospel, the deacon genuflected before the pope to kiss his shoes and to receive his blessing. This curious gesture of kissing the feet was required by the Byzantine court ceremonial. Ministers serving the pope waited on him at the throne and the altar with covered hands, again as demanded by imperial ceremonial. He took communion not at the table but at his throne.

Strangely, the splendor of the imperial court was confined mostly to the entrance rite. Thus the liturgy of the Word was celebrated with less pomp, and the liturgy of the Eucharist with the proverbial *romana sobrietas* which verged on austerity and gravity. During the eucharistic prayer, for instance, the pope stood at the altar alone and recited the prayer with no further ceremonies and without the assistance of hovering and ubiquitous masters of ceremonies. No candles were brought into the sanctuary at the word of consecration, no bells were rung, no incensation of the sacred species was made, and there were no genuflections and signs of the cross. Thus the core or nucleus of the eucharistic liturgy, namely the Word and the Sacrament, remained practically untouched by the drama and pomp of the imperial court ceremonial.

Another quality of the Roman culture which survived the incursion of the imperial ceremonial was the sense of practicality which was deeply rooted in Roman civilization. The papal mass regarded the entrance, offertory, and communion songs as songs of accompaniment. That is why, when the activities they accompanied were over, no less than the pope himself signaled the choir to stop singing. Altar cloths were not spread until the time of the offertory rite, and presumably they were removed after the celebration. The washing of hands at the offertory, which acquired a symbolic meaning during the early Middle Ages, seems to have been dictated by table hygiene.

We gather from this description of the Roman eucharistic celebration before the eighth century that there were two distinct cultural forces at work. One was the ceremonial of the imperial court, and the other was the native Roman quality of sobriety and practical sense. Some have expressed reservations about the elite character of the celebration or the political overtones of the insignia used during

the liturgy. Surely this type of inculturation need not become a paradigm for the Church today. Though the liturgical insignia of bishops
no longer suggest political power but only ecclesiastical leadership,
one wonders if there are no viable contemporary alternatives. A missionary bishop considered substituting the miter with the plumed
headdress worn by tribal chieftains, but alas this form of inculturation
does not free the Church and the liturgy from the entanglement with
Constantinian court ceremonials. There is more to inculturation than
the change brought about by external adaptation. The miter and the
plummed headdress send the same signal: Church authority patterned
after the imperial system rather than the earlier concept of shepherding.
And certainly liturgical leadership in Word and Sacrament for which
bishops are ordained should not be turned into a caste system.[29]

This period, however, seems to tell us that when the Church in Rome,
and the same must be said of Constantinople, decided to inculturate
the shape of the Eucharist, she chose what was noble, beautiful, and
significant in the culture of the people. The period under discussion
should not in any way be so idealized as to suggest to the Churches
of today to assimilate only what is elite and exclusive in their culture. What it suggests is that, regardless of the socio-economic con-
dition of the people, the eucharistic celebration should be noble, dignified, and beautiful. And nobility of spirit, dignity, and beauty are
not an exclusive possession of the elite and the powerful.

The Early Eucharistic Furnishings

By tradition the Eucharist is a domestic liturgy in meal form. This
leads us to conclude that from the beginning the Church used for the
Eucharist the dining table and vessels at home rather than the altar
and temple vessels for sacrifice. It was largely due to the theology of
the Eucharist as the *anamnesis* or sacramental memorial of Christ's
sacrifice that the Church adopted the sacrificial language of the Old
Testament: altar, temple, sanctuary, priest. This does not mean that
the Jewish or pagan altars, which were normally square structures of
stone or marble upon which victims were slain or burnt, were intro-

---

[29]   See Gordon W. Lathrop, *Holy Things: A Liturgical Theology* (Minneapolis, MN: Fortress
        Press, 1993), 180-203.

duced into the homes, the *domus ecclesiae*, or the basilicas. Yet in the thinking and language of early theologians the eucharistic table was an altar by extension, because upon it the Church celebrates the *anamnesis* of the once-for-all sacrifice of Christ.

What type of vessels did the early Church use for the Eucharist? It seems that in the first century the eucharistic bread was kept in baskets, since these were the normal bread containers used at home.[30] Matthew 14:20 and John 6:13, which are eucharistic pericopes, speak of twelve *kophínous* or wicker baskets in which the leftovers from the five loaves shared by the crowd were gathered together. One of the frescoes in the catacomb of Callixtus in Rome portrays seven baskets containing the eucharistic bread. Wine, on the other hand, was stored in pitchers or jars. These were often earthenware, though some were made of metal. It is likely that communal cups, rather than individual ones, were normally used during family meals. They were made from a variety of materials, including glass. The wealthy might own drinking goblets made of precious metals. We can gather from 1 Corinthians 10:16-17 that a communal cup was used during the Eucharist, in order to underline the unity of the assembly. In short, being a domestic celebration, the Eucharist was served in normal house vessels: breadbasket and drinking cup.

By the early third century, wicker baskets were being abandoned for glass and metal patens. Originally patens were dish-shaped vessels large enough to hold loaves of bread. The *Liber Pontificalis* XVI and XVIII informs us that Pope Zephyrinus made a rule for the Church that glass patens should be used for the Eucharist, while Pope Urban I donated 25 silver patens.[31] Likewise we are told that Emperor Constantine donated to the Lateran Basilica seven golden patens, each weighing thirty pounds, and sixteen silver patens, each weighing also thirty pounds. *Roman Ordo I* reports that for the fraction at papal mass the paten was carried by two subdeacons, which seems to suggest that the paten was large and heavy.[32] It is possible that

---

[30]   Edward Foley, *From Age to Age: How Christians Celebrated the Eucharist* (Chicago: Liturgy Training Publications, 1991). The author deals with eucharistic vessels in several parts of the book, which I use gratefully for the information it offers.

[31]   Duchesne, *Le Liber Pontificalis* I, 139 and 143.

[32]   *Les Ordines Romani du haut moyen âge* II, no. 103, 100.

patens from such materials as glass, pottery, and wood continued to be used as late as the eighth century. A curious practice is mentioned by the same *Roman Ordo*: the loaves of bread offered by the faithful were deposited in linen sacks (*sindones* or *saccula*), and at communion the eucharistic bread was again put in linen sacks for distribution to the assembly.[33] The type of vessel for the wine also underwent evolution. Although the eucharistic cups could be made of glass or ivory, and this continued well into the Middle Ages, by the third century they were increasingly made from precious metals. Some of them might even be decorated with images. The principle of a communal cup would make us believe that the size of the cup was determined by the size of the community. Yet again at the seventh-century papal mass recorded by *Roman Ordo I* a "main cup" was used, thus implying that there were other cups, probably for the communion of the assembly. In A.D. 303, in Cirta in North Africa, Munatus Felix, high-priest of the emperor, had the "house where the Christians customarily met" searched. From this account we may surmise that the house was owned by the community, for they customarily met there, and that it was rather amply furnished for worship. Bishop Felix surrendered the possessions of the community, which were mostly for the celebration of the liturgy. The inventory included two golden chalices, six silver chalices, six silver jars, a silver dish, seven silver lamps, two torches, seven short bronze candlesticks, eleven bronze lamps, and several items like tunics and slippers for men and women, presumably for Baptism.[34] Surely the Church in Cirta could not have been poor by any standard, perhaps because the community was generous in providing expensive vessels for the eucharistic celebration.

We may conclude that the table and vessels used for the Eucharist by the early Church reflected her theology of the Eucharist as the Supper of the Lord. Being a meal, it is partaken of by God's family in the setting of a home. The shift from wicker baskets and glass cups to adorned patens and chalices of silver and gold does not at all detract from the original domestic setting of the Eucharist. It merely sug-

---

[33] *Ibid.*, no. 71, p. 91; no. 115, p. 104.

[34] *The Shape of the Liturgy*, 24-26.

gests that some communities counted among their members wealthy patrons who donated generously. It also points to the growth of a theological and cultural awareness, which became prevalent from the time of Constantine, that to the dignity of the Eucharist corresponds the dignity of a cultic meal.

Summary

From the foregoing discussion what clearly emerges is the domestic tradition surrounding the celebration of the Eucharist in the early Church. The place of celebration was the home or a building that could be transformed into a house where the community could gather to hold the "family" meal. Temples, synagogues, and catacombs did not provide the appropriate space for such a meal. The temple was principally for sacrifices, the synagogue for the Word, and the catacombs for the dead. The Eucharist, on the other hand, was a meal that was best celebrated at home, according to the apostolic tradition of breaking bread, *kat' oikon*, from house to house. Even when the *domus ecclesiae* evolved into the royal basilica, there remained a consciousness that the Eucharist was essentially a meal.

We cannot sufficiently stress the importance of the domestic origin and character of the Eucharist. It is the context in which the meal aspects of the eucharistic celebration evolved: architectural space for fellowship meal, furnishings and vessels like dining table and cups, music, table blessing or eucharistic prayer, presider. All these components of the celebration point to the domestic nature of the Eucharist. This domestic character of the Eucharist is the Church's countercultural message today to a world broken by individualism, anonymity, and absence or even denial of family values. In situations like this the image of the Church as "family" gathered around the table of the Lord to listen to the Word and break the bread in fellowship stands both to accuse the world of its fragmentation and to lead it to unity.

It is, of course, true that already in early patristic period the Eucharist was regarded as the *anamnesis*, the ritual memorial in the form of a meal, of Christ's unrepeatable and unique sacrifice on the cross. There has always been an awareness that the Eucharist was more than a fellowship meal. Christians gathered at home to break bread, but did so in order to recall the mystery of the Lord who offered himself in sacrifice on the cross. By this act of *anamnesis* they experienced the presence of the risen Lord as the Word of God was proclaimed, as the bread was broken, as each shared one's faith experience. In a sense they recalled the passion and death of Jesus in their eucharistic assembly, in order to experience his risen presence.

The theology of eucharistic sacrifice successfully imprinted its mark on the thinking and language of early Christian writers. The eucharistic table was increasingly referred to as altar because of its theological association with Calvary. Yet the exterior form of the table remained that of a table for a ritual meal; it was covered with white table cloth as befits a solemn meal. It did not develop into a stone or marble altar for sacrifices in the Jewish or pagan religions, even if at times it might be difficult to recognize it as a dining table.

Likewise the vessels were basically those used at home: breadbaskets and drinking cups. The financial resources of the community often dictated the type and quality of the eucharistic vessels: gold patens and cups, or curiously also linen sacks. Though they came in various materials, shapes, sizes, and decor, these vessels alluded to the original domestic setting of the Eucharist. The shift from house church to basilicas surely had its effect on the style of celebration. The domestic setting, that "private" character of the Eucharist idealized by Dix, disappeared, but even in Constantinian basilicas the vessels, for all their imperial quality, were meant for a meal.

Besides the domestic and meal aspects, language influenced the liturgical shape of the Eucharist in the context of the local Church's culture. Language expresses the people's cultural patterns; it reveals their hidden thoughts and manifests the values they cherish as a people. The extent and depth of inculturation in the eucharistic liturgy is evident in the language of the prayer formularies and in the rites. For the Roman people of the classical period, culture was defined by their proverbial identifying marks, namely sobriety and rhetorics. These became the identifying marks of most of the Roman eucharistic texts as well. The popes who authored them succeeded in incorporating into the liturgy the thought and language patterns of the Roman people, that is, those who belonged to the class of the elite and the educated. The language of these prayers was elevated and dignified, but not easily accessible to many because of rhetoric. The question that comes to mind is, what kind of language should we use in the liturgy to foster the sense of hospitality, of a welcoming language that can address people across social status and educational attainments? Liturgical language should be a vehicle of unity, not class distinction within the household of God.

The acquired political status of Church leaders also profoundly influenced the ceremonial of the eucharistic liturgy in basilicas, especially at the entrance rite, though the rest of the liturgy kept the Roman tradition of sobriety. After the drama of the entrance rite, the mass continued with a simplicity and gravity that seemed to ignore the imperial splendor and magnificence of the basilica. This was especially the case with the liturgy of the Eucharist, which was marked by austerity. Hence, the core of the Eucharist, namely Word and Sacrament, retained the original Roman cultural pattern of sobriety and noble simplicity. Or were these the qualities of a domestic celebration which survived the incursion of the imperial court ceremonials?

We can conclude that at an early period the Church began to inculturate the eucharistic celebration in the setting of the local people's language, values, dwelling-places, and meal traditions. The key, it seems, for understanding and appreciating this early example of inculturation is the domestic character of the Eucharist. Through inculturation the Church brought the Supper of the Lord to the homes of the faithful.

LITURGICAL MUSIC AND ITS EARLY CULTURAL SETTINGS[1]

Anscar J. Chupungco

In his classic work, Joseph Gelineau offers a penetrating insight into the nature and role of music in the liturgy.[2] His basic distinction between music *in* the liturgy and music *of* the liturgy clarifies what liturgical music is all about. It is not any kind of music which occurs during a liturgical celebration, regardless of whether or not it corresponds to the spirit of the liturgy or to the part of the celebration. Liturgical music is the music whose lyric or text comes directly from the liturgical *ordo*. Edward Foley defines it as "that music which weds itself to the liturgical action, serves to reveal the full significance of the rite and, in turn, derives its full meaning from the liturgy."[3] The definition shows the three components of liturgical music. First, it is woven into the liturgical rite and becomes an element of the celebration. The singing of the *Gloria* or the *Sanctus* at the prescribed time is part of the community's liturgical action. The offertory song while the gifts are brought to the presider is not merely for the sake of musical accompaniment; when performed, it becomes an element of the offertory rite, a liturgical action. Second, liturgical music has a symbolic nature and role: it reveals the meaning of the liturgical action. This means that its text corresponds to what goes on during the celebration and expresses its deeper meaning. The text is basic to the notion of liturgical music. Third, liturgical music derives its full meaning from the liturgy. The purpose of liturgical music cannot be isolated from the purpose of the liturgy itself: it is com-

---

[1]   An elaborated form of this chapter appears in the author's book, *Tradition and Progress*, copyright Pastoral Press, 1994.

[2]   *Voices and Instruments in Christian Worship* (Collegeville, MN: Liturgical Press, 1964), 59-65.

[3]   "Liturgical Music," *The New Dictionary of Sacramental Worship* (Collegeville, MN: Liturgical Press, 1990), 855.

posed and performed for the service of the liturgy. We may say that it has a ministerial role, outside of which it loses its meaning.

The aim of this chapter is to review the development of liturgical music in the early Church (prior to the eighth century), with special attention to the influence exerted upon it by culture as well as the prevailing theological thinking of the times.[4] For greater clarity of exposition the material is arranged here chronologically rather than thematically.

Liturgical Music in the First Century

Scholars advance the opinion that the type of music for the liturgy which the Church adopted in the first century was borrowed principally from the synagogue and home. This type of music became the model for centuries to come. We may explain this by the first Christian community's closer association with the synagogal and domestic forms of worship than with the cult of the temple. The synagogue provided them with the liturgy of the Word, while the Eucharist was a sacred meal they celebrated at home. Word, sacrament, and home are the three chief elements of early Christian worship. The temple in Jerusalem did not serve the Church's forms of worship, since it was not the normal place for the proclamation of the Word, nor was it the place for family meals. The first disciples continued to worship in the temple (Acts 3:1), and perhaps offered there the prescribed sacrifices (Acts 20:16). But their typical form of worship as a Christian community was synagogal (Acts 19:18) and domestic (Acts 2:46; 20:7-12). Even after the Nazarites, as Christians were then called, no longer attended the synagogue services, they continued to read

---

[4]   For historical material I depend on the following authors (in alphabetical order): B. Cole, *Music and Morals* (New York, 1993); E. Foley, "Liturgical Music," *The New Dictionary of Sacramental Worship* (Collegeville, MN: Liturgical Press, 1990), 854-70; Idem, *From Age to Age: How Christians Celebrated the Eucharist* (Chicago, Liturgy Training Publications, 1991); Idem, *Foundations of Christian Music: The Music of Pre-Constantinian Christianity* (Nottingham: Alcuin/GROW Liturgical Studies, 1991); E. McKenna, "Styles of Liturgical Music," *The New Dictionary of Sacramental Worship*, 870-81; J. McKinnon, *Music in Early Christian Literature* (Cambridge, 1987); Johannes Quasten, *Music and Worship in Pagan and Christian Antiquity* (Washington, D.C.: Pastoral Press, 1983) (originally published as *Musik und Gesang in den Kulten der heidnischen Antike und christlichen Frühzeit* (Münster Westfalen: Aschendorff, 1973).

the Jewish Scriptures at home gatherings. In short, the Word and the Eucharist, which constitute the nucleus of Christian worship, were musically influenced by the synagogue and the home. On the other hand, after its destruction in A.D. 70, the memory of the temple and its music was lost in the mist of time.

The temple did not interest the young Church probably because the Church did not possess the kind of organization and instruments the temple had. Even in the time of Jesus, professional singers and instrumentalists rendered their services during temple celebrations. Instrumental music was part of temple ritual actions. The *shofar* (horns and trumpets), for example, announced the entrance of priests. Harps and lyres, on the other hand, were proper to Levites. These stringed instruments were allied to the art of poetry, and thus were suited to accompany the psalms and other temple songs. They had a way of sustaining the lyric of the song and focusing attention to it. That is why harps and lyres were regarded as properly liturgical instruments. 1 Chronicles 25:1-3 tells us that "for the liturgy, David and the senior army officers set apart the sons of Asaph, of Heman, and of Jeduthun." These were "prophets" who accompanied their singing with lyre, harp, and cymbal. The Chronicler attributes prophetic characteristics to liturgical chant performed "to the sound of the lyre." Bells, tambourines, and cymbals were also used to accompany liturgical singing. But flutes, pipes, and oboes were considered lay instruments to be used at family or social affairs, especially marriages and funerals. Temple liturgical singing was performed by a trained choir which numbered at least twelve adult male singers.[5]

Psalm 150 names some of the instruments used in temple liturgical services: "Praise him with the sound of trumpet, praise him with lute and harp, praise him with timbrel and dance, praise him with strings and pipe, praise him with the clashing of cymbals."

The Church of the third and fourth centuries had little or no sympathy for musical instruments, because these were often associated with pagan worship or else with immorality. The Church of the first century, on the other hand, could not afford them; instruments would

---

[5]   *Voices and Instruments in Christian Worship*, 148-52.

have been regarded as luxury items for a small group of believers gathered in a private house. The question of immorality or pagan worship would not have been raised, since musical instruments were part of the temple service. Nonetheless, we cannot categorically exclude the use of all musical instruments from domestic liturgies. It is probable that by and large the lyre or the harp was used to accompany songs. But there seems also to be a theological reason, possibly in the subconscious of the Christian community, why musical instruments did not form part of the liturgy. Was it the awareness that the Christian cult derived from the synagogal and domestic, rather than temple, tradition? We know that the synagogal liturgy definitely excluded the playing of musical instruments, except the horn to signal the feast.

The temple was staffed by professional instrumentalists and singers. The synagogue, on the other hand, used local talents and resources. Until the destruction of the temple in Jerusalem, when the dislocated professionals moved to the synagogues, the synagogal service, which centered on prayer and the Word, had no place for musical instruments and choirs. Its chief activity revolved around the proclamation or reading of the Word and the recitation of the *Shema* (*cf.* Deuteronomy 6:4-7,9) and the *Amida* or eighteen benedictions. A consideration of major significance to the history of liturgical music is how these elements of synagogal worship, namely the reading and recitation of liturgical formularies, were rendered. Scholars tell us that in ancient times reading or public speaking and singing were not as clearly distinguishable as they are today. In other words, the scriptural reading and the blessings and prayers must have been proclaimed with some degree of melody. Foley explains that "the audible nature of all reading presumed rhythmic and melodic features that today would be more quickly classified as music rather than as speech. Public speaking, too, presumed a kind of chanting in cadence that fell someplace between modern categories of speech and song."[6]

This manner of reading and speaking in public is a musical genre known as "recitative," as opposed to "air." It is performed through cantillation, the recitation of a text with musical tones or set of me-

---

[6] *From Age to Age*, 9.

lodic formulae. It can be described as a type of musical declamation in which both the structure and meaning of the text are respected, in which the purpose of the music is to be a vehicle of proclamation. Its reason for being is the lyric or text. As Gelineau has pointed out, the "recitative [unlike the "air"] is so bound up with words, that playing the melody without them would be meaningless. It is the text which gives to the melody the completion of its form; the melody alone cannot subsist without the words which give it existence."[7] This is the musical tradition which the early Church inherited from the Word-centered synagogal form of worship.

The domestic liturgy of Judaism with its preference for music joined to a formulary also influenced the early Church's liturgical music. The blessings chanted before meals, the psalms, and hymns were normal elements of Jewish home liturgies. Although we do not possess documents to prove that the psalms were used by Christians in their assemblies before the third century, christological hymns patterned after Jewish models are found in the New Testament. Ephesians 1:3-14, Philippians 2:6-11, and Colossians 1:15-20 are such hymns. One thing we should remember is that the central position held in the synagogue and Jewish homes by the Word of God and the liturgical formularies—in short, the Word-centeredness of their celebrations—would in turn not have permitted florid musical arrangements to be used in early Christian worship. They would have been regarded as something that detracted from the primacy which the Word or the liturgical text held in the liturgy. The "recitative" would have been the typical musical genre employed by the emerging Church of the first century. As late as the time of St. Augustine, this musical tradition was kept alive. Quasten informs us: "In the West it was primarily Augustine who was intent on not letting melodic beauty become the main concern in ecclesiastical singing. He permitted singing only for the sake of the text."[8]

Liturgical Music from the Second to the Fourth Century

Until the fourth century liturgical music continued to develop in the context of the house church. It was a type of music suited to the

---

[7]   *Voices and Instruments in Christian Worship*, 113.

[8]   *Music and Worship in Pagan and Christian Antiquity*, 93.

setting of a domestic liturgy, of a "private" celebration within the confines of a *triclinium*. For this reason authors believe that the practice of cantillation continued to be the norm, especially for biblical readings and the prayers said by the presider of the assembly. It is likely that at this time the eucharistic prayer was delivered in a recitative tone, possibly patterned on the Jewish tradition of chanting the meal blessing. It seems that the distinction between public speaking and singing had not yet been established. Thus, the two principal elements of the liturgy, namely scriptural reading and the prayers by the presider, were performed according to the earlier tradition of music whose chief, perhaps only, purpose was to deliver or proclaim the Word or the liturgical text.

Besides Scripture and prayer formularies, there were other elements of the domestic liturgy: psalms, nonbiblical songs, and hymns. There is no record before the end of the second century that psalms were used in Christian worship. This does not, of course, indicate, contrary to some authors, that Christians did not recite psalms during worship. The silence of the documents is not sufficient argument against the liturgical use of psalms in the early Church. Rather, because of the Church's strong synagogal tradition, which is probably the basis of St. Paul's admonition to "sing psalms, hymns, and spiritual canticles to God" (Colossians 3:16), we may suppose that from the very start psalms already formed part of Christian worship. Since the "great Hallel" (Psalms 112-117) was an element of the Passover meal, which was a domestic celebration, we can presume that at the Passover season Christians would have revived this Jewish tradition. At any rate, the chanting of psalms is reported by the apocryphal *Acts of Paul* 7,10, written toward the year 190: "Each shared in the bread, and they feasted...to the sound of David's psalms and hymns." Tertullian in his work *On the Soul* informs us that in Christian assemblies "the Scriptures are read and psalms are sung, allocutions are delivered and prayers offered."[9] It is interesting to note that this liturgy was held *in ecclesia inter dominica sollemnia*, which can only mean the Sunday Eucharist. Its *ordo* consisted of scriptural reading, followed by the chanting of psalms, the homily, and prayers—

---

[9] *De Anima* 9,4, *Corpus Christianorum* II/2 (1954), 792.

or, in short, what is known today as the liturgy of the Word. The position of the psalms between the readings and the homily seems to witness to the early tradition of responsorial psalms at the Eucharist.[10]

Nonbiblical psalms, known to scholars as *psalmi idiotici*, began to appear at this time. These were compositions by Christians in the style of the psalms, and hence could be sung like psalms. The earliest example are the *Odes of Solomon* written in the second century. Part of Ode 27 reads: "I extended my hands and hallowed my Lord, For the expansion of my hands is his sign. And my extension is the upright cross. Hallelujah."[11] We may say that nonbiblical psalms answered the Christian need to sing "psalms" that are directly and explicitly Christian. Although we read in Luke 24:44 that everything written in the psalms about Christ had to be fulfilled, it requires some mental process, which is not always accessible to all, to recognize Christ in them. The later tradition of concluding the psalms with the Trinitarian doxology supports the Christian interpretation of the Jewish psalms.

Through nonbiblical psalms, the early Church sang to the Lord in words that proclaim directly his person and mystery. We may imagine that in Christian assemblies the singing of nonbiblical psalms was a rather normal occurrence. It offered an opportunity to individuals to proclaim in song their faith and experience of Christ, comparable to the modern personal witnessing of faith in charismatic gatherings. Tertullian mentions the practice of singing privately composed psalms: "After the ritual handwashing and the bringing in of the lights, each one is invited to stand and sing to God as one is able: either something from the holy Scriptures or of one's own making."[12] With typical irony Tertullian adds, in answer to the pagan accusation of drunkenness in Christian assemblies, "hereby we are able to prove how much one has drunk!" It was indeed an era of spontaneity and improvisation, and we may surmise that the manner of singing

---

[10] A. Verheul, "Le psaume responsorial dans la liturgie eucharistique," *Questions liturgiques* 73 (1992/4), 232-52.

[11] See English translation in *From Age to Age*, 31.

[12] *Apologeticum* 39,18, *Corpus Christianorum* II/1 (1954), 153.

these songs depended to a large extent on the talent of the individual. Tertullian's words "as one is able" (*proprio ingenio*), which Hippolytus also applies to the bishop when he speaks of the eucharistic prayer, seem to confirm this. It is important to remember that the liturgy then was celebrated in a domestic setting, where one would expect a measure of spontaneity.

Hymns also formed part of the early Church's worship, or in the words of Gelineau, they have always been "on the threshold of liturgy."[13] Unlike psalms, hymns are metrical poems divided into stanzas of at least two lines. Each stanza has the same meter, number of syllables, scheme of word accent, and number of verse lines. This trait allows for the singing of each stanza in the same way as the first. When such trait is not observed by the composer, as in the case of the *Gloria* and *Te Deum*, singing suffers because of adjustments made on notation. The singing of the psalms, on the other hand, which are not metered like the hymns, requires modification of the music, however slightly, in order to accommodate the varying meter, number of syllables, and word accents. In the situation of the domestic church it would appear that hymns were sung by the assembly, rather than by a choir of singers. The letter of Pliny the Younger to Emperor Trajan in A.D. 112 reports that the assembled Christians sang hymns alternately among themselves; that is, the assembly must have been divided into two groups. Pliny writes: "They were accustomed to meet on a fixed day before dawn and sing alternately among themselves a hymn to Christ as to a god".[14]

A famous hymn to Christ, in Greek, dating from the early third century was composed by Clement of Alexandria, whom authors suspect to have been influenced by second-century Gnostic hymns. In translation it reads: "King of saints, almighty Word of the Father, Highest Lord, Wisdom's head and chief, assuagement of all grief; Lord of all time and space: Jesus, Savior of our race."[15] The only example of a musically annotated hymn dating from the third cen-

---

[13]   *Voices and Instruments in Christian Worship*, 183-91.

[14]   English text in R. Cabié, *History of the Mass* (Washington, D.C.: Pastoral Press, 1992), 22.

[15]   English text in *From Age to Age*, 32.

tury was discovered in a papyrus from Oxyrhyncos in Egypt. Musicologists have been able to transcribe its melody, which is definitely not of the "recitative" genre, but is closer to what is called "air." Composed in Greek, the fragment in translation reads: "...neither the stars, sources of light, nor the springs whence flow the raging torrents are silent! While we sing the praise of Father, Son, and Holy Spirit, let all the powers cry out: Amen, Amen! Power and glory to the sole giver of all good things: Amen, Amen!"[16] Unlike the nonbiblical psalms which could be composed on the spur of the moment or at the inspiration of the singer, hymns had established text and music which rendered them easily accessible to the assembly.

During this period we notice the absence of reference to special singers, psalmists, or cantors. The reader and the presider, of course, chanted or cantillated their parts, but the assembly sang the rest, especially the psalms and hymns. Before the fourth century the shape of the liturgy was still very much a domestic affair in which there was as yet no need for a trained or professional choir. Furthermore, it is useful to bear in mind that the entire liturgy was musical. The readings and prayers were cantillated, and the psalms, both biblical and nonbiblical, as well as the hymns were sung. No part of the liturgy would have been spoken. When one proclaimed the Word, one did not simply speak; one cantillated the text. Such was the musical context in which the liturgy of the Church began to evolve from the second to the fourth century.

Obviously this musical tradition is foreign to many cultures today. Some find the chanted greeting "The Lord be with you" as amusing as would be a chanted "good morning." Yet we should probably be wary of easy cultural analogies. The liturgy is a ritual action which has developed a cultural pattern distinctly its own. Chanting greetings and prayers, or even biblical readings, should not surprise us any more than the required singing of "happy birthday to you." No one would think of merely reciting the lyric of this song.

---

[16]   The text and musical notation of this hymn are reproduced in *Voices and Instuments in Christian Worship*, 55.

Which instruments did the early Church use for liturgical services? Gelineau writes: "We cannot say definitely that during the patristic era Christians never made use of certain instruments, such as the lyre, to accompany their liturgical singing. Certain passing allusions or repeated prohibitions even lead to the conclusion that this was a well established practice".[17] Yet we come across strongly worded prohibitions of use in the liturgy of certain musical instruments, like the flute and the music pipe or *aulos*. Clement of Alexandria, who died in A.D. 215, condemns the use of trumpets, *aulos*, lyre, horn, and cymbals. "These instruments," he writes, "should be excluded from the sober repast [of Christians]; they are more fitted to charm animals than people, or people who are deprived of their reason." Clement goes on to interpret the musical instruments mentioned in Psalm 150 in a purely allegorical sense. In actual practice they are of no use except for inciting to war, stimulating the passions, inflaming lust, or arousing anger. And he concludes by saying that "we make use only of a single, peaceful instrument, the *Logos*, by which we honor God".[18] Sometime at the beginning of the fifth century the Syrian Pseudo-Justin wrote: "Singing is not a childish matter, but singing to the accompaniment of inanimate instruments, dancing, and shaking rattles is. Hence, in churches the use of instruments and other childish things have been excluded from songs, though singing is retained."[19]

As late as the fourth century we meet a certain reticence in the use of musical instruments. John Chrysostom in his homilies on Psalm 149 explains that God permitted the Jewish people to use musical instruments "out of regard for the weakness of their spirit, and because they had hardly emerged as yet from the cult of idols."[20] On the other hand, Augustine of Hippo makes an allegorical interpretation of the instruments in Psalm 150 in his treatise on the same psalm: "It is you who are the trumpet, the psaltery, the harp, the tympanum, the

---

[17]   *Voices and Instruments in Christian Worship*, 150. See *Music and Worship in Pagan and Christian Antiquity*, 72-75.

[18]   *The Pedagogue* II, 4, *Sources Chrétiennes* 108 (1965), 93.

[19]   *Questions Addressed to the Orthodox* 107, *PG* VI, col. 1353-55.

[20]   *Homily on Psalm* 149, *PG* LV, col. 494.

chorus of dancers, the strings, organ and cymbals of jubilation, well sounding because concordant. It is you who are all these. There is no allusion here to anything despicable or ephemeral, or which would be mere amusement."[21]

Thus, while the first-century Church did not use the musical instruments for temple services because of her synagogal tradition, the Church from the second to the fourth century excluded such musical instruments as flutes and castanets from the liturgy because of their association with the worship of idols, licentious meals, and the theatre and dances of lascivious character. Cole makes the following reminder: "It has to be kept in mind that those Fathers who were negative about the music of their period were not making aesthetic judgments about pure music as we know it, a recent art by historical standards. Rather, most of these Fathers condemned the drunkenness and lewd dances which in many instances were associated with it."[22] In fact, the various patristic references to musical instruments until the fifth century ran the gamut of all the possible attitudes: from approval, to reticence, to an allegorical acceptance, and to condemnation. It was only in the Middle Ages that the Church in the West introduced organs, harps, guitars, flutes, bagpipes, cornets, and other instruments to accompany the voices in polyphony or religious processions.

Liturgical Music from the Fifth to the Eighth Century

"Moving worship from the house church to the basilica meant not only a change in the architectural space but also in the acoustic space."[23] Unlike the *domus ecclesiae*, the basilica, which the Christians of the Constantinian era adopted for their public worship, was an imperial hall which encouraged grand, almost theatrical, celebrations. If we consider that the bishop of Rome adopted the imperial insignia and was treated according to the ceremonials of the imperial court, we can understand the profound influence of the basilica on

---

[21]   *Enarration in Ps. 150, PL* XXXVII, col. 1965-66.

[22]   *Music and Morals*, 51.

[23]   *From Age to Age*, 49.

liturgical music. Just as the emperor was greeted by a choir as he entered the civic basilica, so was the bishop of Rome. In contrast to the simple musical tradition of the house church, choirs had to be trained for the specialized ministry of singing. It was during the pontificate of Sergius I (687-701) that there appeared in Rome what later came to be known as the *schola cantorum*. These singers were clerics who were trained from infancy to a very high technical standard of chant-singing. To them we owe the composition of the Roman chant which later developed into the so-called Gregorian chant.

A development that has had repercussions on the role of women in church choirs is the clericalization of the *schola cantorum*. Quasten tells us that "as the boy choir superseded the cantor, so individual boys from the choir gradually took the place of the lector, whose office was often connected with that of the cantor."[24] He mentions, among other regulations, the decretal of Pope Siricius, who died in A.D. 398, requiring those who wished to dedicate themselves to the service of the Church from childhood to begin as a lector. The linking of the *schola cantorum* to the office of lector clericalized the choir. Hence a boy lector, chosen from the boy choir, in effect became a cleric. This was probably the background for the prohibition by the Synods of Auxerre in the years 561-604 to admit laymen and women into the *schola cantorum*. The ministry of singing in choir during liturgical functions became a clerical reserve to which women had no access.

Quasten notes that during the first two centuries women took part in liturgical singing as members of the assembly. In the third century, heretics began to establish choirs of women separated from the rest of the assembly. Among heretics women enjoyed the exalted ranks of prophets, lectors, deacons, and singers. Was this the reason why a century later some of the Church Fathers, among them Cyril of Jerusalem, reacted against women's choirs and sometimes also against women's participation in congregational singing? But this negative attitude was not universal. Ambrose defended it by affirming that singing the psalms was fitting for every age and for both sexes. On

---

[24] *Music and Worship in Pagan and Christian Antiquity*, 90.

the other hand, Ephrem founded choirs of virgins and taught them to sing hymns and responses to counteract the heretical choirs of women. According to Quasten, the exclusion of women from singing as choirs and finally from singing as members of the assembly was motivated by the Church's struggle against heresies and the liturgical practices of heretics like the establishment of women's choirs. His thesis, however, does not necessarily exclude the factor of clericalization. At any rate, the question cannot be viewed from the angle of culture but of Church discipline.

While the liturgy of the house church did not require trained musicians, the imperial liturgy encouraged professionalism in music. The *Roman Ordo I*, which describes a papal mass in the seventh century, speaks of a schola led by a *prior scholae* or head cantor. It was the *schola*, and it would seem the schola alone, that rendered the entrance, offertory, and communion songs.[25] It is not clear from this *Ordo* whether the assembly sang anything at all, though we have no reason to believe that the responses to the greetings and the psalms, and perhaps the *Gloria* and the *Sanctus*, were not chanted congregationally. The point is that the ambience of the basilica necessitated the composition of a more elaborate type of liturgical music at the expense of popular participation.

Yet, notwithstanding the imperial character of the liturgy at this period, liturgical music retained the traditional "recitative" form or cantillation in the proclamation of biblical texts and the presidential orations. And this is significant, because it shows that the original core, namely the centrality of the Word, was preserved in the process of change in "acoustic space."

It was toward the sixth century when the Roman Church began to develop its liturgical chant and continued to do so until the thirteenth century. This ancient Roman chant was ascribed in the middle of the ninth century to Gregory the Great who died in A.D. 604, and thus it came to be known as Gregorian chant. According to Gelineau, the original stratum of the Roman chant "is made up of the recitatives of

---

[25]   *Les Ordines Romani du haut moyen âge* II, ed. M. Andrieu (Louvain, 1960), no 60, p. 83; no. 85, p. 95; no 112, p. 107.

readings and prayers, the verses of psalms, the acclamations and the dialogues, and some of the most ancient of the hymns."[26] This recitative quality of the original Roman chant, which exalts the lyric rather than the melody, is what defines this music as liturgical. Thus, he affirms that "beyond all doubt the perfect wedding of text to music is one of the most remarkable characteristics of Gregorian chant."[27] As examples, Gelineau mentions the Roman tones for the Gospel reading, the prefaces, the opening prayers, *Gloria XV* and *Sanctus XVIII* in the collection *Liber Usualis*, and the *Te Deum*. Their music, he explains, is allied with the Jewish cantillations, and can claim to be rooted in the early tradition of liturgical music. It is a syllabic type of music, which means that normally there would only be one or at most two notes per syllable. This type of chant was especially suited for congregational singing.

The rise of professional singers during the Constantinian era led to the evolution of the ancient system of cantillation to complex ornamentation and melodic developments. Such musical genre required professional soloists or choirs with advanced vocal techniques. They excluded the participation of the assembly. Examples of these in the Gregorian corpus are the neumatic[28] pieces, like several introits and communion antiphons, and the melismatic[29] graduals that are prolix in musical ornamentation. In these instances the interest is no longer in the text but in the melody. Thus liturgical music evolved from the "recitative" to the "air," in which the melody and the rhythm become autonomous entities, that is, independent from the text.

Another trait of this period is the flowering of hymnody. We know that hymns were an ancient element of Christian worship. According to Adolf Adam, "from the fourth century on, *hymns*, which in early Christianity usually had quite simple texts and melodies, showed advances in textual and musical quality."[30] Ambrose of Milan is

---

[26] *Voices and Instruments in Christian Worship*, 195.

[27] *Ibid.*, 118.

[28] Several notes for a single syllable.

[29] An extended melody for a single syllable.

[30] *Foundations of Liturgy: An Introduction to its History and Practice* (Collegeville, MN: Liturgical Press, 1992), 82.

regarded as the father of Western hymnody, and it is possible that his hymns were sung to well-known secular tunes of the time, as with Martin Luther's some centuries later. Some hymns were presumably sung during the eucharistic liturgy, and more so in the divine office from the time of Benedict of Nursia in the sixth century.

Liturgical hymnody did not always and everywhere receive the sympathy of Church authorities. Hymns were popular, because the assembly found their melodies simple and engaging. No amount of prohibition could put a stop to the practice of singing hymns during public worship. In A.D. 563 the first Council of Braga, canon 12, decreed that except for the psalms or other biblical passages from the Old and New Testaments, no poetic compositions, that is, hymns, may be sung in liturgical gatherings. The preoccupation here was, of course, to hold at bay heretical doctrines which could easily creep into such poetic compositions. But such measure did not stifle the production of liturgical hymns. From the fourth century we witness a demand for hymns. Adam estimates that "about 35,000 hymns in all were composed" after the fourth century.[31]

The flowering of hymnody was symptomatic of the gradual decline of active participation of the faithful in the liturgy, particularly the Eucharist. Singing hymns meant singing *during* the liturgy, rather than singing the liturgy itself. The rise of professional singers at first confined the role of the assembly to the recitative parts of the liturgy. But even these began to be abandoned in later centuries, in favor of the more ornate and talent-demanding genre called melismatic music. Thus the assembly had to content itself with hymns, which were not necessarily constitutive of the liturgy. Today, however, hymns are no longer extraneous to the liturgy. Apropos the local churches with native musical tradition distinct from the Western, Gelineau writes: "It is particularly desirable that in mission countries native compositions should be encouraged rather than the imported tunes of European hymns, for they can suit the musical idiom of the country and the poetry which belongs to the language concerned"[32]

---

[31]   *Ibid.*, 82.

[32]   *Voices and Instruments in Christian Worship*, 205.

Summary

In the Jewish as well as other ancient cultures, proclamation and public speaking, because of their solemn character, were not merely read or spoken. They were cantillated. This was the practice in the synagogues from which Christian worship inherited it. It consisted of reciting a text with musical tones or with a set of melodic formulae. For the early Christians, whose liturgy centered on the Word of God and prayer formularies, cantillation was the best available form of music, because it transmitted more effectively the message of the text. As a musical genre it highlights the words and enhances their meaning. The proliferation of musical notes, on the other hand, has the tendency to obscure the text, while calling attention to the melody. The early Christian music stressed the primacy of the text and placed itself at the service of the Word. It shared in the Church's ministry of preaching the Word.

From the beginning the liturgy did not consist only of biblical readings and prayers formularies. Psalms, which were sung in synagogues and homes, must have made their way into the homes and gatherings of Christians. And we can presume that the first converts continued to sing them in the way they were sung in synagogues and domestic religious celebrations. As early as the third century nonbiblical songs, which had been composed in the manner of psalms, became a popular element of Christian worship. Through them any individual could witness in song to the mystery of Christ and one's faith-experience. From the earliest times hymns also formed part of Christian gatherings, as they formed part of the Jewish worship. Matthew 26:30 tells us that after the Last Supper, Jesus and his disciples sang a hymn before they went out to the Mount of Olives. Hymnody was a normal element of people's musical as well as lyrical culture. When Pliny the Younger reported that Christians sang hymns to Christ as to a god, he implied that they were doing what the pagans would normally do during their worship, that is, sing hymns. There was no reason to arrest them for this.

Yet the *psalmi idiotici* and hymns were not always looked upon with sympathy, because their lyrics did not originate in Scripture. Was it perhaps a matter of prudence in the face of possible incursions of heresy through private authorship? What could be safer, doctrinally, than the Word of God? At any rate, the Church's reticence and pro-hibition to use nonbiblical texts did not discourage the proliferation of hymns for the liturgy. Hymnody is a strong element of people's musical culture. When the greater portion of the eucharistic liturgy was turned over to the clergy and the professional musicians as their exclusive domain, the assembly had to content itself with singing hymns. Often they did not reflect the meaning of the liturgical rite. Nevertheless, it is in hymns where we are able to perceive most clearly the role of culture in the development of liturgical music. For hymns embody the people's poetic spirit and lyrical talent.

The transition from the *domus ecclesiae* to the Constantinian ba-silica affected liturgical music, as it did the liturgical rite, in a dra-matic and lasting way. Unlike the domestic type of celebration, the solemn liturgy in the splendor of the spacious imperial hall required professional singers and trained choirs. To match such solemnity, splendor, and artistic quality, liturgical music began to be ornamented with neums and melisma, which rendered them inaccessible to the majority of the assembly. It did not take the Church very long to abandon the "recitative," that musical tradition which is so conge-nial to the Word-centered liturgy of the Church and to active partici-pation.

WORSHIP AND CULTURE IN THE LUTHERAN REFORMATION

Gordon W. Lathrop

The chapters herein on worship and culture in the New Testament have their own cultural context. They are situated within late twenti-eth-century, "post-modern" global culture. They are thus marked by the interest in honoring specific, local, often forgotten cultural mate-rials. At the same time, they are characterized by a quest for an authentic human unity, for what can genuinely draw us together against the xenophobic ravages of heightened tribalisms. Such char-acteristics have come to expression in the biblical studies here through resistance to the idea that the sacraments, at their origins, were *ex nihilo*, without cultural content, by the treasuring of specific local Jewish transformations of Hellenistic meal practice and Iranian wa-ter reverence, and by the quest for that critical Christian center which, while differently expressed in different major New Testament writ-ings, has the capability of uniting us in our diversities today as it may be perceived to have united diverse Christians then. Post-mod-ern biblical scholarship is often interested in "splitting,"[1] in discern-ing the very great differences between groups. It also needs to look again at some careful "lumping," at finding authentic lines of unity.

But the context of these studies has also been the global Lutheran tradition. The writer is a Lutheran. The conversation of which his papers are part seeks to find help in the Lutheran tradition for the present cultural moment. How may worship among Lutherans honor the diverse, even suppressed, local cultures? How does worship find lines of authentic unity across real differences?

In fact, the themes which have been the principal motifs of these chapters are Lutheran themes. The sense that real ecclesial continu-

---

[1]   About "splitters" and "lumpers," see Paul Bradshaw, *The Search for the Origins of Chris-tian Worship* (London: SPCIC; and New York: Oxford University Press, 1992), ix.

ity is to be found in the central signs, the idea of the "broken symbol," and the paired welcome and critique of cultural material are traceable to the Lutheran Reformation itself. These themes are corollaries of the doctrine of justification by grace through faith, applied to liturgy. They also can be considered as a faithful way to read the biblical witness.

The intention of this chapter is to trace in the Lutheran Reformation those ideas about welcome and critique and about the strong-but-broken symbols which we have traced to the New Testament.

Cultural Setting of the Lutheran Reformation

The Lutheran Reformation arose at a cultural crossroads. The northern European setting of its beginnings was marked by continuing *medieval* patterns encountering *the renaissance spirit* in scholarship and the arts, by new strength in *local cultural symbols*—German language and customs, for example—encountering the old but still lively dream of *Roman imperial unity*, and by the newly strong *cities* as the primary place for all of this cultural "traffic."[2] The manner in which various sixteenth-century ecclesial reformers dealt with culture and with the cultural conflict swirling about them can be instructive for us today.

All of these leading cultural characteristics of the early sixteenth century in Europe can, of course, be traced in their ritual forms, their liturgical implications. Thus, the received medieval pattern of worship, the palimpsest of the liturgy, was itself a culture, a system of social communication which reinforced the given social order. Its Latin books and tradition, its system of overlaid symbols, widely recognized if diversely interpreted, even its welcoming of vernacular preaching and communal singing into one part of its *praxis*—all of this presented an embracing scheme of universal meaning for its participants. However, all things did not necessarily hold together in this scheme. The renaissance spirit, the quest for the "ancient" and

---

[2]   Important studies include Bernd Moeller, *Reichstadt und Reformation* (Berlin: Evangelische Verlagsanstalt, 1987) and the papers collected in Steven Ozment, ed., *Religion and Culture in the Renaissance and Reformation, Sixteenth Century Essays and Studies*, xi (Kirksville, Missouri: Sixteenth Century Journal Publishers, 1989).

the "original," was itself giving birth to new cultural symbols. The quest for the new could be joined with the sense that there was a forgotten, classical, liberating past which placed the human being at greater value than did the medieval synthesis. As that renaissance spirit was becoming "protestantism," it could apply a concern for cleansing to the liturgy, searching for the "purity" of the early Church, choosing to do things the way the sixteenth century conceived that they were done in *Christian* classical times.[3]

Meanwhile, local cultural symbols, especially the German language and customs, were increasingly strong. This *germanitas*, linked to the emergent power of local rulers or of a local peasant populace, often affected ritual life. Local saints' legends and festivals, local magical practices, and vernacular singing were all quite alive, even if marginal to the concerns of church leaders. At the same time, the dream of universal unity was also still alive, symbolically albeit weakly expressed in the Holy Roman Empire. The Lutheran insistence, at Augsburg in 1530 before the Emperor Charles V, that the reformers had not "abolished the mass,"[4] indicates that liturgical matters as well as doctrine were widely taken to represent the hoped-for universal unity. In the midst of all this, the new strength and independence of the cities sometimes demanded that allegiance to the city should itself be central.[5] In many such cities the citizens were required annually to renew their vows of fidelity to the city during large public rituals.

Conservation and Innovation

In the midst of these politically charged, cultural-ritual currents, the Lutheran form of the Reformation was, in dealing with matters of worship, deeply conservative. "Follow me; I have never been a destroyer," said Luther, asserting his position amidst the cultural con-

---

[3]   On the origin of the idea of pure origins and successive histories of degradation in early protestant conceptions of the fate of Christian worship, see Jonathan Z. Smith, *Drudgery Divine: On the Companion of Early Christianities and the Religions of Late Antiquity* (Chicago: University of Chicago Press, 1990), 13-14.

[4]   Augsburg Confession, 24.

[5]   See Thomas A. Brady, Jr., "Rites of Autonomy, Rites of Dependence: South German Civic Culture in the Age of Renaissance and Reformation," in Ozment, 9-23.

flict.[6] In various ways, Luther repeated this assertion again and again, saying that his goal was not to abolish the *cultus* but to put it in *"rechten schwang."* [7]

His urgent recommendation of the pattern of the western mass[8] and the baptismal rites,[9] of the lectionary and the church year,[10] of matins and vespers,[11] of the *Te Deum*[12] and the litany,[13] of translations of Latin hymnody and extensions of medieval *leisen*,[14] and his defense of vestments, images, gestures and church arrangements,[15] all demonstrate the truth of his assertion while also showing the depth of the cultural conflict.

The Augsburg Confession and many influential church-orders, preeminently those of Johannes Bugenhagen in Germany and of Olavus and Laurentius Petri[16] in Sweden demonstrate the same conservative concern. Thus, the Augustana, after conservatively teaching the means of grace (Articles 4 and 7), the necessity of Baptism (9), the real presence of Christ in the Lord's Supper (10), the retention of private absolution (11 and 12), the expectation of canonical ordination (14), the usefulness of the liturgical calendar (15), and the commemoration of the saints (21), asserts: "no conspicuous changes have been made in the public ceremonies of the mass, except that in certain

[6] *"Volgend mir, ich hab es jo nye verderbt,"* is Luther's assertion in the first of the Eight Sermons Preached at Wittenberg, *Invocavit* 1522, *Weimar Ausgabe* 10,3:8; *Luther's Works*, (American Edition) 51:72. Henceforth, the Weimar edition of Luther's works will be noted as WA, the American Edition as LW.

[7] *Concerning the Order of Public Worship*, 1523: WA 12:35; LW 53:11.

[8] WA 12:205-220; 19:72-113; LW 53:19-40, 61-90.

[9] WA 12:51-52; 19:537-541; LW 53:96-103, 107-109.

[10] See his postils and WA 26:222-225; LW 40:298-301.

[11] WA 12:35-37; 19:78-80; 26:230; LW 40:307; 53:11-14, 68-69.

[12] WA 35:458-459; LW 53:171-175.

[13] WA 30,3:29-42; LW 53:153-170.

[14] See LW 53:195-197, 208.

[15] See *Against the Heavenly Prophets in the Matter of Images and Sacraments*, 1525; WA 18:62-125, 134-214; LW 40:79-223.

[16] For Bugenhagen and the brothers Petri, see Luther D. Reed, *The Lutheran Liturgy* (Philadelphia: Muhlenberg Press, 1947), 88-94, 110-116.

places German hymns are sung in addition to the Latin responses" (24).[17] This conservation was especially focused on the means of grace, on the faith that through real things on this earth, with real histories, God gives us that grace which creates and enables faith.

At the same time, the Lutheran form of the Reformation was, in dealing with worship, critical of the tradition and critically open to innovation. This openness to new cultural phenomena was demonstrated more by Luther's *sorting* of the tradition than by the creation of entirely new forms of worship. But this method of sorting owed a great deal to the current renaissance cultural symbolization; in that sense it was "new." Luther shared with renaissance scholars the conviction that it was possible to find and to accentuate those matters which were original and central. Thus, while "retaining the mass," while not making any "conspicuous changes" in the liturgy, Luther did attack the major and minor canons of the mass, the offertory prayers and the sacrificial prayers of the "consecration."[18] These were relatively inconspicuous to the people but of immense importance to the regnant conception of priesthood and to the entire hierarchical structure of the medieval liturgy. Also, Luther placed a great accent on the importance of preaching,[19] on curtailing the daily masses,[20] and on German language and style.[21]

In Luther, as also in the Augsburg Confession, the renaissance quest for "the original" was received, but usually the interest in "the pure form of the early Church" was transformed into an interest in the Gospel alive in the received means of grace. For Luther, the undertaking of such "sorting" was dominated by the biblical counsel of St. Paul: "test everything; hold fast to what is good."[22] This was not so much an idealistic historical quest but an inquiry for that critical center of the received tradition which would actually nourish faith.

---

[17]   Theodore G. Tappert, ed., *The Book of Concord* (Philadelphia: Fortress Press, 1959). 56.

[18]   WA 12:206-208; LW 5:20-22.

[19]   WA 12:35; LW 53:11.

[20]   WA 12:37; LW 53:13.

[21]   See *The German Mass and Order of Service*, 1526, WA 19:72-113; LW 53:61-90.

[22]   1 Thessalonians 5:21; *cf.* WA 12:208; LW 53:22.

Luther, too, could speak longingly of some imagined, simple liturgical patterns, enacted on supposed New Testament models,[23] but he had the good sense to know that "I have not yet the people or persons for it" and "if I should try to to make it up out of my own need, it might turn into a sect."[24] At their best, all critique of the old and all reception of the new were for the sake of faith, not for the sake of a recovery of the pure ideal.

In any case, the new was never to be compelled or legislated. For Luther, the old plus the Word is the new. The new *required* is simply the old in other guise. The dream of universality is not to be imposed. Thus, in speaking against the liturgical requirement of utter simplicity imposed by his former university colleague, Andreas Carlstadt, Luther asserted that the pope and Carlstadt were really "bed-fellows:" the pope requires that ceremonies be done; Carlstadt requires that they *not* be done. Indeed, the *requirement* is at the center of their teaching. Luther writes: "We, however, teach neither, and do both."[25] Similarly, he concludes his proposal for the ordering of a German mass with these words:

> Among Christians the whole service should center in the Word and Sacrament. In short, this or any other order shall be so used that whenever it becomes an abuse, it shall be straightway abolished and replaced by another, even as King Hezekiah put away and destroyed the brazen serpent, though God himself had commanded it be made, because the children of Israel made an abuse of it. For the orders must serve for the promotion of faith and love and not be to the detriment of faith. As soon as they fail to do this, they are invalid, dead and gone; just as a good coin, when counterfeited, is canceled and changed because of the abuse, or as

---

[23] The so-called "third kind of service;" WA 19:75; LW 53:63-64.

[24] LW 53:64

[25] LW 40:131; *cf.* WA 18:113; LW 40:130-131: "For in the cloister we observed mass without chasuble, without elevation, in the most plain and simple way which Carlstadt extols Christ's example. On the other hand, in the parish church we still have the chasuble, alb, altar and elevate as long as it pleases us.. We do as the papists, but we do not tolerate their teaching, commandment, and constraint. We refrain from doing like the Carlstadtians, but we do not tolerate the prohibition."

> new shoes when they become old and uncomfortable are no
> longer worn, but thrown away, and new ones bought. An
> order is an external thing. No matter how good it is, it can
> be abused. Then it is no longer an order, but a disorder.[26]

At their best, the cultural conservatism and the cultural radicalism
of the Lutheran Reformation were set in a lively balance intended to
serve both faith and love.

Liturgical Hermeneutics

The liturgical heritage of the Lutheran Reformation, then, is found
not so much in specific liturgical solutions as in a critically conservative liturgical hermeneutic proposed to all the churches. It is fascinating to note that Luther's primary liturgical writings, the *Formula
Missae* and the *Deutsche Messe*, are not really liturgical books but
guides to the use of the existing liturgical books. Luther gives us not
a liturgy but critical guides to the use of the liturgical tradition. The
Saxon Visitation Articles of 1528 and the many church-orders largely
continue that pattern, sorting out and proposing to the churches ways
to use the tradition evangelically. The Augsburg Confession, too,
gives us the means of grace for the sake of faith at the heart of "rites
and ceremonies of human institution" (Article 7). It does not reject
the latter but orders these received ceremonies to the newly perceived
center. This hermeneutic, this distinguishing of what is central from
what is additional—though the latter is often good and is not thrown
out!—is the "greatest and most useful art"[27] known in the Church.

There were other options in responding to the cultural moment. Thomas Münzer, for example, published a full liturgical book, music
and texts and all, not a guide to the use of the tradition. And while
Münzer's book was itself, at first, relatively conservative, simply
translating the Latin texts into German and largely making use of
traditional Latin chant melodies, it presented itself as the new requirement. Münzer and other reformers were to go on to yet other,
more radical, new requirements. Similarly, Zürich's town council

---

[26]   LW 53:90.

[27]   WA 6:355; LW 35:81.

came to require certain worship patterns by law. In the Zwinglian reform the sacraments came to resemble the urban allegiance oaths: they were demonstrations of the believers' Christian loyalty, not believable signs of God's gracious will toward us. When the Wittenberg town council tried a similar legally enforced reform, Luther radically objected, restoring all the old practices and calling for reform to be made by preaching and by teaching and by love, not by compulsion.

Luther's action in this specific case and his own general contribution to the Lutheran liturgical hermeneutic ought not be seen as fear of change, nor as some kind of political astuteness. Rather, Luther demonstrates a genuine interest in the nature of our relation to God as depending on faith fed by the means of grace, not works fed by law. Also, Luther shows a genuine rejection of purity as a mark of the Church's life, another form of that very rejection we have traced so significantly in the early history of both Baptism and the Lord's Supper. The Lutheran liturgical hermeneutic, the "yes and no" both to the tradition and to the new cultural material, is another example of tension and paradox in central Lutheran thought.

Conclusion

Both the New Testament and the Lutheran Reformation propose a pattern for the relationship between worship and culture. Lutherans should study and know the great catholic liturgical tradition as one of our own cultures. We should engage in sorting and criticizing it, however, because continual inculturation and critique belong centrally to the tradition itself. We should continually welcome new cultural symbolism to the assembly of the Church—as the Lutheran Reformation welcomed German or the spirit of the renaissance—but we should do so critically, welcoming such symbolism to serve and not to supplant the central liturgical pattern of the Church, to join the palimpsest of cultures and to be itself transformed in the service of the Gospel. The best instincts of the Lutheran Reformation place the Gospel and the means of grace which serve the Gospel—not culture—at the center of our worshiping assemblies. Then cultures come into appropriate focus: they may be loved, honored, welcomed, criticized, transformed, redeemed.

Lutheran World Federation, 1993

CARTIGNY STATEMENT ON WORSHIP AND CULTURE:

BIBLICAL AND HISTORICAL FOUNDATIONS

Preface

This statement was prepared at the first consultation of the Lutheran World Federation's study on "Worship and Culture," held in Cartigny, Switzerland, in October 1993. Those invited to participate comprise the LWF's ongoing international study team for the project; the participants represent all continents of the world. At this initial consultation, the study team focused on the biblical and historical (early Church and Lutheran Reformation) foundations of the relationship between worship and culture. The study team will meet again in March 1994, in Hong Kong, to explore contemporary issues and questions of the relationship between culture and liturgy, church music, and church architecture. Following the Hong Kong consultation, it is envisioned that the study will move into a regional phase, in which regional study teams will encourage and assist in the identification and exploration of particular issues related to worship and culture as they exist in the LWF's regions, sub-regions, and member churches; this exploration is to be at the pastoral as well as the theological level. Phase III of the study is to synthesize and reflect globally on the regional findings; phase IV is to conclude the study with a wide variety of seminars and workshops to implement the learnings of the study, as each region and LWF member church decides is helpful.

The contents of this Cartigny Statement, therefore, are conclusions only of the study team's initial consultation, with its specific focus on biblical and historical foundations; it is not a final statement on the topic as a whole.

1.   Introduction

1.1   With gratitude to God, the LWF study team on Worship and Culture acknowledges the efforts of the Church throughout the ages to adapt to current and local situations. We ourselves are also particularly grateful that the Lutheran World Federation and its member churches have given us a mandate to begin a new study on this central aspect of our Christian life.

1.2   We began our work with the conviction that even during our own times the Word of God must be interpreted within the context of a changing world. Through the Holy Spirit, Jesus Christ is present in our own diverse cultural contexts today, just as his presence was incarnated in the life situation of the first century.

1.3   We acknowledge the need in our time to make worship both authentic to the Word of God and relevant to given cultures. The Church is called upon to continue the on-going task of reformation, so that the Gospel might faithfully be proclaimed among the various cultures of today's world. In the final analysis, the Church is an assembly of believers in a given place and time where the Word of God is preached according to the Scriptures and the Sacraments administered following the letter and spirit of the Gospel (cf. Augsburg Confession 7). It has been our Lutheran tradition — indeed, it belongs to the Christian tradition as a whole — that the Word of God should be rendered understandable to all and that the Sacraments should be accessible to all believers. This is understood in the context of God's grace and what Christ does for us.

1.4   In the incarnate Christ, the witness and service of congregations become meaningful to our societies. The Church in its worship, which is the central expression of celebrating our life in Christ, should be seen as an ongoing incarnation of the Gospel.

2.   First Questions

2.1   As member churches of the Lutheran World Federation from across the world begin to explore how the Gospel can be rooted in cultural patterns, it is clear that such an exploration is not a luxury, but an imperative. Further, it is clear that the process of localizing worship is not something new, but rather is an age-old ecclesial inclination attested by well-known examples from the past.

2.2   But the rich and complex record of the faith compels us to take more than a cursory look at the past. It seemed right, then, to engage ourselves in a more comprehensive search for the roots and methods which could provide directions and energy for present opportunities and challenges.

2.3   The process for the first consultation grew from a profound recognition that Jesus Christ himself is God incarnate in human culture. This pre-eminent inculturation led us first to the New Testament where we could discover how the liberating Word for the world met culture. Then we were propelled into a study of the early Church, where the Word continued to be incarnated in several different cultures; and finally the consultation focused on the Lutheran Reformation as a particular time when that creating Word was experienced anew, challenging and transforming culture. The ecumenical importance of this process led to the involvement in our deliberations of several non-Lutheran participants.

2.4   A sense of the dynamic life-giving relationship between worship and culture derives from more than an examination of theological development. Therefore, this study by definition searches for illumination from the histories of liturgy (text and action), church architecture, and church music as well, giving the study that kind of breadth required by current cultural contexts.

2.5   The deliberate intent to discover how the Church in the past has sorted out the issues and processes attending the worship/culture dynamic has yielded considerable insight and prospects for future fruitful interaction. Examples: (A) The Church, as a continuing incarnation of Christ in the world, is always taking root in culture as that place where Christ can be experienced anew. To recognize the cultural component of the Church's worship, however, is to reckon with the rich presence of God's diverse creation in the references and materials of Christian worship. A focus on the cultural leads the Church toward a more responsible relationship with creation itself. (B) Asking inculturation questions of the Church's history has made it clear that there are identifiable core elements of Baptism and Eucharist which perdure through nearly every time and place. (C) The Church's liturgy is most authentic when it resists crystallization by permitting the Gospel to interpret and direct the contextualization process.

2.6   The focus on history, therefore, quite naturally draws attention to contemporary issues, as Christian communities live the Gospel in worship in their various cultures. At the Hong Kong consultation in 1994, the study team will turn toward specific contemporary concerns, seeking to find common methods and mutual encouragement as the churches carefully attend to these issues.

3.   Models and Methods

3.1   An examination of the history of the Church, from its inception in the Hellenistic-Jewish milieu to the current modern contexts, reveals that it has struggled continually with how to relate Christian worship to the cultures in which it is located. The process of understanding and answering this question has been alternately called contextualization, indigenization, localization, and inculturation. Each of these terms has been used in different ways, in different places in the world, and it should be noted that no one single term adequately expresses the process.

3.2   Nonetheless, it remains the case that the Christian assembly for worship, with its music and its spatial environment, stands at the intersection of Christian faith and cultural patterns. Out of this complex interplay of Christianity and culture, three areas for consideration readily become apparent — the cultural, the countercultural, and the transcultural. The task of relating worship and culture, then, involves asking the following three questions:

3.3   First, what are the cultural elements in Christian worship (including liturgical texts, gestures, vestments, furnishings, art, music, and architecture) which give expression to the particularity of the gathered people? Cultural elements have been used in worship throughout the history of the Church (for example, the adaptation of basilican architecture in the Constantinian church) to help engage Christian worship with a particular context, while yet remaining faith ful to the Gospel. In the same way, the churches in every generation and in every context must ask what cultural elements can/should be used in their worship in order to help locate the worshiping community in its particular cultural context.

3.4   Second, what are the countercultural elements in Christian worship which challenge the culture in which it is located? The Church throughout its history, by its faithful proclamation of the Gospel, has challenged the status quo and the social injustices of its day (for example, Christ and his disciples sharing meals with the socially unaccepted people of their day). In the same way, the churches in every generation and in every context must ask what in their worship can/should be countercultural, challenging the culture in which it exists and ultimately facilitating its transformation.

3.5   Third, what are the transcultural elements in worship which place it clearly within the universality of the Christian liturgical tradition? The Church throughout its history has consistently observed certain core elements within its worship as a way to identify itself with the universal tradition of the Church which transcends time and place (for example, the use of water in Baptism). In the same way, churches in every generation and in every context must ask in what ways their worship practice can/should transcend their particular culture, placing them within the universal Christian tradition.

3.6   Therefore, the task of relating worship and culture is ultimately concerned with finding the balance between relevance and authenticity, between particularity and universality, while avoiding eclecticism and/or syncretism. While it is clear that each church in its cultural context will need to ask these questions for itself and find answers appropriate to its own situation, it is also clear that this inquiry will require each church to attend to the experiences of the other churches and to the treasures of other cultures.

3.7   An examination of the tradition, from the Biblical witness, the early Church, and the Lutheran Reformation, reveals the core of Christian worship to be Word, Baptism, and Eucharist. The pattern, or ordo, of entry into the community is teaching and baptismal bath. The pattern of the weekly gathering of the community on the Lord's Day is the celebration centered around the Word and eucharistic meal.

These core elements are clearly evident in the historical witnesses of the Christian worship tradition. Further, it is evident that the purpose of this pattern of worship is faithfully to receive and faithfully to proclaim the Gospel of Jesus Christ.

3.8   One helpful model, then, which is evident throughout the history of the Church, is found where the worshiping community is able to receive and use the important elements of the culture (and thus be localized in a particular context), while at the same time critically shaping these elements so that they may bear witness to the Gospel of Christ who transcends and transforms all cultures (and thus be rooted in the universal Christian tradition). "See, I am making all things new" (Revelation 21:5; NRSV).

4.   Prospects

4.1   The consultation studied processes of interaction between worship and cultural settings in the New Testament, the early Church, and the Lutheran Reformation. It identified the use of different models and methods and recognized in these patterns an on-going process.

4.2   The study team wishes to invite the churches to join in this study of the common roots of Christian worship, believing that study offers important tools for the analysis of their worship (liturgy, music, architecture, art, and so on) within their various cultural settings.

4.3   The study team will continue its work by examining contemporary relationships between worship and cultures. In specific topics for further consideration, the study will seek to clarify the interrelationship between form and content in liturgy; the use of language, gestures, symbols, and music in varying cultural contexts; and the shaping of worship space, with the goal of the inclusive participation of all people — exploring what is cultural, countercultural, and transcultural in these elements.

4.4   The sacramental practices for Baptism and the Eucharist need to be examined and adapted to recover their full meanings, within the churches' current diverse cultural contexts, in order that the gift of God's grace may be offered to all.

4.5   The churches are challenged to be creative as they develop forms of worship which are both authentic and relevant, responding both to their cultures and to the Gospel. Through the power of the Holy Spirit, the churches can find for themselves and offer to the many societies of the world an alternative model of life.

A CONTEMPORARY LUTHERAN APPROACH TO WORSHIP AND CULTURE: SORTING OUT THE CRITICAL PRINCIPLES

Gordon W. Lathrop

In his "Treatise on the New Testament, that is the Holy Mass" of 1520, Martin Luther proposes that the ability to distinguish what is central and constitutive in the Eucharist from what is additional and secondary in its celebration is "the greatest and most useful art."[1] Since, in the same treatise, he asserts that Christ appointed "but one law or order for his entire people, and that was the holy mass,"[2] this sorting of the central and the secondary is, for Luther, immensely important to the life of the Church. The center of the Lord's Supper—and, thus, of the very existence of Church—is the gift of Christ

---

[1]   WA 6:355; LW 35:81: "*die groeste nutzlichste kunst.*"

[2]   WA 6:354; LW 35:80-81. The full quotation is: "Christ, in order to prepare for himself an acceptable and beloved people, which should be bound together in unity through love, abolished the whole law of Moses. And that he might not give further occasion for divisions and sects, he appointed in return but one law or order for his entire people, and that was the holy mass [*nit mehr den eyne weyss odder gesetz eyngesetzt seynem gantzen volck das ist die heylige Mess*]. (For although Baptism is also an external ordinance, yet it takes place but once, and is not the practice of an entire life, like the mass.) Henceforth, therefore, there is to be no other external order for the service of God except the mass. And where the mass is used, there is true worship [*recht gottis dienst*]; even though there be no other form, with singing, organ playing, bell ringing, vestments, ornaments, and gestures. For everything of this sort is an addition invented by men. When Christ himself first instituted this sacrament and held the first mass, there was no tonsure, no chasuble, no singing, no pageantry, but only thanksgiving to God and the use of the sacrament. According to the same simplicity the apostles and all Christians for a long time held mass, until there arose the various forms and additions, by which the Romans held mass one way, the Greeks another. And now it has finally come to this: the chief thing in the mass has been forgotten, and nothing is remembered except the additions of men!"

in the proclaimed Word and in the thanksgiving-bread and blessing-cup of the Church's gathering. None of the additional, peripheral materials—forms of music, vesture or ceremony, for example—lovely and important as they may be, can be made into laws, into the only right ways to get to God. When such ceremonial materials are presented as if required by God, as if necessary for grace, the Church itself is threatened, even destroyed.

It is not that one does without music or ceremony! Luther clearly says, "I neither wish nor am able to displace or discard such additions."[3] Indeed, Luther himself praised music, created and reworked hymns and the music of the liturgy, and seems to have rather loved some aspects.[4]

No, what he longs for, rather, is to distinguish these formal and ceremonial matters from the center which is thanksgiving and Christ's gift, to require them to serve that center, and to forbid them—or their absence![5]—from becoming a new law or a ground for boasting.

This major critical principle of the Lutheran liturgical hermeneutics, a corollary of the doctrine of justification, the application of that doctrine to worship, stands also as a major resource for current Lutheran thought about worship and culture. It proposes to the many Lutheran churches of the world that, in worship, the center must be clear: the assembly gathers around the gift of Christ in Word and sacrament. At the same time, it urges us not to make a law out of western or northern cultural forms. It welcomes the gifts of the many cultures of the world: their languages, their music, their patterns of festivity and solemnity, their manners of gathering, their structures of meaning. None of these is to be despised. All are to be honored. But Lutheran liturgical hermeneutics also urges that these cultural patterns must not become their own new law or usurp the place of the center; they must rather come into the "city" to gather around the

---

[3]   See above, note 1.

[4]   *Cf.* WA 18:113; LW 40:131: "...in the parish church we still have the chasuble, alb, altar and elevate as long as it pleases us."

[5]   So LW 40:131: "We do as the papists, but we do not tolerate their teaching, commandment, and constraint. We refrain from doing like the Karlstadtians, but we do not tolerate the prohibition."

"Lamb" (Revelation 21:22-27); they must be broken to the purpose of the Gospel of Christ. Cultural patterns of all sorts—southern and northern, western and eastern, rural and urban, specifically local and increasingly world-wide—are welcome here. But they are not welcome to take the place of the Lamb. They are not welcome to obscure the gift of Christ in the Scripture read and preached, in the water used in his name, and in the thanksgiving meal.

This much is clearly implied by the "greatest and most useful art" of Lutheran liturgical hermeneutics. This agenda for the relationship of liturgy and culture in our present time can be seen as a faithful reading of the seventh article of the Augsburg Confession:

> It is also taught among us that one holy Christian church will be and remain forever. This is the assembly of all believers among whom the Gospel is preached in its purity and the holy sacraments are administered according to the Gospel. For it is sufficient for the true unity of the Christian church that the Gospel be preached in conformity with a pure understanding of it and that the sacraments be administered in accordance with the divine Word. It is not necessary for the true unity of the Christian church that ceremonies of human institution should be observed uniformly in all places.[6]

But how shall we actually apply this principle of Lutheran liturgical hermeneutics? What gifts of the cultures should come into the assembly of Christians? And how are these gifts to be used or "broken" to the purpose of the Gospel?

Unlike Luther or Melanchthon, the writer of the Augsburg Confession, we cannot uncritically adopt the renaissance conception of historical development as a pure and simple early core subsequently clouded by "additions." We have seen that the very beginnings of the Christian practice of Baptism and the Eucharist were marked by the use of complex local cultural phenomena. But, at their best, in the

---

[6]   Emended from Theodore G. Tappert, ed., *The Book of Concord* (Philadelphia: Fortress Press, 1959), 32.

proposals of the Gospels and of Paul, these were cultural phenomena criticized and turned to a new purpose. It is not so much Luther's
or Melanchthon's historical assertions we adopt as their method of
critique and distinction, their theology of Christ's gift in the midst of
our diverse ceremonies.

The Center

But then the very beginnings of Baptism and the Eucharist may give
us a key for our on-going work. If the suggestions of these chapters
are correct,[7] Christian practice welcomed the cultural symbolism of
an eschatological resistance movement: full body washing to be ready
for the day of God, for example. But it rejected repeated washings,
self-washings, such washing only for men, because it reinterpreted
the "day of God" to be the presence and gift of the crucified Christ,
thereby reinterpreting "purity" to be nearness to him. The symbol
was now a "broken symbol."[8] The resultant washing became the
way to enter into Christ's community, his "body." The use of this
washing in new situations led Christians to unfold the power of such
entrance into Christ by adding a long period of teaching the faith
before the baptismal bath and the use of anointing, the laying on of
hands, exorcisms, clothing and fire, and the leading to the eucharistic meal at the time of the bath. Such use of the "Word," of the
"name" of God as God is known in Christ, of *teaching* next to the
bath, and such welcoming to Christ's table were necessary in order
to make clear that this washing was the washing of *Christ*, was the
gift which calls us all to faith. The other "additions" were all a kind
of ceremonial astonishment, in new cultural situations, that washing
could be washing into life and grace before God in Christ.

Similarly, Christian practice welcomed, at its heart, the food symbolism found in some instances of the Hellenistic-Jewish cultural
synthesis: that meal which, by its prayers over bread at the beginning and over wine at the end of the meal, proclaimed the creation
faith of Israel. But it rejected the closed circle of pure men as the
appropriate community of such praise because it found the deepest

---

[7]   See the chapters on Baptism and Eucharist in the New Testament.

[8]   See above, "Baptism in the New Testament and its Cultural Setting," note 49.

gift of the sacramental meal to be the very presence of the crucified Christ. In Christ, all people—women, outsiders, Gentiles, children, sinners, a multitude coming from east and west—are brought before the God who made and saves all things. Indeed, in the celebration of this meal *of Christ*, the Christians came to join to it that reading and preaching of Scripture which tells of the crucified risen one, to do this Word-and-meal service especially on Sunday, and to accent especially the bread and wine of the thanksgiving, giving the rest of the food away. These were developments which accented the meal's Christological meaning. For a while, Christians made use of culturally available, relatively neutral forms: the use of the local baths or of stone-held "living" water and the use of rooms for reclining at table. As the Church grew and shifted in cultural location, baptisteries were built and reclining disappeared.

The juxtaposition of the event of Jesus Christ to old washing rites and old meal practice, at a specific historical and cultural moment, has given to the Church a *center* and a *method*. The center is this: Christian assemblies gather around a washing rite now done in Jesus' name, around the Scriptures read so that the cross and resurrection which bring all people to God may be proclaimed, and around the thanksgiving over the shared bread and cup. These things are not optional, if the assembly wishes to be Christian. They are indeed fragments of an old, first-century culture, floating down to us over the ages. But transformed by the gift and promise of Christ, they are also the means of grace, the central ways we may hear and encounter the Gospel, concrete witnesses in material reality of our historic salvation.

By God's great mercy, these central things are also richly accessible in new cultural situations: they are stories, a water-bath, a meal. As long as the central patterns of their use and the critical character of their transformation in Christ are maintained, they may indeed be done in new ways, appropriate to new cultural situations. The Scriptures will be read in whatever local vernacular is appropriate for foundational stories. Baptism will be exercised in such a way that the local community can recognize that this great washing matters profoundly, is overwhelmingly gracious and is inextricably bound to Christian preaching and teaching about God. The eucharistic meal will be shared in ways that connect to local meal practice, especially when that practice is festive and richly hospitable. In any case, the central things will be done strongly and clearly.

The recovery of the centrality of these things in all of our churches will be exactly the recovery of that center which will enable and encourage the healthy use of cultural gifts in our worshiping assemblies. The first agenda item for a renewed Lutheran interest in worship accessible to local culture will be renewed scriptural knowledge and strong biblical preaching, new clarity about baptismal teaching and baptismal practice, and the establishment of the Lord's Supper as the principal service in all churches every Sunday. Then there will be a reliable place, a center filled with Christ's gift rather than, say, western nineteenth-century cultural fragments or the untransformed apotheosis of anyone's own present society, around which all of our cultural gifts may be gathered.

But, at the same time, the juxtaposition of Jesus Christ to the ancient cultural material of washing and meal also yields the Church a method for that gathering. New cultural material, entering into the assembly around Christ, coming into the meeting around the central things, will need to be received with the same love and sympathy *and* the same criticism accorded to that washing which hoped for God's Day and to that meal which expressed the faith of Israel. The Church's method will need to be marked by both welcome and critique, by the open gate and the warning ("Nothing unclean may enter there!" Revelation 21:27), by *yes* and *no*.

Yes

If strong local religious meanings were operative in the original Christian uses of the bath or the meal, they can continue to be welcome in the Church in new situations. A quality in music or a kind of instrument which traditionally suggested to local ears a significant connection to the spirits may now be used to sing to God in Christ by the power of the Spirit. Ways to gather, to arrive together in a meeting, or ways to orient the meeting toward the directions of the earth which are locally experienced as enabling an important meeting—these may now be used to communicate that this meeting is before the God who created the earth and who gathers us together into unity. Many other locally significant practices—festal garments or the taking off of the shoes, an empty and chairless room or a richly decorated one, dancing, the use of locally significant colors and materials, the observance of local times, local ways of setting a table and local festive vessels—all may be welcome here. Christians will be especially drawn to authentic and strong symbols, meaningful objects and practices which intensify and, often, subvert ordinary experience, calling ordinary experience toward transformation.

Just as we always need local words to be able to speak, we will always need something of local metaphors simply to gather. In the early centuries, the churches took the form of "supper clubs" to the Greeks, though they were obviously much more than that and though their "supper" was finally moved to the morning. In modern North America, the churches are seen as "volunteer religious societies," groups which care for essentially private spiritualities, a conception especially available in Enlightenment-engendered democracies which eliminated any state church. Here, too, the churches must be much more than the culturally available category, although accessibility to the people in the culture may begin with this category. This category, of course, must be appropriate to the Gospel and not in fundamental opposition to it. The form of a church in a given culture will need to start somewhere between "house" and "open gathering." It cannot be "men's club" or "warrior society" or "sacrificial cult" or "temple."

Christians may have a special interest in seeing that insights that have belonged to minority cultures and have been enshrined in their languages and symbolic systems should not be lost. Dominant cultures, especially those with widespread economic power and most especially that growing international culture called "consumerism," can be afflicted with blindness and amnesia regarding the necessity of harmony between the human community and the surrounding natural world, or the urgency of strong local community for the maintenance human well-being. Sometimes the Christian yes to indigenous cultural practices will look like a certain "romanticism" insofar as it maintains practices which are nearly forgotten and on the edge of disappearing: "yoiking" in Sami, for example, or the use of certain tree leaves to sign cleansing and reconciliation in West Africa, or the use of pollen and sage in prayer on the North American plains, or the use of ancient instrumentation associated with small tribal groups in Asia. But the very rareness and indigenous quality of these practices may enhance their power to suggest the holy to our present time. The otherness of the practices may assist us all in subverting the power of uncriticized dominant cultures. And their age may stir everyone's memory toward forgotten values, forgotten symbols. After all, the old Jewish washing of which Christian Baptism was made and the meal-thanksgivings spoken in praise to the *melech ha-olam* ("king of the universe") amidst the lands of Caesar's rule were also minority symbolizations, resistance symbolizations.

The cultures of churches which were missionary-founded and which have gradually mixed local language and some local musical style with received western patterns are also to be respected and honored. These patterns are frequently experienced as belonging to the beloved history of Christianization, and that experience sometimes includes overtones of liberation. In some places, people who became Christian were not included within the purview of classical cultural systems and only found dignity in the received western Christian patterns. On the other hand, continuing fierce adherence to old western patterns may carry something of the sense that the local culture is defeated, lost, failed. That may be especially sensed because of the dominance of western technology and economy in so much of the current world. But the Christian community cannot allow economic and technological victories to determine its values. Christians have long been taught to value that which "the world" despises, beginning with the cross of Jesus Christ. Hidden in "failed" symbols may be values urgently needed in the modern world.

International "youth culture" may present its own special problems. To the extent that rock music and MTV represent a widespread criticism of dominant cultural values, the kind of criticism to which young people of every age are frequently called, the Christian community needs to take it seriously. Such music frequently sings out longings for global peace and for the care of the earth. That does not mean that "rock," with its accent on star performers and community as group-conformity, is immediately usable in Christian worship, but something of its symbolizing may come in. Christian musicians, who know the Gospel and the spirit of the liturgy, need to experiment with such welcoming. But the rock music culture is also a colossal and international business, a vast example of consumerism, and its seeming subversion of dominant values may be only a shallow pretense. Young people of our day need to be invited deeper. Sometimes they need to be invited to remember cultural treasures of their own which both they and the world-wide community need.

In any case, since God created all things, since all things hold together in Christ, since all things have been reconciled to God by the blood of Christ's cross (Colossians 1:17,20), all things are welcome in the Christian meeting. Human cultures are none other than the rich variety of human beings passing on their traditions about how the community lives with each other and with the earth. By the doctrines of creation and redemption, Lutherans say yes to these cultures.

No

But they also say no. Lutherans also confess that we are all together caught in sin, in alienation from God, in the Fall. When "all things" are placed at the center, instead of the One in whom they hold together and are reconciled, they fall apart. Festivals, new moons, sabbaths—or the four directions, local leaves, certain ways of gathering or singing, the ways the missionaries did it, the drum or the organ, European hymnody, youth culture, television culture—cannot be insisted upon (Colossians 2:16-22). Nor can local purity laws: "do not handle; do not taste; do not touch." What matters is Christ, who liberates us from all laws which pretend to present us to God. What is central is the body of Jesus Christ, in comparison to which all other ritual practices are like shadows. "Nothing unclean may enter there."

So all things are welcome in this assembly, but they are welcome to enter into the economy of "the grace of our Lord Jesus Christ, the love of God, and the communion of the Holy Spirit" (2 Corinthians 13:13). They are not welcome to make themselves the center. Cultural practices, which reflect a people's identity, cannot be so used that that identity is made the primary matter, excluding all people who do not share that identity. For this reason, national flags or cultural heroes or local rulers may sometimes "come" to church, but they may not be made the center of church nor be given a place which reflects a power uncriticized by the all-redeeming cross of Christ. The welcoming of the cultural treasures of the peoples into the praise of the mercy of the Holy Trinity will need to reflect a profound sense of the doctrines of *creation*—that all things are made by God and owe praise to God alone, of *sin*—that all things are fallen and in need of God, and of *justification*—that, by the cross, all things have been once-and-for-all reconciled to God. Cultural treasures cannot be used to reintroduce the assembly to legalism nor to the necessity of making sacrifice in order to please God.

While cultural symbols which suggest spirit or godliness to local participants will be welcome, they will also need to be criticized. The Christian community is not just interested in *God*, any god, it is interested in the gracious God known by the power of the Spirit in the crucified and risen Christ. Suggestions of "god" or "spirit"— whether they are made by stained glass windows and organ music or by drum-beats and dancing—will need to be broken to that purpose.

Furthermore, the welcoming of cultural treasures into the assembly of Christians will always need to show forth the dignity of the baptized people of God, redeemed and beloved ones in Christ who have been made to stand whole in him. No practice can be excused as "my culture" which trivializes or shames members of the body of Christ or any of the "little ones" for whom Christ died. Women and men, young and old, members of dominant and of minority groups, rich and poor, locals and foreigners are to be honored alike here and not to be segregated according to some "cultural" way of dividing people. Patterns of ritual purity are to be rejected. The baptized are never made "unclean" by the bodily functions of God's good creation nor by contact in love with those whom a culture may regard as unclean. Circumcision of men or mutilation of women are not to be used as divine requirements, and the latter should be resisted altogether. Cultural practices are not to be made grounds for boasting.

Indeed, *every* culture—including any culture of protest—needs to be subverted in order to come to clarity as an economy of symbols held together by God's mercy in Christ. Such a need for subversion may be hardest to see in one's own cultural system or systems. That is why we need each other so badly, in conversation across the *oikoumene*, between fellow Christians asking each other questions and calling each other to faithfulness. Especially is it true that cultures which have long been associated with the Church and have left their own gifts imprinted on the "palimpsest" of traditional liturgy may seem impervious to such subversion while profoundly needing it. Western patterns of hierarchy, of androcentrism, of the valuing of wealth, of "community" in intimacy or of musical and artistic standards are not to be identified, without further criticism, as "Christian." Also from the north and the west, "nothing unclean may enter."

There is no one absolutely pure and godly music, for example, commanded by God or required by the Church, by which alone we may sing ourselves into heaven. There are only a variety of human musical traditions, some better suited than others to enable the community to gather around the Word and the sacraments, suggesting harmony and dialogue, diversity and unity, holiness and accessibility in their singing.

A Method of Juxtaposition

The best way of critically associating the good gifts of our cultures with the purpose of the Christian assembly, then, may well be by a method of juxtaposition. It is essentially such a method which Luther's "art" proposes to us. What is brought in must be capable, in clarity and harmony, of serving the gathering of this people as they find the Word and the sacraments at the center. What is brought in must accord with this center, enhance it, serve it, not obscure it. Music must be critically juxtaposed to the Word and to the need to gather around the eucharistic table in praise. Means of entrance and arrangements in the space of assembly must be juxtaposed to baptismal dignity and to the unity of the shared table. Suggestions of "spirit" must meet that Holy Spirit which enlivens the Scripture when it is read and preached as given to us in the crucified Jesus.

Two means will especially serve this method of juxtaposition. The cultural symbols—music, ceremony, environmental arrangement, gestures, vestments, arts—will come to Christian purpose most clearly as they serve the flow of those very simple ancient patterns of Baptism and Eucharist which belong to their origin. We teach; we bathe; we welcome to the table. We gather; we read and interpret the Scriptures; we pray for all the world; we set the table, also taking a collection for the poor; we give thanks and eat and drink; we are sent in mission. These things may be done slowly or rapidly. They may be done in received ancient patterns or in rich local elaborations or in some combination of the two. But it is these things which the Christian assembly does and which will form the clearest framework for the juxtaposition of cultural materials to the gift of Christ.

And the cultural symbols will bring their own strongest gifts to voice when they can be set next to the biblical Word, full of the power of God's saving grace, and be used to illuminate the continuing strength of that Word. Thus, in ancient baptismal rituals, a cup of milk and honey given to the newly baptized probably arose from the symbolization of the mystery cults. In the Church, however, it became the taste of the promised land (Exodus 3:8), now available to all people in Christ, and the sweet taste of God's grace, the pure milk of the Word of Christ (1 Peter 2:2-3), through the juxtaposition of the Scripture. The cultural practice was reoriented, and the biblical Word was given a strong local resonance.

The examples of this juxtaposition of symbol and Scripture could be multiplied. In current practice, among the Gbaya people of Cameroon and the Central African Republic, the leaves of the *soré* tree, long of immense symbolic importance in Gbaya culture, may be used in Christian baptismal, reconciliatory, or burial rites, since now Jesus Christ is the true *soré* tree; he is the source of the tree of life yielding leaves for the healing of the nations (Revelation 22:2).[9]

It may be, however, that the actual *use* of the cultural symbol may be too strong, too impervious to breaking for the purpose of the Gospel, too evocative of the untamed spirits. That is a pastoral decision which sometimes must be made. Sometimes the juxtaposition of cultural symbols to Christ and their subversion to grace occur first and, perhaps, best *verbally*: This *communion* cup is our milk and honey, an old preacher might have said. This word of Jesus Christ in your ears, this water poured out on your body, is our *soré* leaf. "Jesus Christ is our *soré*-cool-thing," say the Gbaya Lutheran Christians. Such juxtapositions serve to enhance the center while evoking God's great love and mercy for the concretely local.

---

9   See Thomas Christensen, *An African Tree of Life* (Maryknoll, N.Y.: Orbis Books, 1990).

Such reflections may lead us, finally, to sort out five critical principles for the welcoming of cultural elements into the Christian assembly and for the evaluation of the current symbolization utilized there:

> 1. Is this a strong and real symbol or complex of symbols with a deep social resonance? Does it carry hope and human identity in its use?

> 2. Does it accord with the Christian doctrines of creation, sin and justification? Or, rather, can it be subverted to serve them?

> 3. Does it accord with the baptismal dignity of the people of God? Is it capable of being genuinely and graciously communal?

> 4. Set next to the biblical Word, does it illuminate God's gracious, saving purpose? Is it best exercised as a verbal symbol?

> 5. Can it serve and sing around the central signs of Christ, around Word and sacrament used especially on Sunday? With its use, are Word and sacrament still *central*, more clearly and locally *central*?

There should probably be one other principle listed. It is *love*. To speak about evaluating current symbolization or introducing local cultural symbols in worship is inevitably to talk about change. Such change cannot be made while despising the people of the assembly. If it is, then Christ is dishonored; the spirit of the liturgy is violated and all is lost. Liturgical change cannot be made a matter of a new law. But listening to the actual cultural circumstances of each local community, listening to the questions raised by the international community of churches, loving and teaching, calling people to the importance of the central things, encouraging local gifts to be celebrated around those central things, juxtaposing all of our ceremonial patterns to the gift of Christ in those things—these are methods that can be used.

In fact, *juxtaposition* has been the method of the liturgy down through all the ages.[10] Word has been set next to sacrament, teaching to bath, texts to preaching, thanksgiving to eating and drinking, praise to lament, presider to assembly, hospitality to reverence, the local to the universal. When the basilica was adopted as the Christian building, it was most faithfully used as long it still had something of the domestic about its central table and table-prayers. When the winter solstice festivities of the Mediterranean world were adopted as a Christian feast, the observance had a *double* character: waiting (Advent) and celebrating presence (Christmas). When the Lutheran churches encouraged more singing in church, they did so in at least two ways: chant and chorale. And why? Because "here on earth we can never rightly say the truth of God with just one word, but always only with two words."[11] Because Christ only, not some pure or right ceremonial practice, is our way to God, and that will be clearest if each practice is set next to another and the whole is made to bear witness to him. Because even the bath and the meal need to be set next to the Word of Christ and be transformed by it in order for us to see how great is God's gift of grace on, in, and under materials drawn from human culture.

We all, in each place, need to receive and continue this history of juxtapositions. The whole cultural "palimpsest" of the liturgy is ours: Jewish washings and meals, Roman festivals, imperial vestments and buildings, North African and Syrian prayers, European hymns, African and Asian instrumentation, North American inclusivity. We need, however, to sort its treasures, to make sure the Gospel of Jesus Christ is really being heard and known in Word and sacrament. Also, we need to make sure that the Gospel is being heard *here*, in each local place, saving and transforming the concrete cultures which are none other than the *people* whom God loves and welcomes to mercy. As that transformation continues to occur, new gifts will emerge that have more than local meaning—a song will be sung that will spread to all the churches, a gesture will be used that many peoples discover that they need in order to more profoundly understand God's good earth and God's great, saving, life-giving love.

---

[10]   See Gordon Lathrop, *Holy Things: A Liturgical Theology* (Minneapolis: Fortress Press, 1993).

[11]   A. Köberle, *Rechtfertigung und Heiligung* (Leipzig: 1929), 295.

In the second century, Justin, our earliest recorder of the great patterns of juxtaposition which are the Christian liturgy, wrote an assertion which must continue to be true: "There is not one single human race, whether barbarians or Greeks or whatever they may be called, nomads or vagrants or herders living in tents, among whom prayers and the giving of thanks are not offered through the name of the crucified Jesus."[12]

---

[12]   Dialogue with Trypho, 117.

LITURGY AND THE
COMPONENTS OF CULTURE

Anscar J. Chupungco

Over the centuries the Church, both in the East and the West, has been in constant dialogue with the culture of every race and nation. One remarkable result of such a dialogue is that the Church often assimilated various components of culture into the liturgy. We may say that it became one of the Church's ways of incarnating the Gospel in the life and history of peoples. Or to state the matter more simply, by assimilating new cultural components into the liturgy, the Church allowed the liturgical shape to be influenced by culture. Thus, soon after Christianity had been transplanted into the Greek and Roman soil, the liturgy came to be rooted in a culture other than and in addition to the Jewish.

One need only consider the shape of Baptism and Eucharist to realize how in the course of time these Jewish-Christian rites became so Hellenistic, so Roman, so Franco-Germanic, that it is not always easy for us to define their original core. In fact one of the difficulties encountered when working on inculturating the liturgical *ordo* is how to distinguish between what is immutable in the liturgy and what is subject to change.

But perhaps the root of our woes in inculturation is the failure to recognize the basic fact that all liturgical rites are vested in culture, that no liturgy is celebrated in a cultural vacuum. Such a failure leads people to miss the theological meaning and consequence of Christ's incarnation. We know that the incarnation is the paradigm, the model, for the Church. Christ became a human in all things, indeed totally Jewish, except that he was without sin, in order to set an example for the Church, to which he gave the mission to extend the mystery of his incarnation in time and space. To do as he has done: this is what the Church is all about. In short, when people are not sensitive to the cultural shape of liturgical worship, perhaps neither are they sensitive to the economy of Christ's incarnation and the Church's essential mission.

Cultural sensitivity is thus a requirement. While inculturation requires a profound understanding of the nature, components, and laws of the liturgy, there is another side to the question, namely, culture. Culture, like the liturgy, has its nature, components, and laws. And while we assume that not everything cultural can be assimilated by the liturgy and that what is assimilated must undergo a strict critical evaluation, we should keep in mind that culture is not something we play around with or, worse, impose upon in the name of liturgical inculturation. Culture has its own requirements which need to be respected, if dialogue with it is to be honest and fruitful.

Thus, when we borrow a musical rhythm meant to suggest an amorous relationship, for example, for a communion song, it is possible that we are spiritualizing that type of love. But are we not thereby imposing on the musical rhythm a signification it is not meant to possess? Surely every society claims a distinct musical rhythm with which it expresses relationship with God. Or when we take over an indigenous rite of initiation, like the cutting of hair in some societies, as a symbol of Lenten penance in place of the traditional ashes, are we not interfering with cultural patterns? Sometimes we think that in matters concerning inculturation everything is alright provided we jealously safeguard liturgical norms. And we demand, rightly, that propriety should be observed regarding the use of church furnishings outside liturgical functions. Antique altars or pulpits decorating restaurants are not a too uncommon sight in Europe. Such cases of impropriety offend our Christian sense of the divine. In a reverse way, we offend cultural sensitivity when we use cultural components in the liturgy without due regard for their original meaning or purpose.

A Definition of Culture

In the humanistic tradition of the past, culture was synonymous with the vastness of human knowledge. And knowledge referred to ideas and notions— in short, to rational understanding. A person was considered "cultured" depending on the amount of such knowledge one had acquired. With the advent of cultural anthropology, the concept of culture has evolved into something much broader. Although there is no uniform way of defining culture, there is a general agreement among authors on some of its descriptive elements.

First, culture embraces not only rational thought, but also the practical realities of life, like the pattern of constructing homes, of cooking and eating, of planting and harvesting, of paying worship to God. In this respect we can say that the liturgy, inasmuch as it is a pattern of worshiping God, is a cultural reality. Though we claim that in the liturgy there are divinely instituted elements, we know that these are embodied in culture.

Second, culture is anthropo-genetic. This means that while humans produce culture, culture in turn is able to influence them so profoundly, that they become differentiated, that is, they acquire an individuality all their own. Applying this principle to the liturgy as a cultural reality, we can say that while we shape the liturgical ordo, it fashions us by its values and leads us into communion with its divine component.

Third, culture is pluralistic. Monoculturalism, on the other hand, is often the arm of conquest and domination. Cultural pluralism means that there are as many cultures as there are social groups with their particular patterns of thought, language, and rites. If we consider the cultural dimension of the liturgy, we should be able to conclude that there must be as many liturgical ordines as there are patterns of thought, language, and rites.

Fourth, culture is by nature structural: it does not come about casually or by chance. Rather, it is governed by set structures, even if such structures undergo evolution. We should therefore not be annoyed by the fact that the liturgy is structured or governed by norms. Liturgical tradition calls structure *ordo*, which implies a set of normative patterns.

Fifth, culture often runs the risk of becoming an instrument of manipulation in the hands of despots and dictators. Manipulation can show itself the the areas of education, arts and literature, propaganda, fashion, and sports. Liturgy too can be reduced to a forum for propagating and imposing one's personal ideology. The danger is present in those situations in which the liturgical ordo is left to the responsibility of one person or a restricted group of persons without community participation.

The Components of Culture

Culture is sometimes defined according to its components. Cultural anthropologists name three: values, patterns, and institutions.

1. Values

Values are principles which influence and give direction to the life and activities of a community and its members. They are formative of the community's attitude or behavior toward social, religious, political, and ethical realities. The value of hospitality, for example, shapes the active vocabulary of a community and creates pertinent rites to welcome, entertain, and send off guests. The value of family ties brings members back to parental homes for family meetings and annual celebrations. The value of leadership is extolled by titles of honor and pledges of loyalty on the part of the community, and by the corresponding promise of active service by the leader.

The liturgy has also its set of values. These are parallel to human values, although they are obviously seen from a Christian perspective. Hospitality, for example, acquires a distinctly Christian meaning in the baptismal celebration, when the community receives the newly baptized. It is expressed by the openness with which strangers are welcomed by the community into its eucharistic table. The Sunday ministers of hospitality are not mere ushers; they perform the task of Christian hospitality not only toward strangers but also the members of the household. Surely we claim the *domus ecclesiae* as our home, but we do not wish to get in and out of our home anonymously; we need to be welcomed back and seen off at the door.

Another important liturgical value is community spirit, which is a broader version of family ties. In the 1970's, the following remark was often heard from people who found Sunday liturgy utterly boring, if not meaningless: "Why go to church, if one can worship God at home, in the privacy of one's room?" When liturgy is regarded merely as a vertical relationship in which the horizontal can be dispensed with, such an attitude is easily generated. But if the liturgy is viewed as a cultural reality possessing its own value of community spirit or family ties, coming together every Sunday in order to celebrate as a Christian community or family should not be too difficult to understand. Nor does it come as a surprise when people get deeply involved in church matters and remain loyal to the community. Something of the natural order of things is carried over to the realm of the supernatural.

The value of leadership is a basic ingredient of the concept of liturgical assembly. The liturgy is essentially the worship of an assembled community, that particular image of Christ's Church, which is organically structured, or we may also say structurally organized. We refer here to the relationship between the presider and the assembly. Whether we speak of episcopal and presbyteral hierarchy or of the presidency of regional synods, we are dealing with no less than the office of church leadership, and consequently with liturgical leadership. This is a value which is inherent in the very nature of community worship, as it is in every secular assembly and institution, not excluding democratic systems. In our mainstream tradition we cannot conceive of acephalous liturgical celebrations. Even in those liturgies where the hierarchical representative does not preside, there is always a layleader, a *primus inter pares*, yet *primus*.

2. Cultural Patterns

The second component of culture are cultural patterns. These are the typical way members of a society think or form concepts, express their thoughts through language, ritualize aspects of their life, and create art forms. The areas covered by cultural patterns are thus: thought, language, rites and symbols, literature, music, architecture, and all other expressions of the fine arts. We call them cultural patterns because they are rather predictable, in the sense that they follow an established course. Things are thought out, spoken of, and done according to a certain pattern, in much the same way we expect cherries to blossom in spring. Thus every cultural group has its typical way of thinking, verbalizing concepts, expressing values, and so on.

Without intending to generalize or offend people's cultural sensitivities, allow me to present a stereotypical example. If you present the latest and most advanced computer to a Japanese, what do you think will be his or her spontaneous thought? Will it not be something on its technology? How about the Chinese? Will it not be its market value? And the Filipino? Some Filipinos answer that it will be on how to imitate the product cheaply. Each group possesses a cultural trait, a genius, all its own which identifies them, individualizes them as a people and a race.

In passing it might be useful to note that the law of cultural patterns is verified not only in social groupings but in individuals as well. Each of us personally operates according to set individual patterns. Banal things like putting on shoes first on the left foot and then on the right are day-to-day examples. When we think we know a person sufficiently, we tend to comment after hearing or seeing something from him or her, "typical, isn't it?"

Cultural patterns are so named also because they are the society's norms of life into which a person is born and reared. Through the process of what anthropologists call enculturation a person is initiated and trained to behave according to such patterns that these become like second nature to each of the community. That is why, anything which happens outside the normal pattern is regarded as something exceptional or anomalous. Although cultural patterns do not eliminate individuality, they shape members of society within the established bounds of social acceptability. For this reason we should have no scruples distinguishing one society from another, one racial group from another. The extent with which we accept the profound influence cultural patterns have on members of a society or race is shown when we say things like, "don't be surprised he does things so; he's German, that's why." Comments such as this are not necessarily judgmental; rather they express a perception, namely that cultural patterns have the power to shape the life of an individual, as they conform him or her to the image society has of itself and its members.

Cultural patterns are at the root of social and racial identities. The typical way in which members of a group think, speak, and ritualize allows us to distinguish one cultural group from another. Thus, each cultural group has its thought, language, and ritual patterns with which to express the values of hospitality, community spirit, and leadership.

a. Thought Pattern: It is helpful to engage in a process of introspection in order to indentify one's own cultural patterns. What comes immediately to mind when a guest or a stranger is announced? We are dealing, in other words, with thought patterns, with concepts and images that spontaneously arise in the mind. Typical of the biblical world is theophany: God visits his people in the person of strangers. The sixth-century Rule of Benedict directs the porter of the monastery to welcome guests as Christ himself, and to answer those who knock at the monastery door with the exclamation, "thanks be to God." But one cultural group has this curious imagery: "A guest who stays for more than three days begins to smell like fish."

b. Language Pattern: From thought pattern we pass to language pattern. What words and phrases do we readily associate with the value of hospitality? What are the first words we address to a guest? A number of cultural groups, especially in Asia, waste no time with set formularies like "welcome," "how are you," "I hope you had an enjoyable trip," "have a seat," and so on depending on the situation. Instead the host's first words are: "have you eaten yet?" Language patterns reveal what is uppermost in the mind of a welcoming host: concern for the well-being of guests. Throughout the duration of a visit guests are given the reassurance of being welcome and cared for with words like "feel at home," "you are family," or "yell when you need something."

c. Ritual Pattern: From language we turn to rites. The value of hospitality is ritualized according to established patterns. Handshake, embrace, slight bow of the head, hands pointed toward the forehead, kissing the right hand of the elders or placing it on one's forehead are some of the ritualizations of welcome and leave-taking. Guests who are familiar with these ritual patterns expect to receive them from their host. It is not surprising that no less than Jesus was offended when his host Simon failed to kiss him and offer water for his feet as he entered his house. In the ancient world footwashing was a sign of hospitality and certainly a source of physical comfort for those who travelled on foot. As late as the sixth century the Rule of Benedict required the abbot and community to wash the feet of incoming guests. Different cultural groups have different rituals of entertaining guests. Some of these are really details of social refinements, the ignorance or omission of which constitute a *faux pas* in hospitality. Examples are the ritual of introducing the guests, the assignment of places at table, the order of serving the food. Sometimes the children are told by their parents to perform for the guests by singing, playing a musical instrument, reciting a poem, or dancing. In a sense the host will not spare anything to please the guest. It is not unusual in some cultures for a family to bring out the best it can afford in terms of food and lodging, or alas get into unnecessary debt because of hospitality. Guests are sacred and the ritual patterns of hospitality are often as extravagant as the furnishings used for sacred worship.

Ritual patterns of hospitality manifest themselves not only when guests are welcomed and entertained, but also when they are sent off. Leave-taking can be as elaborate as the rite of welcoming. In some cultures saying farewell can last forever. This is so because the host, out of a sense of hospitality, tries to hold back the guest, even if at times this might prove inconvenient for those who have a schedule to keep or a plane to catch. The rites used for welcoming are normally also those for leave-taking, but the formularies express various sentiments from the prayerlike *"adieu"* or *"adios,"* to the hopeful *"arrivederci"* or "see you soon," and even to the apologetic "I wish I could have done more."

Cultural patterns of hospitality are the typical way a group of people think or form concepts and images about guests, speak to them and about them, and perform rites to welcome, entertain, and send them off. How do these things affect the liturgy? If we regard the liturgy as a cultural reality, though with a divine component, and consider that one of its values is hospitality, it becomes evident that the liturgy too follows a system of cultural patterns. In other words, the liturgy has its peculiar way of thinking and speaking about hospitality and of expressing it in ritual form. We find this in its ordo which, due to its consistency and predictability, is called typical, that is, an exemplar to be followed. The ordo contains the typical way the liturgy handles the value of hospitality.

Though we can ultimately trace our liturgical origins to the Jewish tradition, we have to accept the fact that in the West the Christian liturgy has been ulteriorly influenced by the Roman cultural patterns. The western liturgies, as they are known today among Roman Catholics, Lutherans, and Anglicans, are a conglomeration of cultural patterns from the Jewish to the Christian medieval times. Nonetheless they all possess a distinct and typical style of formulary and rituality which we can identify as being typically Roman: sober, concise, direct, and practical. It is this kind of cultural patterns that has, by and large, shaped the patterns of hospitality in the western liturgies.

A strikingly Roman pattern affecting hospitality in the pre-Vatican II liturgy is the abruptness with which the assembly is sent off. In concise and direct words the Roman assembly was told: *ite, missa est.* In modern English we would simply announce, "meeting adjourned." Under the influence of this Roman pattern the liturgical assembly is quickly blessed and sent away in three words. Some even call this rite of leave-taking the rite of dismissal, which can be quite offensive and is absolutely lacking in social refinements. Something apropos needs to be said here. That people do not find offense at being dismissed is a sure sign that they do not take the words they hear seriously enough or they have formed the habit of not regarding the liturgy as a cultural reality. The Roman genius for brevity applied to the leave-taking in the liturgy can cause uneasiness among societies where it takes considerable time and art to say good-bye. It is understandable that some liturgists try to elaborate this part of the liturgy in an effort to incorporate into it another pattern of hospitality.

The rite of communion needs to be reviewed in the context of hospitality. That the presider takes communion ahead of the assembly can be explained by the office of leadership. But the kind of imagery it creates can be quite culturally outrageous. The presider, in the sight of all, eats and drinks first, and only then distributes communion to the rest.

Perhaps the most significant expression of liturgical hospitality is in the greetings "The Lord be with you" and "Peace be with you." These greetings, which are said at various moments in the eucharistic celebration, serve as words of welcome, as reassurance of Christ's presence. Some presiders replace them with more contemporary formulas, or else juxtapose them, thereby giving the wrong impression that these Christological greetings do not have the same value of hospitality that contemporary greetings such as "Good morning" or "Good evening" have.

d. A Note on Other Values: The same considerations can be made regarding the value of family spirit. We perceive this liturgical value in words like "family" and "household of God," which are used frequently to describe the assembly gathered together. The biblical imagery of sharing in one bread and one cup heightens the value of family. The very name of the church building, *domus ecclesiae* or the house of the church, suggests a pattern of thought and language. The architectural disposition of the building as well as the order of the gathered community, with the presider and the ministers in the sanctuary and the assembly in the nave, seems to be patterned, however, on the arrangement observed among Roman families when they were at meetings. In a cultural ambit wherein the *paterfamilias* reigned supreme, such an arrangement loudly affirmed a cultural pattern regarding the family.

As regards the value of leadership, the liturgy observes a clear thought, language, and ritual pattern. The image of the bishop in the writings of Ignatius of Antioch is that of God, while the presbyters surrounding him reflect the college of apostles. In the liturgy the office of leader is traditionally symbolized by the president's chair, probably influenced by the Roman *cathedra* or seat of authority. The liturgy also reserves certain functions to the leader of the assembly. Traditionally these are the presidential prayers, especially the eucharistic prayer, and the homily or sermon. From the time of Emperor Constantine, bishops (particularly the bishop of Rome) and to a degree also the presbyters and deacons, acquired political rights and with them the corresponding imperial court ceremonials. Bishops could use the throne, be greeted with a choral song as they entered the basilica, have their feet kissed, and so on. Thus, the liturgy's pattern of leadership, which had been previously focused on shepherding, as we read in the third-century *Apostolic Tradition*, gradually shifted to a pattern of leadership which was more sociopolitical in character.

e. Conclusion: From the foregoing discussion we are able to conclude that the liturgy operates according to cultural patterns. It has its way of projecting its values through a particular use of language, rites, and symbols. It is helpful to keep in mind that the cultural patterns which are operative in the Western liturgy do not come from a single source. They form several strata, the result of centuries of contact with different cultures. We have been focusing on the value of hospitality. Perhaps we can rightly say that the western liturgy was marked and should continue to be marked by hospitality, by openness to other cultures, by friendliness toward the cultural patterns of the people who celebrate it. All this gives us the assurance that our effort to inculturate the liturgy is not alien to the history of the liturgy itself. Incarnation does not belong to the past: it is life for all local churches today.

3. Institutions

The third component of culture are institutions. These are society's traditional rites whereby it celebrates the different phases of human life from birth to death. Thus we speak of initiation rites, rites of marriage and parenthood, rites of taking offices of leadership, and rites connected with sickness, death, and funerals. Other institutions are society's celebrations to mark the beginnings of the seasons of the year, especially spring and summer for shepherds and farmers respectively, and to commemorate memorable legends in its mythology or events in its history. These rites are feasts which engage the family, the neighborhood, or the entire community. They are celebrated with great regularity and fervor, and with a fidelity to traditional rites that put liturgical rubricists to shame.

The *Pesachim* says of the child who protests against the passover meal observance: "The impious child asks, What ceremonies do you perform, and why do you impose this observance every year? Since he excludes himself from the observance, he should be answered thus: It is because God granted great favors to me. But he has not granted them to this impious child who, if he had been in Egypt under Moses, would not have deserved to be delivered from that land." In other religions the efficacy of the institution depended on the exact and minute observance of ritual details. Such is the power and influence institutions have on the life of communities.

The liturgy has also its institutions. It possesses special rites to accompany the faithful in important events in life, from birth to maturity in the faith, to critical moments like marriage, call to leadership, and life's decline. All of these institutions respond to a particular situation in the life of the Christian community and its members. Likewise they have been profoundly influenced by the values, cultural patterns, and institutions of various cultures. They are, in other words, institutions in the cultural sense of the word.

The liturgy has other institutions, celebrated at various times of the year according to a calendar system, an institution in itself, which is known as "liturgical year." A few feasts originate in the Jewish world of Jesus and his disciples: Sunday, Easter, and Pentecost. In the course of time a great number have been added from both religious and secular feasts: Epiphany, Nativity, John the Baptist. Others have a political coloring, introduced in times of uneasy relationship between Church and politics: Christ the King and Joseph the Worker. And lastly some feasts were occasioned by turbulence and calamities: Michael the Archangel, Rogation Days. The Church instituted such feasts, as any human society would. The difference is that we deal here with Christian institutions: they celebrate the mystery of Christ and the Church, though they do so in the context of the culture and traditions of the celebrating assembly.

Summary

The liturgy is not celebrated in a cultural vacuum but in the living cultural expressions of the worshiping assembly. This principle has urged us to delve into the cultural components of Christian worship. The awareness of the cultural dimension of the liturgy led to the need to examine the very components of culture itself. This is an exercise which is prerequisite to inculturation. For it is not sufficient to know only the nature, purpose, and laws of Christian liturgy. We are required to have a certain amount of familiarity also with the culture that will enter into dialogue with the liturgy. We also reached the conclusion that to know the theology of the liturgy more profoundly, we must know its cultural traits as well. As in the mystery of the incarnation, we are led to the knowledge and love of the invisible God by the knowledge of the God made human.

We described in summary form the traits of culture as contemporary anthropologists understand it, comparing such traits with the cultural characteristics of the liturgy. In a sense, provided exception is made regarding its divinely revealed or instituted elements, Christian liturgy can fall under the category of a cultural reality. This is so, because it has the same components that are identifiable also in culture.

These components we called values, cultural patterns, and institutions. The liturgy also has human values which it projects as Christian values: hospitality, family spirit, leadership. These values are expressed in established patterns of thought, language, rites, and symbols, according to an *ordo* or a typical liturgical way of speaking and performing the rite. Finally we examined some of the institutions whereby the liturgy concretely celebrates the mystery of Christ and the Church in the vesture of cultural values and patterns. The values, cultural patterns, and institutions in the liturgy are not monocultural: they belong to various cultures in the world and form a cultural conglomerate. Christian liturgy welcomes the values, cultural patterns, and institutions of peoples and races, so long as they can be vehicles of Christ's message. This, in the final analysis, is what the incarnation is all about.

*   *   *

For Further Reading

M. Chomsky, *Syntactic Structures* (The Hague, 1964)

A. Chupungco, *Shaping the Easter Feast* (Washington, D.C., 1992)

C. Di Sante, "Cultura e liturgia," *Nuovo Dizionario di Liturgia* (Rome, 1984) 341-51

M. Eliade, *Patterns in Comparative Religion* (London, 1958)

E. James, *Seasonal Feasts and Festivals* (New York, 1965)

J. Lyons, *Semantics*, 2 vols. (Cambridge, 1979)

L. Luzbetak, *The Church in Cultures* (Pasadena, 1977)

T. Krosnicki, *Ancient Patterns in Modern Prayer* (Washington, D.C., 1973)

F. Keesing, *Cultural Anthropology: The Science of Custom* (New York, 1958)

R. Panikkar, "Man as Ritual Being," *Chicago Studies* 16 (1977) 5-28

D. Power, *Unsearchable Riches: The Symbolic Nature of the Liturgy* (New York, 1984)

K. Richter, *The Meaning of the Sacramental Symbols* (Collegeville, 1990)

J. Shaughnessey, ed., *The Roots of Ritual* (Grand Rapids, 1974)

T. Tentori, *Antropologia culturale* (Rome, 1980)

A. Terrin, *Leitourgia. Dimensione fenomeonologica e aspetti semiotici* (Brescia, 1988)

A. Triacca and A. Pistoia, eds., *Liturgie et anthropologie.* Conférence Saint-Serge. XXXVI Semaine d'études liturgiques (Rome, 1990)

V. Turner, *The Ritual Process* (Chicago, 1969)

CONTEMPORARY QUESTIONS ON CHURCH ARCHITECTURE AND CULTURE[1]

S. Anita Stauffer

There is an irony about the contextualization of church architecture. On the one hand, it is the most immediately observable kind of contextualization that is possible. On the other hand, it is often the last type of contextualization to occur, because it usually involves considerably more expenditure of money, and takes longer to accomplish, than contextualizing liturgy or church music. Nonetheless, questions around the contextualization of worship space must be a priority for the churches, both because people are so greatly influenced and formed by what they see, and because contextualization can never be profound unless it involves the worship space as well as the liturgy and music.

Terms

It is important to note that the term *architecture* is used here in a very broad sense, not in the strict architectonic sense. It refers here not only to the structure and form and plan of a building, but also to everything that comprises the worship space—the entire environment for worship, including the liturgical centers (font, altar, pulpit or ambo), the aesthetics, the iconography, the furnishings, the ornamentation, the colors of vestments and paraments, and the materials. All of these elements relate to culture. For example, color symbolism differs greatly by cultures. White is used in the Western Church as a symbol of joy and the light of Christ, while in many Oriental cultures white is the color of grief.

---

[1]   An earlier form of this paper, including an historical section, appeared as "Inculturation and Church Architecture" in *Studia Liturgica*, 20:1 (1990), 70-80. When presented in Hong Kong, this paper was illustrated with slides; specific references to the places shown have been deleted here.

The terms *contextualization* or *localization* are preferred because they are broader than the word *inculturation*. In considering architectural issues, one must give attention to ethnic, geographic, and climatic influences, and to such factors as local building materials. For example, in planning a church in an earthquake-prone area, obviously the instability of the ground must be kept prominently in mind in designing the structural system.

Two Functions

A space for Christian worship serves two functions—the practical and the symbolic. On the practical or utilitarian side, the space gives shelter for worshipers and provides that which is necessary for the celebration of Word and sacrament: font, altar, pulpit or ambo, and a place for the people to sit or stand. However, the worship space itself is also a symbol. The ideal is a synthesis of the utilitarian and the symbolic.[2] Luther recognized this dual purpose when he wrote: "Today in our churches we have an altar for the administration of the Eucharist, and we have platforms or pulpits for teaching the people. These objects were built not only to meet a need [*necessitatis*] but also to create a solemn atmosphere [*solemnitatis*]."[3]   Peter Brunner has commented on this passage from Luther:

> This distinction and association between *necessitas* and *solemnitas* is reminiscent of the two sides that must be distinguished in the architectural problem of church construction. *Necessitas* corresponds to the technical-rational side, which grows from the practical needs, *solemnitas* corresponds to the particular artistic side of the problem, ac-

---

[2]   See Stanley Abercrombie, *Architecture as Art: An Esthetic Analysis* (New York: Van Nostrand Reinhold Company, 1984), 103-105; Roger Scruton, *The Aesthetics of Architecture* (Princeton, NJ: Princeton University Press, 1979), 6 and *passim*; and Harold W. Turner, *From Temple to Meeting House: The Phenomenology and Theology of Places of Worship* (The Hague, Netherlands: Mouton Publishers, 1979), 325-326.

[3]   Luther, "Lectures on Genesis" (1535), in Jaroslav Pelikan, ed., Volume 1, *Luther's Works* (St. Louis, MO: Concordia Publishing House, 1958), 95. In the Weimar edition of Luther (42:72:17-20), the text is: "*Hodie in templis habemus altare, propter communionem Eucharistiae, habemus suggesta seu cathedras ad docendum populum. Haec non necessitatis tantum causa, sed etiam solennitatis facta sunt.*"

cording to which the spacial form becomes a symbolic reference to the hidden pneumatic event of worship.[4]

Current Questions and Issues

The interdisciplinary nature of this subject is staggering, including as it does such diverse disciplines as liturgics, theology, ritual studies, cultural anthropology, topistics,[5] aesthetic philosophy, and various other subdisciplines of art and architecture. Current situations of churches around the world render the topic even more complex, given the realities of cultural evolution, cultural diffusion, and cultural pluralism—as well as the different sociological dynamics between indigenous populations and immigrant populations. It is important, however, to attempt to address the issues and identify some of the pertinent questions.

It should be noted that some congregations, especially in Africa, worship out-of-doors. Still, however, there is some arrangement of the people, perhaps in relationship to a hill or a tree or group of trees, and there must be places at which the core liturgical actions are done. The way a worshiping assembly arranges itself around liturgical centers, and in relationship to the natural world, expresses something about their culture as well as about their theology of worship.

1. What is the core of Christian worship, and what does that core require spatially?

The core has been identified as Word, Baptism, and Eucharist.[6] That core assumes a body of Christians assembled around Jesus Christ, who is manifest and present in that core of Word and sacrament.

---

[4]   Brunner, *Worship in the Name of Jesus* (St. Louis, MO: Concordia Publishing House, 1968), 348, fn. 297. The original German by Brunner is *Zur Lehre vom Gottesdienst der in Namen Jesu versammelten Gemeinde*, in *Leiturgia, Handbuch des evangelischen Gottesdienstes*, Volume I, edited by Karl F. Müller and Walter Blankenburg (Kassel: Johannes Stauda Verlag, 1954).

[5]   See E. Victor Walter, "The Places of Experience," in *The Philosophical Forum*, XII:2 (Winter 1980-1981), 159-181. Topistics is "the holistic study of places" (163). See also his book, *Placeways: A Theory of the Human Environment* (Chapel Hill, NC: University of North Carolina Press, 1988).

[6]   Cartigny Statement on Worship and Culture 3.7.

Christians come together to hear the Word of God proclaimed, to be baptized, and to share the Lord's family feast. Thus, worship requires a place for the people to assemble (whether outdoors or indoors), a place from which to proclaim the Word, a pool in which to baptize, and a table on which to celebrate the sacramental meal.

What does Lutheran theology say about the meaning of these core actions of assembly, Word, Baptism, and Eucharist? To take just one example: if Lutherans are to give serious attention to Luther, then his repeated writings about the meaning of Baptism must be pondered. For example:

> Baptism...signifies two things—death and resurrection, that is, full and complete justification. When the minister immerses the child in the water it signifies death, and when he draws it forth again it signifies life.... It is...indeed correct to say that Baptism is a washing away of sins, but the expression is too mild and weak to bring out the full significance of Baptism, which is rather a symbol of death and resurrection. For this reason I would have those who are to be baptized completely immersed in the water.... The sinner does not so much need to be washed as he needs to die, in order to be wholly renewed and made another creature, and to be conformed to the death and resurrection of Christ, with whom he dies and rises again through Baptism.[7]

Some congregations today are taking Luther's paschal understanding of Baptism, based on Romans 6, so seriously that they are providing fonts in the shape of a Greek cross, with water deep enough for the immersion of both adults and infants. Other congregations have taken the profound meaning of Baptism equally seriously, but on the basis of their African heritage and traditional African respect for the earth, have constructed fonts as pools which look like natural

---

[7]   Martin Luther, "The Babylonian Captivity of the Church" (1520), in Abdel Ross Wentz, ed., Volume 36, *Luther's Works* (Philadelphia: Fortress Press, 1959), 67-68. For similar statements, see the *Large Catechism*, Fourth Part (English text in *The Book of Concord* [Philadelphia: Fortress Press, 1959], 444-445); "The Holy and Blessed Sacrament of Baptism" (1519), LW, Volume 35 (1960), 29; and "The Blessed Sacrament of the Holy and True Body of Christ, and the Brotherhoods" (1519), LW, Volume 35, 50.

bodies of water. The core is the same, and immersion is enabled—
but the form, the external dressing, is different. Culture is in dialogue with liturgical core.

Or consider the first act of Christian worship: that people come together, they gather. The very act of a corporate assembly dictates
that a Christian worship space be quite different from a Hindu or
Buddhist temple, where the purpose is merely for *individuals* to do
cultic acts. In Hinduism and Buddhism, there is no *corporate* (in the
sense of the church as the *corpus*, or body, of Christ) ritual action
comparable to what there is in Christian worship. Thus, the purposes of a Christian church and a temple are totally different,[8] and
that precludes modeling a Christian church after a Hindu or Buddhist temple.

2. How does a people define its own cultural tradition?

How broad, or how narrow, is this definition? With what period or
periods of history does a people identify? To what extent do people
recognize the cumulative nature of their cultural legacy?[9] These are
questions of historical or traditional cultural patterns and their present
value to a people.

For example, to what extent is contemporary European culture influenced by its Gothic inheritance?[10] To ask a more complex question, to what degree is the culture of North Americans of northern
European descent shaped by the northern European architectural
heritage? Most people in North America (as well as other parts of
the world, due to missionary influence) think churches should have
spires and pointed arches and windows. Whether or not they realize
it, their idea of a church has been influenced by twelfth-century Gothic

---

[8] See John F. Butler, "Nineteen Centuries of Christian Missionary Architecture," *Journal of the Society of Architectural Historians*, 21 (1962), 14; and John F. Butler, *Christian Art in India* (Madras, India: Christian Literature Society, 1986), 16-19.

[9] See Frank C. Senn, *Christian Worship and its Cultural Setting* (Philadelphia: Fortress Press, 1983), vii.

[10] Frédéric Debuyst moves beyond the Gothic in considering contemporary French culture and its relationship to church architecture, in his *L'Art chrétien contemporain* (Paris: Nouvelles Editions Mame, 1988).

churches.[11]   Does it matter that Gothic architecture may have had Germanic and Nordic pagan origins?[12]

Another example of twelfth-century European architecture which emphasized verticality and interior darkness is the Norwegian stave church. Built of wood, stave churches were influenced both by domestic and ship-building techniques, and by the early Christian basilical plan. To what extent do contemporary Norwegian Christians claim this part of medieval culture as their own? Anscar Chupungco has written that "No traditional cultural form vanishes completely from the consciousness or the subconscious of the society which it nurtured over generations and on which it imprinted a particular character. That is why museum pieces are not utterly alien to the daily life of a nation."[13] To what extent should the form of "museum pieces" such as stave churches influence the design and decoration of Norwegian churches today?[14] Cultures evolve—constantly. To what extent does a people identify with its history and cultural roots? How do people decide what to claim as their own cultural heritage? Such questions have relevance for their architectural implications for churches. In China, for example, is the ancient practice of *feng shui* applicable and appropriate in the design and placement of Christian churches, or would its use represent syncretism?

Or, to what extent should African heritage be reflected in the design of a worship space for a contemporary African-American urban congregation in the United States? Recently an inner-city congregation in Chicago was forced to construct a new building because the roof of their old church had collapsed under the weight of snow. They formed a committee of parisioners to work with a liturgical consultant in studying both the liturgy and their culture. They identified

---

[11]   Regarding European architectural prototypes and American church adaptations, see Bartlett Hayes, *Tradition Becomes Innovation* (New York: Pilgrim Press, 1983).

[12]   Butler, "Nineteen Centuries...," 5.

[13]   Chupungco, *Cultural Adaptation of the Liturgy* (New York: Paulist Press, 1982), 76.

[14]   Regarding Norwegian church architecture, see Arne Saether, *Kirken Bygg og Bilde: Rom og liturgi mot et tusenårsskifte* (Asker, Norway: Utgitt På Eget Forlag, 1990).

themselves as African-Americans, but with the accent on "American." Still, they wanted to reflect something of their distant-but-important African heritage. The circular shape of the resulting worship space echoes the design of an African hut.[15] A similar design principle has been used in southern African churches which echo the design of tribal kings' huts. One could inquire as to what it means to worshipers there to be in spaces which are reminiscent of the dwelling places of tribal rulers, and associated questions about earthly versus heavenly authority.

3. What is the relationship between the Christian faith and the cultural patterns of a given people?

Certainly it is clear that the fourth-century Church in the West had some respect for Roman culture, since the Church adopted and adapted not only Roman architectural forms but also vesture and ceremonial. But what is the degree to which Christianity in different parts of the world today is or ought to be countercultural and/or transcultural? Are there certain inherited or current cultural forms or influences which are inappropriate for use in a Christian worship space? Are there some architectural or decorative forms which would undermine the symbolic meaning of a church building? Are there cultures or subcultures whose values are contradictory to the liturgy and the theology it enacts?

Much of the United States population today is highly influenced by the entertainment culture of Hollywood. One of the results is that worship is often seen not as participatory liturgy, but as a "program" to be observed passively—something to be watched, a time to be entertained. The architectural manifestation of this is worship spaces which resemble theatres, with theatre seats, sloping floors, and chancels which look like stages. Does not this form of architectural inculturation not twist and warp what worship is? Within the context of the American entertainment culture, Christian liturgy must be countercultural.

---

[15] See David Baldwin, "There Is a Sweet, Sweet Spirit in This Place," *Faith and Form*, XXV (Fall 1991), 24-26.

National identity is a part of many cultures. However, is there not something contradictory about placing signs of national identity, such as national flags, in a space used to worship the God who transcends national boundaries—even in countries which have a state church? Do not flags as symbols of national particularity make the Christian confession of catholicity (in the Apostles' and Nicene Creeds, for example) less convincing? How can the Church counteract the increasing tendency for people to consider their national, ethnic, cultural, tribal, or caste identity more important than their Baptism into the whole communion of saints?[16]

It is also important to recognize the different dynamics between Christians who live in a predominantly non-Christian society, and those who live in a so-called Christian society. There is an enormous new church in Yamoussoukro, Ivory Coast, which closely resembles St. Peter's Basilica in Rome. The post-Renaissance style hardly seems at home in the Ivory Coast of Africa. But perhaps the intention was laudable: to provide a place of Christian identity in a country in which only 10% of the population is Christian, and 90% is either Islamic or animist. The design intention was to be countercultural, although one might ask whether the resulting building was quite the best form to be so.

In a nation in which the predominant religion is animism, or Buddhism, or Shinto, or Hinduism, Christians may express the need to divorce themselves from architectural forms which they identify with the non-Christian faith. Indeed, the missionary influence may have caused such people to identify western architecture with Christianity. On the other hand, it may be important for Christian church buildings to reflect something of local culture even in such a land,

---

[16] See Samuel P. Huntington, "The Clash of Civilizations?" (*Foreign Affairs*, 72:3, Summer 1993), in which he identifies seven or eight major civilizations in the world today: Western, Confucian, Japanese, Islamic, Hindu, Slavic/Orthodox, Latin American, and possibly African (25). He defines civilization as "the highest cultural grouping of people and the broadest level of cultural identity people have short of that which distinguishes humans from other species" (24). A civilization "is defined both by common objective elements, such as language, history, religion, costume, institutions, and by the subjective self-identification of people" (24). Huntington argues that the great world conflicts of the future will be cultural, not national.

but using such cultural forms is not always easy. In a nation like India, it is difficult to make a distinction between Hindu religion and Indian culture. The dilemma was described in a report of a seminar on Christian art in India, held at Gurukul Lutheran Theological College in 1976:

> Over the centuries all of the arts have been utilized fully and skillfully in the Hindu religion. The difficulty for Christians is to find artistic expressions which do not carry heavy overtones of Hindu belief.
>
> The obvious reaction to this situation was to adopt the Western artistic forms. These have now come to be 'indigenous' for many Indian Christians.[17]

Thus, another question becomes obvious.

4. What is the meaning of an architectural form or a visual design, and how does that meaning relate to a particular cultural context?

What are the typical architectural forms in a given culture, and what meaning do they have in that cultural context?[18] That is, what are the cultural building patterns of shape, orientation, structural systems (e.g., post-and-beam construction, or arch construction), symmetry vs. assymetry, the relationship of the vertical to the horizontal, and the use or non-use of axiality? Once such culturally typical architectural forms have been identified, they can be analyzed with regard to their cultural meaning, and then their appropriateness for use in church buildings and worship spaces.

---

[17]   Quoted in Herbert E. Hoefer, ed., *Christian Art in India* (Madras, India: Gurukul Lutheran Theological College and Research Institute, 1982), 39.

[18]   See Rudolf Arnheim, *The Dynamics of Architectural Form* (Berkeley, CA: University of California Press, 1977); and Francis Ching, *Architecture: Form, Space, and Order* (New York: Van Nostrand Reinhold, 1979).

It is important to remember that architecture "never simply exists; it also communicates; it has content; it conveys messages."[19] Much hinges on how a church building is interpreted by those who come there for worship. For example, what are the symbolic messages conveyed by African churches which use a variant of the traditional conical thatched roof and bichromatic geometric wall painting? Or, what meanings do Navajo Christians in the United States find in church buildings modelled after traditional hogans or tepees? Does the central plan simply convey a generic holy place, or does it also carry symbolism of indigenous Navajo religion? To what degree, if any, do pre-Christian sensibilities get imported into Christian spirituality when pre-Christian building types are used as models for Christian churches?

Similar questions can be explored regarding the symbolism of art for a worship space. For example, what is the meaning of a cross or corpus surmounting a lotus flower, a traditional Hindu and Buddhist symbol? In traditional Buddhist iconography, for example, Buddha is shown resting on the lotus.[20]

Such issues are not new, of course. Similar questions could be asked about the third-century mosaic from the Christian necropolis beneath St. Peter's Basilica in Rome, in which Christ is depicted as Helios, the sun god. Did such art help early Christians understand the Lord's identity in terms they could grasp from their culture, or did it confuse them? Was the mosaic an example of religious diffusion, or was it syncretism? In all such examples, historic or contemporary, one must ask what was or what is the symbolic meaning system, and how was/is it decoded? How are symbolic meaning systems influenced by culture? How by theology? Such inquiry leads to questions of the interpretation of images.

---

[19]   Abercrombie, 125.

[20]   See Daniel Johnson Fleming, *Christian Symbols in a World Community* (New York: Friendship Press, 1940), 37.

5. What are the functions of religious images, and how do they relate to various cultures?

There is a wide range of types of religious images, and they are interpreted in different ways.[21]   One type is the aforementioned mosaic of Christ as the sun god—there was an attempt to interpret Christ in the artistic vocabulary of classical Greek or Roman culture and religion.

A second type is exemplified in images in which Jesus and others[22] are depicted with approximate historical accuracy—for example, sculpture or painting in which Jesus is shown as a relatively young middle eastern Jewish man.

A third type is exemplified in images in which Jesus and others are depicted in ways with which a given culture or ethnic group can relate, rather than in ways which are either classical or historically accurate. This type of image is perhaps the most frequent; consider all of the paintings in which Jesus is shown as a fair-skinned European. Theologian Geoffrey Wainwright terms this "the iconographic tradition which 'translates' Jesus to the artist's time and place."[23] All too frequently, European and American missionaries to other parts of the world have used images depicting Jesus as a white Anglo-Saxon man. In reaction to that, the same type of image has arisen in other cultures in which, for example, Jesus is depicted as an African, or a Chinese.

A fourth type of image is the abstract. For example, Islamic culture rejects representational images in favor of the abstract. What does that imply for the iconography in Christian worship spaces in an

---

[21]   For a scheme somewhat different from mine, but which has informed me, see Margaret R. Miles, Images as *Insight: Visual Understanding in Western Christianity and Secular Culture* (Boston: Beacon Press, 1985), 34.

[22]   Images of Jesus are more problematic than images of other persons, because of his divine-human nature; some types of images emphasize his divinity, while others emphasize his humanity.

[23]   Wainwright, *Doxology: The Praise of God in Worship, Doctrine, and Life* (New York: Oxford University Press, 1980), 365.

Islamic context? Should the art be contextual (and thus abstract), or countercultural (and thus figural)? In considering art and iconography for a Christian worship space in a given culture, it is important to know how these four types of images function in that culture.

6. *What are the aesthetics of a given culture, and how does the aesthetic system relate to a sense of the Holy?*

How is beauty understood in a given cultural context?[24] This is to ask an extraordinarily complex question.[25] To begin, one must explore languages. What is the word for *beauty* in various languages, and what does the word mean? In English, there are subtle but clear differences between *beautiful*, *pretty*, and *lovely*. Beyond the linguistic questions, what is considered beautiful varies by culture. There is no universal sense of aesthetic quality.

The second part of this inquiry is, how is holiness understood? And what is the relationship between beauty and holiness in both cultural and Christian contexts? From the beginning of Christianity, there has been a connection between beauty and worship of the Holy One, and that connection has been expressed architecturally in different eras and different cultures. Reflecting neo-Platonism, the twelfth-century French Abbot Suger, who was responsible for the influential Gothic renovation of the church of Saint-Denis near Paris, wrote: "By way of material beauties the mind is elevated to true Beauty...." (that is, to God).[26] The eminent American Lutheran architect Edward Sövik frequently reflects in his writings the same neo-Platonic

---

[24] See Jacques Maquet, *The Aesthetic Experience: An Anthropologist Looks at the Visual Arts* (New Haven, CT: Yale University Press, 1986); and Enrique Dussel, "Christian Art of the Oppressed in Latin America (Towards an Aesthetics of Liberation)," *Concilium*, 132:2 (1980), 40-52.

[25] For one summary of various Western (and, to a lesser extent, Eastern) approaches, see James Alfred Martin, Jr., *Beauty and Holiness: The Dialogue between Aesthetics and Religion* (Princeton, NJ: Princeton University Press, 1990). Regarding the medieval period in the West, see Umberto Eco, *Art and Beauty in the Middle Ages* (New Haven, CT: Yale University Press, 1986). Another approach, focussed on modern Western culture, is Gregor T. Goethals, *The Electronic Golden Calf: Images, Religion, and the Making of Meaning* (Cambridge, MA: Cowley Publications, 1990).

[26] Quoted in Georges Duby, *History of Medieval Art*, Volume I (New York: Rizzoli, 1986), 201.

influence, as well as Rudolf Otto's definition of the Holy.[27]   Sövik has said, for example, that "Beauty is the portal to transcendence."[28] Later he elaborated: "There is no other viable symbol for the Holy but the beautiful. For beauty, like the Holy, is a mystery. It is perceived not by reason but by intuition. It is at once remote, beyond understanding, and immediate.... Beauty is the metaphor of the Holy."[29]

Perhaps here is a truth for both East and West. However, it is necessary to explore in each cultural pattern what beauty is, how it relates to the Holy, and how beauty can be used in the design of places for Christian worship, in terms of art and design as well as the use of natural beauty in flowers.

One question related both to beauty and to a sense of the transcendent is the use of light, both natural and artificial. In a given culture, what are the patterns of light and darkness vis-a-vis beauty and the Holy? How can light and darkness be used in places for Christian worship in these contexts?

7. *How can architectural provision be made for the different musical instruments used in Christian worship in different cultural settings, as well as for different cultural traditions of movement?*

A pipe organ, for example, requires different architectural provision than a group of indigeneous instrumentalists in south India or Africa. In addition, different types of music and musical instruments may well demand different acoustical provisions.

As well, movements of various sorts require architectural accommodation. In Africa, for example, if forms of dance are to be included in worship, spatial provision must be made.[30]

---

27   Otto, *The Idea of the Holy* (London: Oxford University Press, 1950).

28   "The Environment for Sight, Sound and Action," in *Dialog*, 25:4 (Fall 1986), 276. This paper was originally presented at a consultation on architecture for worship, sponsored by the Lutheran Church in America. See also Walter Huffman and S. Anita Stauffer, *Where We Worship* (Minneapolis: Augsburg Fortress, 1987).

29   "The Mirror of the Church," *Faith and Form* (Fall 1988), 17.

30   See Boka di Mpasi Loudi, "Freedom of Bodily Expression in the African Liturgy," *Concilium*, 132:2 (1980), 53-64.

*8. In multicultural congregations, how can the cultural heteroge-
neity be reflected in architecture and iconography for worship?*

It is common now in both North America and Europe for congregations to be pluralistic, that is, to include persons from diverse cultural and ethnic backgrounds. It is important that no one feels excluded. That becomes quite challenging in terms of architecture and
art, especially when the cultural makeup of congregations changes
and evolves.

*9. What are the dynamics of change within cultures, and what are
the implications of that change for the place in which people
worship the God who is eternal?*

This is a question especially relevant to immigrant congregations,
wherever they may be, because the people's need either to identify
with or to reject their traditional cultural architectural forms changes
over time as assimilation occurs. Newcomers to a country may
"gradually lose the language and cultural characteristics of their native
land and adopt the language together with the dominant cultural characteristics of the new nation"[31]—at least that has been the historical
pattern with immigrants to the United States; only time will tell if
that pattern continues.

Conclusion

These nine questions are some which need to be asked and explored.
They are deliberately posed here as questions rather than answers.
However, there is one principle which can help "sort" the answers
regarding the relationship between culture and liturgical architecture: The architecture and art of a worship space should speak both
the universality of the Gospel and the church catholic, as well as the
particularity of a congregation's own cultural background(s) and
identity.

---

[31]   Joseph P. Fitzpatrick, *One Church, Many Churches: The Challenges of Diversity* (Kansas
City, MO: Sheed & Ward, 1987), 142-143.

A Christian congregation gathered for worship needs a visual sense of belonging to the whole *communio sanctorum*, the whole Church of every time and every place—as well as a visual sense that their worship space is hospitable to them, whatever their own cultural identity. The Gospel is relevant to all cultures, while at the same time it transcends and seeks ultimately to transform all earthly cultures. A worship space, like the liturgy itself, must not be captive to any given culture. God alone is the Holy One. Jesus Christ alone is at the center of a worshiping assembly. The baptized people of God must respect all people of various world cultures, while at the same time not allowing any culture itself become an idol. The contextual, the countercultural, and the transcultural all have a place in architecture for Christian worship.

DYNAMICS OF LITURGY AND WORLD MUSICS: A METHODOLOGY FOR EVALUATION

Mark P. Bangert

Large-scale festivities for the Protestant Church of Bali normally involve Balinese dancing and the gamelan orchestra. Attending one of these events leaves one with the sense that here is the inculturated worshiping church at its best.

In liturgies for church-wide festivities, teen-age female dancers, usually about a dozen in number, offer their choreography through a sign language which is both understood by the worshipers and capable of carrying the message of Gospel. The fifteen or more members of the gamelan orchestra, all dressed in brightly colored costumes, sit to play their instruments, which include a variety of metallophones, xylophones, and gongs. Dancers and musicians carry on a dialog, each urging the other on. Coming at the beginning of the liturgy it is a kind of call to worship in an envelope recognizably Balinese, and, one suspects, appealing to the deep cultural roots of the people.

Experienced observers still thrill to the exotic sounds of the gamelan scale patterns even as they cannot fail to be impressed by the musical and choreographic intricacies, all in a way reflective of Balinese life and faith. But if they remain for more of the liturgy, they will hear all the people together sing hymns which are either Western in style or direct Western imports. With that, some of the exuberance over inculturation can dissipate.

What goes on here among the more than sixty thousand people who belong to the Protestant Church of Bali lifts up a variety of opportunities and challenges facing churches both young and old. Like churches all over the world, these Balinese worshipers utilize their own musical resources, while they are simultaneously charmed by a hymnody from another culture. While the gamelan and its dancers are indeed marvelous examples of inculturated worship, they nevertheless are performance-oriented and non-participatory. Does the gamelan really belong in the liturgy? If so, should it be balanced by other indigenous music which is more capable of carrying the assembly's song? Do the carvings which adorn the gamelan instruments, carvings which portray old Balinese understandings of the ying/yang struggles between good and evil, represent a theology at odds with Christian teaching? Questions such as these are or probably will be asked by the Balinese Christians themselves.

Their struggles and joys in their own music give us all energy to search for those common dynamics which emerge when worship takes on musical form, no matter where one is in the world. To do that is a daunting, perhaps impossible, task, since the hundreds of micromusics[1] across the world offer few universals. Contrary to the popular adage, music is not a universal language. Work in micromusics across the world has taught us that. Common denominators are at a minimum, but a search for what can be said about all music, especially vocal music, can still be fruitful.

Before we begin such a search, there is time for happy wonder. Across this world Christians are breaking out in song which is birthed from the wombs of their own culture. It is happening in Africa, in Bali, in India, in Thailand, in Taiwan, in Bangladesh, and in Latin America. When Martin Luther, following Augustine's lead, boldly asserted that music was part of the creation, he probably was not thinking of *bhajans* from India, for instance, but his theology welcomes that new song too.

As younger churches explore their own musics, and as older churches re-examine assumptions about liturgy and music in a world grown musically complex, it is possible to lift up some common dynamics

---

[1]   The term "micromusic" refers to a musical system and repertoire belonging to a subculture. For instance, within the Western European musical culture one can distinguish Scandinavian music, but within Scandinavian music the music of the Sami people (formerly Laplanders) can be considered a micromusic.

which can serve all Christians seeking to channel the musical impulse in their worship. We begin with a concern for the ecology of music, will continue by exploring the inner connections between text and music, then propose a grid for structural analysis of music in worship while sorting out the possibilities and problems connected to meaning in music, and finally conclude with a word about the muse itself. It will become clear that individual parts of the plan take major facets of Luther's theology of music and apply them to the challenges and opportunities of worship set in the micromusics of the world.

Ecology

Music may not be a universal language, but it is present in one form or another in every culture on this earth. There is a wondrous array of micromusics across the globe, all related in one way or another to the world's five major musical systems: Graeco-Roman/European, Persian, Chinese, Indian, and Indonesian. A major musical system is differentiated by a developed complex of notation and by a history of written theoretical materials. Each one of these systems has developed in its own way, and each displays some mutual influences. One of the Javanese scales systems, for instance, is based on an equidistant pentatonic division of the octave. That same octave division is thought by some to have shaped the scale systems of Eastern Africa, though Eastern African music shares family traits with the Graeco-Roman system too.

In spite of these complexities, it can be said that all the world's peoples sing, that in all societies music is used in religious ritual, that in all cultures music is used to transform ordinary experience, and that for all peoples music is an emblem of identity.[2] Why one culture chooses a particular division of the octave, or why it sings in its own peculiar way, are matters which are due to a variety of factors, perhaps best summed up by the observation that a given society develops its music in accordance with the character of its social system.[3]

---

[2]   Bruno Nettl, *et al.*, *Excursions in World Music* (Englewood Cliffs, New Jersey: Prentice Hall, 1992), 6-7.

[3]   *Ibid.*, 11.

None of the congruences mentioned so far represents some common technical building block. The musical products themselves will not yield common, unifying elements. Therefore any search for commonality among musical systems is more promising when it is centered in the musical impulse itself. Among all peoples there is evidence for such a musical impulse. It is a human characteristic which invites us to think of it as part of God's design for creation. How that musical impulse is expressed, however, and, more importantly, why it works itself out are matters which will also interest those of us who wish to explore the relationships between worship and music.

Because we have now intersected with one of Luther's principle theological observations, his view of music's origins is worth a closer look. Luther was trained in music at the University of Wittenberg. The study text for music there was written by Jean de Muris (14th century), also a strong proponent of the universality of music. Muris, following the medieval quardrivium of arithmetic, geometry, astronomy and music, believed music to be founded on mathematical principles. He was only following Pythagoras, of course. Nevertheless, Luther learned that number was at the base of everything; therefore, music as audible number was universal, a part of creation, and since creation was good, music too must be a gift from God. That excited Luther, and the excitement has been with Lutherans ever since.

Whether one locates the universality of music in the musical impulse or in created numerical law, the point remains the same: music is a part of creation and therefore is meant by God to be a good thing. Basing the origins of music in the musical impulse opens doors immediately to its many cultural manifestations. The musical impulse, that musical imagination present in all peoples, needs to be cared for as if one were caring for a good gift of creation meant by the Creator for the welfare of people. To lose any micromusic is to lose a manifestation of the musical impulse as if losing a species of creation. Like other parts of the creation, the musical impulse suffers from the effects of sin. It can be made to serve perverse ends. Alert Christians will want to respond to attempts which threaten the fragile ecology of music in this world. In an article on the popular music industry one Australian commentator issues this alarming observation:

MTV: This giant advertising network has ensured that white Anglo-American popular music has consolidated its international hegemony visually as well as aurally.[4]

Most major record stores today offer a section on "World Music," a category originating in 1987 and which holds displays of recordings bringing together micromusics in a hybrid way. To some it might mean new and interesting combinations of sounds and systems; on another level it means the mining of musics, as raw resources, from Latin America, Africa, and Asia, to serve the entrepreneurial hungers of pop music producers. If this busy process of mining were producing some notable results would be one thing; rather, this "commodity fetishism" has nothing more to show than a "shallow array of surfaces."[5] In the last century missionaries delivered the Gospel via cultural structures and methods in retrospect blatantly imperialistic. That same kind of imperialism is at work again. This time its results are more insidious since current electronic gadgets enable the projection of Western musical will across time zones to any place in the world.

Luther's basic insight about music, nature, and creation can and must be taken up anew in our midst. Care for the micromusics of this world should lead us to resist profit-motivated plundering of earth's wondrous sounds, to tell the real story of MTV, and, above all, to nurture local musics without and within the church.

Text Longing for Melody

A baby's crying may not be music to its parents, but it is clear that the body's mechanisms which facilitate crying are the very same mechanisms which are employed for singing. The outcry, the shout, the acclamation, the amorous sighs of lovers, litanies of pleading, even children's games seem always to long for melodic expression. Heightened speech or zealous communication moves quickly to mu-

---

[4]   Tony Mitchell, "World Music and the Popular Music Industry: An Australian View," *Ethnomusicology* 37/3 (Fall 1993), 310.

[5]   *Ibid.*, 335-36. See also Marshall Blonsky, *American Mythologies* (New York: Oxford, 1992), 17ff, for a lively discussion of "surface" in popular culture.

sical utterance. It is possible to speak of a self-contained continuum which moves from whispering on one end to song at the other. All oral communication occurs somewhere on that continuum, and, when impassioned, it advances to another place on the continuum. If, as some hold, the liturgy is a repository of outcries, shouts, acclamations, and outbursts of love, then worship is never without music.

Because it is sounded with pitches and can claim its own rhythm, spoken text is essentially musical, potentially melodic. Spoken text so often also seems to yearn for melody. Why this longing occurs is not clear. Could it be that heightened speech is longing for a certain fullness which melody can begin to provide? Or could it be that this longing occurs because melody is itself the tool by which the text with some of its nuances is preserved and remembered for further use?

Perhaps all of that. The unity of text and music Luther brilliantly recognized as a pillar of theology. He wrote from a culture still essentially oral, but he seemed to anticipate the imminent revolution in printing when he differentiated between word/language/message, on the one hand, and tone/speech/voice on the other. The former are about concept, grammar, and structure, while the latter refer to nuanced delivery, rhythm, and sound. A full and complete communication includes sound and is therefore existential. Luther perceived that, theologically speaking, for the Word to become flesh at any time requires some kind of musical delivery.

> Thus it was not without reason that the fathers and prophets wanted nothing else to be associated as closely with the Word of God as music. Therefore, we have so many hymns and Psalms where message and music [*Sermo et vox*] join to move the listener's soul.... After all, the gift of language combined with the gift of song was only given to man to let him know that he should praise God with both words and music, namely, by proclaiming [the Word of God] though music and by providing sweet melodies with words.[6]

---

[6]   Martin Luther, "Preface to Georg Rhau's Symphoniae iucundae," *Luther's Works*, American Edition (Philadelphia: Fortress Press and St. Louis: Concordia Publishing House, 1955), 53:323-24. Hereafter this edition will be referred to as LW.

Therefore theology and music cannot be separated; a desire to articulate the Gospel always leads to a musical expression. Music is also on the scene once the Gospel is heard, for it is the primal and quintessential way by which one can express joy, the first response to the announcement of the Gospel. In a very profound way music is understood by Luther to be the natural form of the Gospel.[7] For these reasons Luther exclaims that next to theology he "gives music the highest honor."[8]

We must take seriously once again the longing of Gospel text for melody. It seems there are no choices here, not *whether or not* the Gospel will be dynamically inculturated musically, but *how* the Gospel will be inculturated musically. This is at the heart of being Lutheran: that is, Word is taken to be an oral thing, an enfleshed event, seeking a voice (*vox*), longing for fulfillment in song, hymn, or dance.

As the musical impulse gives flesh to these longings within the world's cultures, a colorful array of musical possibilities emerges. Some examples follow to illustrate the variety of ways the Gospel takes on musical form shaped by cultural inclinations.

First is an example of music which has transformed a bit of the text, from the liturgy used by a diocesan seminary near Arusha, Tanzania. At the conclusion of the mass the priest dismisses the people and they respond, in Swahili: "*Asante, Bwana, Jesu, kwa mema vako*" ("Thanks, Lord Jesus, for all your gifts"). Set to music in this Tanzanian example, the song is typically African, employing the familiar call/response pattern. In this version, the call parts are improvised to highlight the occasion. Note that the song begins without any official signal.

A second example takes us back several centuries to the time of J.S. Bach. Most Lutherans have some allegiance to this great composer but do not know exactly why he figures so prominently within the

---

[7]   Walter Blankenburg, "Luther und die Musik," *Kirche und Musik*, ed. Erich Huebner and Renate Steiger (Göttingen: Vandenhoeck & Ruprecht, 1979), 23.

[8]   Luther, "Preface," 323.

Lutheran family. He and others of his contemporaries took seriously Luther's linkage of Word and music and pressed the concept yet again by creating musical sermons, now known as cantatas. For the last section of such a cantata written for Christmas Day, Bach chose to sum up his message with a stanza from Luther's Christmas hymn, *Vom Himmel hoch* ("From Heaven Above"): "Ah, Dearest Jesus, holy child/ come, make a bed soft, undefiled/ within my heart that it may be/ a quiet chamber kept for thee." The four lines of the stanza are interspersed with trumpet and drum fanfares to make clear that this little child is at the same time monarch.

A third example illustrates how prayer and meditation long for melody as well. One form of popular religious music in India is the *bhajan*, a song which encourages meditation and contemplation through a loving rehearsal of God's names. Among Christians the *bhajan* is often used as music to be sung while the Eucharist is distributed.

Finally, text linked to melody is frequently employed by Christians as a mode of private or small-group worship. In the area surrounding Udon Thani in northeast Thailand, Christians carry the memory of the assembly from meeting to meeting by singing and playing religious folk songs, some in a dialogical form (called *Maw lum*). These songs are group-events, for they encourage participation from several people at the same time.

Text longing for melody is more than a useful observation to explain what *has* happened among Christians in many times and in many places. As a theological insight it wants to be implemented as the mode for proclaiming the Gospel in any culture and as faith's first response to the Holy Spirit.

Critical Impulses and Emerging Recipes

As soon as liturgical text finds melody, it seems, passioned guardians of the cult mobilize the critical impulse. Beginning jarringly with the prophet Amos (5:23f), persisting doubts about music continued with Clement, Tertullian, Augustine, appeared in the proceedings of ecclesiastical councils, in the famous bull of Pope John XXII (*Docta sanctorum Patrum*, 1324-25), drove the very radical thought of Zwingli, hovered over the Council of Trent, preoccupied Lutheran orthodox theologians and Lutheran pietists, and influenced the worship practice of Lutheran missionaries. Reluctance about music has been fueled by a fear of syncretism, or by scruples regarding God's own appreciation of the music, or by a fear of being distracted from more important parts of worship, or by a fear that the liturgy will lose its purpose, or even by a fear of what was believed to be music's own seductive powers.

Those who are awaking to the blessed possibilities of planting worship within the myriad micromusics of today's world often move with hesitation, slowed by the same old worries. Dare we ignore that critical impulse? Does it have substance? Is there something we *should* say about music in worship? Can it simply be given free reign? Is there some way it can be safely channeled?

With all of his enthusiasm about music, Luther also responded to the impulse to receive music critically. He was vitally concerned about song and its influential role as the vehicle of life in the Christian worshiping community. For what other is his concern for the vernacular than to make it possible for all the people to mouth the Word? For what other are his hymn paraphrases of the Ordinary (*Kyrie, Sanctus*, etc.)—some of the very first hymns composed and much loved—than a way to get all the people together singing the liturgy? So he admonished parishoners: "Sing with the congregation and you will sing well."[9] When he sought to engage George Spalatin for writing new hymns he advised: "in order to be understood by the people use only the simplest and the most common words."[10] Instinctively he knew that a reformed worshiping community needed a song which followed some overriding principles. That they should be anchored partly in the worshiping assembly makes him more contemporary than what we might at first think. But for him and for us, the development of critical principles rests on how we understand music to have meaning.

Given that the musical impulse shows up in human societies throughout the world, it should be possible to discover a common dynamic

---

[9] Luther, "An Exposition of the Lord's Prayer for Simple Laymen," LW 42:60.

[10] Luther, "To Georg Spalatin" (1523), LW 49:69.

which escorts and energizes that impulse into musical event. As long as there might be agreement on the definition and meaning of music, such a supposition might hold promise. But there is no single and intercultural concept defining what music is. Definitions vary across the world, for music's contours are understood to range from noise to organized sound to language to game to dance and to social action.[11] If there is no consensus on music's contours, there can be little agreement on its meaning.

Attempts at finding universal meaning are instructive. Within western musicological thought (and sometimes it seems meaning is a distinctly western preoccupation), meaning in music, according to Leonard Meyer, is thought to be delivered via one of two broad pathways. Some hold that there is no meaning in music outside of the musical structures themselves (e.g., a chord has meaning only as it relates to another, and it has no other meaning). If someone should claim meaning for music outside these purely analytical connections, such a one *brings* meaning *to* the musical event. Meyer identifies people in this category as "absolutionists."

The other approach, according to Meyer, holds that the structures and tools of a musical system innately bear extra-musical meaning (e.g. upwards melodic movement implies tension and therefore excitement, anxiety, joy, etc.). "Referentialists" is what Meyer labels people who hold this view.[12]

Within the Referentialists camp there are smaller tribal gatherings, some worth mentioning because they are home for many who think and speak of church music. For one such sub-group, music is referenced to natural law, which then suggests that meaning in music is to be found in the cosmic laws which are held to be mirrored in the musical event. Beginning most clearly with Boethius (470?-525) this view on meaning has dominated the Church's thinking on music for

---

[11]   Jean-Jacques Nattiez, *Music and Discourse: Toward a Semiology of Music*, trans. by Carolyn Abbate (Princeton: Princeton University Press, 1990), 55 and 58.

[12]   Leonard Meyer, *Emotion and Meaning in Music* (Chicago: University of Chicago Press, 1956), 1-6.

over a millennium. Martin Luther took on this tradition. We have noted Martin Luther's fondness for connecting music to the laws of the universe.

Natural law partisans, however, have struggled for years with the bothersome imperfections which acoustical principles impose especially on the West's favorite way of dividing the octave. Using the interval of the perfect fifth as the primary interval, western theorists derive the twelve pitches of the scale by building a series of fifths. Theoretically this series should lead back to the original pitch, but instead it leads to an imperfect unison, one slightly off-key. That nagging imperfection mars a search for musical meaning in what one might suppose to be perfectly balanced law.

Another clan holds that the significance of music derives from its ability to reference an alternate time system, since musical time, or one's perception of it, usually differs from clock time, or one's perception of it. Music offers one a world of virtual time, which provides insight apart from clock time.[13] Insofar that music can offer such an experience it becomes a means by which humans can symbolically transcend the strictures of the clock. This is its meaning, say some.

A third group of Referentialists seek meaning in music through feelings which, many claim, accompany participation in the musical event. Victor Zuckerkandl, one contemporary proponent of this theory, explains that a melody has "something" which a random series of notes does not, and that "something" is a dynamic quality which creates a feeling over and above the simple existence of the notes.[14] Yet, for the sake of argument, if such a feeling does arise from a musical event (and some would say feelings are brought *to* the event), it is likely culture-bound. While perhaps not demonstrable, it is difficult to imagine that a given song will generate the same feeling in every human beings.

---

[13]   Jonathan Kramer, *The Time of Music* (New York: Scribner's, 1988).

[14]   According to John Shepherd, *Music as Social Text* (Cambridge: Polity Press, 1991), 63.

While great debates about these matters continue among western commentators in particular, a breath of fresh air has blown into the heated discussions from ethnomusicologists. Again and again studies of world musics offer a way out of the absolutionist/Referentialists deadlock. Ethnomusicologists urge us to think of music as something much more than the sound event itself or notes on a page. Any usable definition of music, Alan Merriam proposed in 1964, must include its generating concepts, the actual product, and the behavior which accompanies and follows the sound event.[15] Especially with the inclusion of behavior in a definition of music, Merriam provided a way to think more universally about the micromusics of the world.

The far-reaching consequences of this comprehensive definition can be illustrated by John Blacking's study of music among the Venda people of Africa. "Music," he felt confident to summarize, "confirms what is already present in society and culture, and it adds nothing new except patterns of sound."[16] Its chief function is to "involve people in shared experiences within the framework of their cultural experience,"[17] Across cultures it serves "to promote soundly organized humanity by enhancing human consciousness."

Music is "social text," John Shepherd has written.[18] It is to be understood through its sociological dimensions. This focus on behavior, as we revert to Merriam's tri-part definition of music, has gathered notable momentum, and as if ignoring any sure and immanent criticism from the deconstructionists, proponents of the meaning-is-in-the-doing approach to music have begun to look for meaning in the specific societal structures of the musical events themselves.[19] The potentials and challenges of such a search are no more clearly seen than in the so-called Cantometrics Project, begun by ethnomusicologist Alan Lomax and his team about thirty years ago.

---

[15] Alan Merriam, *The Anthropology of Music* (Evanston: Northwestern University Press, 1964), 32.

[16] John Blacking, *How Musical is Man?* (Seattle: University of Washington Press, 1973, 54.

[17] *Ibid.*, 48.

[18] Shepherd, 11-18.

[19] For the influence of Claude Levi-Strauss on Alan Lomax, see Nattiez, 171.

Their discoveries beg attention from anyone wanting to address the relationship of worship and music, for they escort the conversation to a place which enables a reasonable methodology by which critically to evaluate the music of worship.

The Cantometrics Project has been most succinctly described by Jean-Jacques Nattiez:

> [Lomax's] objective is twofold: his first goal is to establish on a global scale, from a comparative point of view stylistic characterizations of 233 specific musical cultures, belonging to 56 cultural areas. In pursuing his second goal he tries to relate the music-stylistic traits he inventories to cultural traits proper to limited areas, to arrive at an explanation of each style in terms of the culture to which it belongs.[20]

Or, as Lomax himself writes, "As people live so do they sing"[21] Song style, he discovered, responds to the following six variables:

1. Productive range [how people work]
2. Political level
3. Level of stratification of class
4. Severity of sexual mores
5. Balance of dominance between male and female
6. Level of social cohesiveness[22]

If there is one single discovery that arises from the project, it is that a culture's favored song style reflects and reinforces the kind of behavior considered essential to its work habits and to its core and prevailing social institutions.

---

[20]   *Ibid.*, 169.

[21]   Alan Lomax, *Folk Song Style and Culture* (New Brunswick, New Jersey: Transaction Books, 1968), 4.

[22]   *Ibid.*, 6.

Lomax and his colleagues concentrated their research efforts on performance characteristics, discovering further that there are several basic frameworks which are determinative:

1. As a joint communication, song requires tacit agreement from its participants to abide by the musical formulas of the group. Performance organizes unity of purpose.

2. Music is socially louder than speech, and it tends to knit its participants together in a unified reaction or action; song, however can silence an individual, or an individual singer can silence the group.

3. Basic to the whole study is the level of participation, particularly the ratio of group to individual or individual to group[23]

Song performances, researchers found, ranged on a continuum between the poles of *individual* and *integrated* (group deliveries). On the one side, an individualized, group-*dominating* performance came about when a solo singer dominated the acoustical space, thereby in effect silencing the group. On the other, a highly cohesive group-*involving* performance made it possible for all to join in acoustically and socially. Each of the pole models displayed certain recurring musical characteristics:

Individualized	*Integrated*
Solo	Choral, multileveled, cohesive
Textually complex	Uncomplicated text
Metrically complex	Metrically simple
Melodically complex	Melodically simple
Ornamented	No ornamentation
Usually noisy voice	Usually clear voice
Precise enunciation	Slurred enunciation [24]

Lomax and team arrived at their conclusions by sampling over 2500 songs and by utilizing an elaborate coding book which permitted

---

[23]   *Ibid.*, 14-15.

[24]   *Ibid.*, 16.

evaluations of 37 characteristics. Among those characteristics are tempo, volume, rubato, glissando, melisma, tremolo, vocal width, nasality, raspiness, consonant production, phrase length, etc. The project also included recognition of dance and movement style, phonemic patterning in sung verse, and conceptual patterns in sung verse. While instrumental accompaniment was included in the coding book when part of the song, instrumental music by itself was considered to be outside the focus of the project.

The study has demonstrated how closely linked music and behavior are and provides information about just what meaning music can have. Worship comprises much more than behavior, but how a worshiping assembly interacts and understands itself is a primary concern for worship leaders and liturgical agents.

One way to utilize the project, then, would be to compile a list of characteristics which describe an ideal worshiping Christian community, and then to see how, according to the cantometrics study, such a community's music might look. Such a proposal immediately poses a problem. A worshiping community is not fully a culture. On the other hand, it does bear traits which suggest it has culture-like qualities. Besides, we are accustomed to describing the Church as countercultural, implying that it is in fact a kind of culture.

Here, then, are some characteristics which might describe an ideal liturgical assembly:

1. Energized by a message, purpose, hope, and power, all of which originate from without the individuals of the assembly; the group therefore does not look to itself for initiative.

2. Carries out its interchanges dialogically both when at worship and when not.

3. Affirms its unity while inviting into its midst a diversity of gifts because they are edifying.

4. Functions by recognizing the equality of male/female, young/old.

5. Embraces degrees of complexity regarding matters of social status, economic position, and educational levels of its members.

6. Provides information relative to the needs and abilities of its members.

7. Is action-oriented, that is, intends to translate worship into individual and corporate daily life.

8. Is conscious of living presently in two time systems, clocktime and the "time to come."

9. Is determined to deal with contextual reality, and resists the inclination to escape from the world.

10. Encourages the "jazz factor"—the unpredictable presence of the Spirit.

Some predictable characteristics of song in such an assembly would be:

1. *The song will be of the integrated type*, that is, it will tend to be choral, multileveled, cohesive, textually repetitious, uncomplicated in melody and meter, with little or no ornamentation, favoring the clear voice and some slurred enunciation. Solo offerings will be welcome from time to time but only as they edify and support the group (1 Corinthians 14). Because the Christian assembly depends upon external initiative, its song will include little from individual claims to special insight, but will rather incarnate what it corporately holds to be true.[25]

2. *The integrated song of the assembly will include some degree of solo/group interaction.* Lomax offers some ways this interaction might occur:

---

[25]   *Ibid.*, 14.

a. *Interlock*: leaderless song, often present in Africa where songs are learned together with customary pitch
b. *Simple social unison*: someone may begin but the part is soon swallowed up
c. *Overlap*: song proceeds on the pattern of alternation between leader and group
d. *Simple alternation*: indicating clear differentiation between group and leader

3. *Instrumental participation will be simple and supportive* (but see no. 1 above). Pure instrumental sections within a song tend to silence the assembly. Basically, orchestral complexity reflects social rigidity,[26] and is therefore not hospitable to the needs of the assembly. If instruments are to be used, the ideal Christian musical expression may be heterophony—at least two sound producers delivering a melody simultaneously but with idiomatic variations.

4. *Melodic embellishment, glissando effects, and other ornamentation devices will occur rarely* since they are more characteristic of solo song. Elaborate songs are found in highly stratified worlds where the fate of every individual depends on a carefully defined relationship to the superstructure.[27]

5. *Vocal style will be free and clear*. Vocal tension accompanies fear related to sexual mores. For example, women who must live according to sexual standards different from men will show tension in their voices.[28]

6. *In parishes of more complex social stratification, songs with heavy information loads will occur more frequently*. Songs dense with information serve worshiping groups who are well-educated, for instance, since the pieces are expected to define with precision

---

[26] *Ibid.*, 154.

[27] *Ibid.*, 151.

[28] *Ibid.*, 195-96.

the bonds which hold the group together. Where Christians are a minority within a larger culture, the same inclination will be at work, for Christians need to know how they differ from their neighbors.[29]

7. *Most songs will be delivered with two simultaneous voice parts (as in octaves) to reflect the equality of male/female, and young/ old.*

8. *Song patterns will reflect the work patterns of the group.* For instance, choir/people alternations on songs indicates a division of labor or a collaborative approach to all tasks.[30] Centralized authority in a single individual, or groups whose labor is delegated to a favored few, will tend to silence integrated group performance.

9. *Worshiping groups which have a high sense of spatial freedom among the individual members will prefer songs with wide interval gaps.*[31]

10. *Some of the songs will incorporate an implicit invitation to dance*, an invitation understood by the majority but not necessarily acted upon in an overt fashion. Lomax observes that "dance functions to establish and renew consensus at moments when a society.... is ready to act in concert."[32] African and African-American Christians readily employ concerted physical movement in worship. Some Thai Christians, too, let song lead to dance. Evidence remains scant for this kind of linkage among Lutherans. One way to account for Lutheran reluctance may be that what is implicit is not automatically permitted. There may be a correlation between lack of dance and Lutheran hesitancy to act upon belief. Within worship, dance should be understood to include all sorts of common movements and gestures.

---

[29]   *Ibid.*, 137-38.

[30]   *Ibid.*, 183.

[31]   The Sami people, formerly known as Laplanders, inhabit areas of the far north in Norway, Sweden, Finland, and parts of Russia. Historically the economy of the Samis has been tied to the reindeer herds necessitating on their part a considerable willingness for mobility.

[32]   Lomax, p. 224.

These ten observations constitute a methodology for evaluating worship set in a musical context. The recurring emphasis on the prominence of assembly song as opposed to individual offering reiterates some of Luther's concerns. Should a parish lean towards a style opposite that described in the ten points, there is reason to examine its self-understanding of worship, perhaps providing that momentous opportunity to redirect its liturgical practice.

Two final observations accompany this attempt to offer a "Lutheran cantometrics." First, these observations are submitted as guidelines for music *within* worship. Many Christians, and Lutherans in particular, also make religious music *outside* of the worship of the community. In such cases an entirely different set of descriptions could be developed to accommodate extra-liturgical needs both of individuals or of the community itself. Examples abound, e.g., the sixteenth-century catechism songs designed to catechize the youth pleasantly, or the folk-based narrative chants currently employed in Northeast Thailand to teach Old Testament stories.[33]

Second, the influential French politician/philosopher, Jacques Attali, would not have us forget that together with all its other characteristics music is also helpful understood as *noise*.[34] Because music is channeled or *controlled* noise, it can exert power over uncontrolled noise. Noise uncontrolled is destructive and therefore violent. But music can overcome such noise, can exercise control, and is therefore powerful.

People who make music actively join forces to silence the violence, and this is, according to Attali, one of music's chief functions. Whenever people are silenced, they are victims of noise and those who manipulate it. The world of MTV, insofar that it silences the individual, is a world of noise. But there is hope. In the midst of society gone mute, there is an occasional commuter who hums along with

---

[33]   These presentations, called *Leh*, follow the pattern of old Thai chants which recount the deep stories of the culture and are punctuated with sort acclamations from the listeners.

[34]   Jacques Attali, *Noise: The Political Economy of Music*, trans. by Brian Massumi (Minneapolis: University of Minnesota, 1985).

the Walkman, and more and more people line up to sing along with the *Karaoke* machine, especially in certain areas of southeast Asia. If music as channeled noise muffles the power of noise (violence), then in a most profound way sung words of the Gospel are both song and a means of God's saving work in the world. To sing in worship, therefore, is to participate in the saving power of the paschal mystery, the death and resurrection of Christ.

The Last Word

We have proposed that a focus on the musical event as behavior releases us from aesthetic theories as a base for evaluating worldwide musical expressions of worship. Behavioral dimensions, especially as they have been broadly studied by Lomax and coworkers, provide a set of expectations for the shape of music in worship. These expectations can serve partially as critique; they can offer some direction; they can even become a kind of emerging recipe, but they can never become a rigid mold, simply because there are too many variables from culture to culture, from assembly to assembly.

One of those variables is the musical impulse itself. Earlier the "jazz factor" was listed as a characteristic of the worshiping community. In jazz music, players and singers best show the style when they "swing" the beat and/or bend the intonation of selected pitches. Square beats (clock-like pulses) invite and enforce conformity, according to certain western understandings of rhythm—but the jazz musician, in search of alternative visions, addresses them with a kind of anticipatory or delayed freedom which attains significance only because of continued recognition of the pulse. Bent intonations are similar in that expected pitches are lowered for effect. Both examples push the edges of accepted musical convention, and are likewise manifestations of the basic musical impulse.

This propensity to push the edges provides any musical system its continued livelihood, and is usually sanctioned by its constituents. For they are the ones who have learned to know the "language" as a series of recognized and accepted units of melody, harmony, rhythm, vocal style, etc., each of which as a matrix is combined with others in new and creative ways resulting in what we know as a composition or improvisation.[35] Occasionally, a composer or improviser will come along who will push the edges in such a way to elicit either great admiration or reactionary disapproval. Usually such matrix reorganization brings with it new insight and behavioral empowerment. A new vision has then emerged.

When within the worshiping community the musical impulse is encouraged fully to unfold, the liturgy may be given a way by which to incarnate its own internal creative urge, an urge which Anscar Chupungco holds as a life-giving inherent imperative.[36] But that can be frightening to some, for it then seems as if the liturgy has lost its hold on the event, leading all too easily to a kind of ritual anarchy driven by the musical impulse. Then one is tempted to apply shackles.

The muse, however, will not be muzzled. It has been said in many ways. When text leads to melody, the dynamics will hold both liturgy and music in tension, making it necessary to place equal emphasis on both *church* and *music*.[37] Ultimately, when all is sung and done, this dynamic tension may be the best icon of the Spirit's presence the community can have.

---

[35] Peter van der Merwe, *Origins of the Popular Style* (Oxford: Clarendon Press, 1989), 93-100.

[36] *Liturgical Inculturation* (Collegeville, MN: Liturgical Press, 1992), 54.

[37] Oskar Soehngen, "*Theologische Grundlagen der Kirchenmusik,*" *Die Musik des evangelischen Gottesdienstes*, vol. 4 of *Leiturgia*, ed. Karl Ferdinand Mueller and Walter Blankenburg (Kassel: Johannes Stauda, 1961), 216-217.

REPORT ON CASE STUDIES

Marcus P.B. Felde

Participants in the 1994 Hong Kong meeting of the LWF Study on Worship and Culture presented and discussed seven case studies. The following is a summary of those studies and discussions.

The case studies, coming from seven different countries, represent not only different cultural situations but different sorts of problems. Discussion of the case studies usually involved two sorts of judgments:

1) what cultural values and patterns might appropriately be addressed by or turned to the use of Christian worship, and

2) whether and how such cultural values and patterns might serve or be contradicted by the core of Christian worship.

Case Study 1
Eucharist in the Latin American Context

Lisandro Orlov of Argentina shared with us some of the ways in which worship has changed in recent years in some of the Latin American Lutheran churches. The Liturgical Commission of the United Evangelical Lutheran Church of Argentina worked out a liturgical agenda, *Celebremos*, which has also been adopted with some modifications and adaptations by Lutheran churches in Brazil, Chile and Colombia.

Liturgical changes were made with keen awareness of the religious culture and also the social reality of Latin America, to the end of "making it possible in the socio-cultural context to bring into being a eucharistic people and culture."

"In Latin American popular religion there exists a certain *ordo*, or liturgical structure, which we ought to recognize," said Pastor Orlov. "There is a deep sense for intercessory prayer, a weak comprehension of the relationship of Gospel and daily life, and a strong sense for eucharistic ritual. In this religious scene, Lutheran identity faces a challenge: in the first place, to amplify the spirit of prayer and to put in place a prayer of thanksgiving [eucharistic prayer] with the recognition of the creative work of God; in the second place, to strengthen preaching which relates to and renews daily life; and third, to celebrate the Eucharist as the living presence of Christ in history and among all peoples."

The liturgy was changed to take account of this analysis of local culture and local needs. For example, the sense that the primary service is eucharistic is emphasized by separating the confession from the rest of the service by the entrance hymn; by celebrating the Eucharist every Sunday; by making the altar a table in the midst of the congregation; and by employing the eucharistic prayer, which "recognizes that the Church is not the owner (master, *dueña*) of the presence of Christ but a servant who cries out for the realization of this promised presence."

The *Kyrie* in its litany form emphasizes the ministry of prayer, and spontaneous participation in the intercessory prayers is encouraged. The assembly also participates more actively in the offering, which is not just gifts of money, but is interpreted as the people of God "offering themselves in, with, and under the once-and-unrepeatable sacrifice of Christ, to be used as instruments in the construction of a society that will be more just, more human, and more fraternal."

"The vocabulary of the liturgy attempts to remain close to that of everyday speech without losing beauty or dignity." Further, out of sensitivity to the lack of credibility of the spoken word in the local context, the scriptural readings are framed with moments of silence.

The music of the liturgy and of the hymns reflects the cultural context as well.

Responses

Participants found much to praise in the Latin American worship renewal represented by *Celebremos* and shared by Pastor Orlov. It was noted that they have apparently succeeded in learning from ancient Christian tradition without being slaves to it, and at the same time in embracing and being hospitable to the culture of Latin America. The result is liturgy that is not merely "correct" by an external standard, but liturgy that works as liturgy is first and foremost supposed to work.

The insistence on every-Sunday Eucharist, Word and sacrament, echoes an ancient tradition. The penitential rite was originally independent of the eucharistic celebration. In early days as well, the social dimension of the Eucharist was strongly stressed by the offertory. Re-connecting the Eucharist to everyday life through the use of common bread and common speech is also an overcoming of a departure from early practice.

We discussed the fact that Lutheran liturgy before *Celebremos* was shaped in part by a Lutheran desire not to appear Roman Catholic. This is not exclusively a Latin American phenomenon, but needs to be overcome. It was suggested that as Lutherans we ought to be sure that the Gospel in the liturgy connects to the everyday lives of people, and thus make a positive use of what is distinctive in our tradition. This might necessitate a greater emphasis on preaching itself. The sensitivity of the new liturgy to the emotional character of the people was appreciated, and comparisons made to other parts of the world.

Case Study 2
Baptism in the Context of African Traditional Religion

Louis Sibiya of South Africa shared insights into some of the cultural values which form a background to Christian practice of Baptism in Southern Africa.

In teaching about Baptism, we talk about being brought into the Christian family. Yet "family" has quite different meanings for an African than for someone in other societies. The extended family of African society extends not only to a very large community of the living, but also to many generations long dead. These are remembered, for example, in the practice of "praises," which keep alive the memory of distant ancestors. Water is also used in African traditional religions "to purge oneself" and at the same time "to transform oneself," in rites of passage. "Circumcision school concludes with the washing away of the clay with which the student had smeared his whole body. After the bath he can rejoin society. But he comes in as a different person with a new and higher status," said Pastor Sibiya. "There are many such cases where only a bath would render the person clean."

"Black stands for darkness, and there is an element of pollution in the color. White, by contrast, is positive.... A white goat is used to appease the ancestors. In a prayer that is said, darkness or blackness is denounced. White is used to call for good luck, blessings, and a bright future." Red (sunrise or sunset) divides the white of day from the dark of night.

Spirit possession is seen positively, when it is possession by an ancestral spirit. But "displaced spirits in the world of the dead cause illness to whoever they possess." Exorcism is a long process which involves not just taking out the evil spirit but also inducing the right (legitimate) spirit. "A person who is prone to possession should not be left empty."

In the light of the foregoing suggestions, Pastor Sibiya suggests the following implications for the order of Baptism. It should take seriously the family of the person to be baptized. Family should be invited, and it should always take place in the midst of the whole congregation, never privately. The choice of sponsors is also important. "An outsider seeking to settle in a strange land must have somebody to vouch for him—usually a relative or a well-trusted friend of the family. In introducing him to the neighbors and the headman, he or she must be able to tell all about the newcomer's family.

Water should be used in a way that is obvious to the congregation. This means perhaps lifting the basin, using more water, or immersion.

Dressing the candidate in white is good symbolism. Exorcism could be retained as in some traditions (Acts 19:13).

Responses

It was noted that African tradition connects with baptismal tradition in some fascinating ways, which, employed properly, could enrich understanding of the sacrament. The sense of the Church as extended family could perhaps be by means of employing the local metaphor. Allusive language may be helpful in several ways.

Use of mud and water was suggestive of possibilities, as it expresses dramatically the cleansing character of Baptism. As an example of similarly enriching drama, reference was made to the *Apostolic Tradition* (ca. A.D. 250) in which the candidate turned first to the West (symbolizing uncleanliness) while renouncing Satan, and then to the East while professing faith in Christ.

The values assigned to black and white were challenged, as having new and disturbing significance in the contemporary African situation. Is it possible that traditional meanings have been subverted to justify the political dominance of white over black? Do we not need to recover for such reasons some of the positive values represented by black in many cultures, for example solemnity (e.g., black evening gown)? In answer it was noted that the color called "black" which represented darkness and evil was not the same color Africans used to describe their own skin color. Nevertheless, this could be a troublesome issue.

The length of time involved in traditional exorcism brings to mind traditions of a longer time of catechesis, and greater seriousness about renunciation of evil.

There was agreement that there are clearly resources in the culture for enrichment of the signs in baptismal practice. (Luther called for the "integrity" and "fullness" of signs.) As in the discussion of the case study from Argentina, it was observed that investigation of ancient Christian tradition can surprise us by showing that early Christians made use of elements of their own cultural contexts in ways that not dissimilar to what we might do today, if we were more sensitive to our own cultures. Initiation in the Central African Republic is a serious ritual that culminates 2-3 years in the bush, a "time of forgetting." The culminating purification rites involve washing in a river, jumping over fire, walking away and not looking back, and burying one's clothes, which may never be worn again. Has Baptism, in comparison to this, become exclusively a matter of words? If this is so, doesn't faithfulness to the core of its meaning and our understanding of what a sacrament is mean that we need to recover some of its bodilyness?

Case Study 3
The Church Year in the Context of Hindu Culture

Adiss Arnold from India brought us a case study which illuminated the issues confronting the Church there as it attempts to deal with the Hindu festival of Deepavali, or Festival of Lights, when it falls on a Sunday.

Both Jewish and Christian calendars over the years have adopted festivals that originated elsewhere. This history stimulates the Indian church to reflect on what there might be for Christians to celebrate on this festival day in India. The myth, the cult, and the celebration of Deepavali need to be understood.

Many myths and legends are related to Deepavali, including Lord Vishnu's victory over the prince of hell; the victory of Vamana (an incarnation of Vishnu) over King Bali; and the victorious return of Rama, another incarnation of Vishnu, after his conquest of an evil power, Ravana. The second of these is characteristic: "King Bali, by his devotion to Lord Siva, had gained so much merit and power that he used it to trouble gods and men. Therefore Vishnu became incarnate as a dwarf, Vamana, and went to King Bali in the guise of a mendicant, asking, as alms, as much ground as he could cover in three steps. The boon being granted, he assumed a huge form and took three steps, with the first covering the earth, with the second the heavens, and with the third treading Bali down into hell. Thereafter, relenting for having treated Bali harshly, Vishnu granted him the kingdom of hell, and three days annually to reign on earth wherever no lamps were lighted. Therefore, [and this is part of the "cult" of Deepavali] people light lamps in every building, to avoid falling again under Bali's power," according to Professor Arnold.

The cult includes rites of expiation to atone for our sins, because the present state is considered a punishment for one's own karma.

What is celebrated is "liberation," the victory of light over darkness. "Deepavali is also a celebration of brotherly and sisterly love. Indian women look forward to the coming of Deepavali as it is during this season they go to their mother's home, where there is real family reunion."

In the context of this Indian celebration, Christian worship is an occasion for proclaiming Christ and his message. Adaptation of Deepavali provides an opportunity to proclaim "Christ as the Light of the world, the Victor who has conquered death and sin, and the one who bestows upon us life here and now."

While Professor Arnold explored the possibilities of responding to elements of Deepavali within Christian worship, he also acknowledged that there are significant difficulties in doing so. Many Indian Lutherans resist any alterations to the liturgies that have been handed down to them, and many Indians of tribal background look at Hindu festivals with hesitation and suspicion. There is some question whether in looking at local culture we should pay more attention to ancient Indian culture, or to modern culture—which is quite different. Youth ask why they should adapt to Indian cultural and religious forms while India is becoming modern and western. And others ask whether those who make such suggestions are implying there is something wrong with present liturgy.

It is also clear that Christian worship will not just find parallels in the values represented in Deepavali. For example, some who are oppressed in present society actually celebrate not the defeat of Bali but the hope of his returning and establishing a just society once again. "At a point of history when the culturally and economically oppressed sections are struggling to regain their identity, how symbols function socially and whose interest they serve are vital questions one should ask."

Responses

This was compared to the case of Christmas, which originated as a christianization of pagan Saturnalia celebrations. In Christian worship, we do not stand outside culture. Rather, as cultural beings ourselves we criticize what is wrong in culture, from within culture, using cultural tools—like times of celebration. The question is how to remove aspects of the celebration that cannot be assimilated but must even be opposed—for example, if the "liberation" celebrated by Deepavali represents to some people the beginning of their oppression. Liturgy should not become an occasion to disadvantage the oppressed.

Perhaps there are deeper, more universal roots of the Deepavali celebration? Something about seasons, changes of the earth? A universal drive for wealth or well-being seems to be expressed here. Perhaps Christians can make this a point of contact, rather than the ambivalent one of liberation.

In engaging the meanings of Deepavali, a theology of the cross will find that Christian texts are paradoxical, not simple. God's love is revealed to us under a contradiction: wealth in poverty, finding in losing, life in death. We cannot simply say that the message of Christianity is just like that of Deepavali.

There is also a need to keep festivals from degenerating into spectacles, in order to preserve the centrality of the paschal mystery itself. Symbols (like the defeat of Bali) will always have several possible meanings. We need to be alert, because of this, and not settle for rigid interpretations of what is going on culturally.

On balance, Lutheran worship tends to be overly intellectual, making too little contact with the other aspects of human life. Taking the opportunities afforded by engaging an important festival is a way to enliven our worship.

Case Study 4
The Sami People and the Worship of the Church of Sweden

Nils-Henrik Nilsson described the history of efforts in the Church of Sweden to make Christian worship more at home among the indigenous Sami (Lapp) people of northern Sweden. The 17,000 Swedish Sami have a way of life which, while it has been changed decisively by modern technology, is nevertheless quite distinctive. In addition to having their own language which is unrelated to Swedish, they have different ancient religious traditions, different music, different ways of organizing their society, and so forth.

The mission work of the Swedish Church among the Sami led to their becoming Christians. However, the development of the Church among the Sami has been hindered in some ways. There are still few Sami clergy, for instance.

Swedish missionaries in the 17th century incorporated very little from Sami culture into worship, except for the language, into which hymns and liturgies were translated. They did accommodate worship life to the nomadic life of the people, gathering them infrequently for worship that lasted for several days. They did not introduce liturgical vestments or "heavy ritualism," which left the door open for later, more indigenous developments.

After evangelical revivals of the 19th century strongly condemned "everything that had connections with the old religion," the 20th century saw a new opening to connections with the past.

Today, it is possible to point to several aspects of Sami worship life which reflect their cultural origins. For example, the *goathe*, or traditional house, is rich in symbolism. There are unwritten rules about how to behave in a *goathe*. Every person and thing has its place. According to Dr. Nilsson, "In the middle is the fire which gives warmth and light. Opposite the door is the kitchen. This place used to be considered holy. One of the gods of the *goathe* lived underneath. When a guest entered he or she was to sit near the door, by the dogs and the wood, until being invited farther in. No chairs were used. One sat on a reindeer skin." Although today Sami live in modern houses, some still use the *goathe* to live in during the summer, and it still holds meaning for them. Today, church architecture among the Sami sometimes attempts by its shapes and its organization to make use of the symbolism resident in the *goathe*.

The traditional singing of the Sami, called yoiking, is becoming accepted in Christian worship. Yoiking is a distinctive form of narrative singing, a way of recalling events and people, or describing nature. Because it was a part of the pre-Christian religion, it was associated by some missionaries with paganism, and was therefore suppressed. Now Christians are free to yoik, even to sing prayers using this unique singing tone.

Liturgical vestments, not introduced in the beginning, are now being made using traditional rich embroidery work, and the traditional bright colors characteristic of the Sami—blue, red, yellow and green.

On the other hand, one cultural element that has entirely disappeared from use is the traditional drum. Before the introduction of Christianity, most families owned one of these. "It was an instrument with which the future could be discerned. Its pictures provided a map of the world of people and gods. The *noaidi* (shaman) used the drum to go into a trance when he had to travel to other worlds or come into contact with the gods."

The chief contribution of the Sami people to the Church of Sweden is considered to be their feeling for creation and nature. "The Sami way of living with its strong feeling of gratefulness for their land and for nature has inspired the Swedes from the 17th century up to our time to turn to God with thanksgiving, with hymns and prayers in worship."

Responses

It seems that in this case (as to some extent with the Indian case study) there is an interest not just in interacting with contemporary culture, but in cultural revival. The Sami appear to be taking an interest in exploring their earlier history and bringing back what is meaningful. This interest in revival of traditional culture is already in itself a cultural reality. Liturgical inculturation inspired by such a spirit is perfectly justifiable; it is not a return to the "museum" but an affirmation of a people's struggle to rediscover part of its traditional identity and heritage.

Care must be taken to respect the meaning of cultural components being brought into use in worship. So, for example, yoiking is by nature narrative, and care should be taken not to simply exploit its melodies. The liturgy has many parts that are narrative. If we do not respect what we appropriate, we are guilty of imposition or dominance.

"Reverent reorientation" might be a way of describing what has been done in this case. Shamanism is not the same as Christianity, and one would not expect that its cultural vehicles could be simply transplanted into the Christian liturgy.

In modeling some church buildings on the *goathe*, a domestic dwelling, the Church has wittingly or unwittingly emulated the earliest Christians. However, can this sort of building be large enough for the purpose of worship? Large enough for the outsider to get in?

How can we avoid exploiting what is simply "interesting" in a culture, "stealing it" to use in our worship, profiteering from nostalgia? Dialogue with a culture is founded on a certain confidence in the "permeability" of cultures to each other, and confidence that the Christian message is for all.

The seriousness of our task was impressed upon us by another participant who has worked with Sami Christians in Norway (Anne Lisbeth Gjøvikli). She shared insight into several areas in which Samis have experienced conflict between their traditions and Christianity. For example, the ancestors had an important role before, but they are neglected by the Christian faith. Christianity also took away from women their traditional ritual role alongside men. The Sami also miss the ecstatic element in worship, which seems dry and intellectual compared to traditional ritual. In retrospect, we may see that many of these conflicts were unnecessary, and only communicated disdain for the people. Because of this, there is a need for the Church to be reconciled to these people, to understand them and assure them of their value.

Case Study 5
Indigenous Music in the Context of a Missionary Church

Mabel Wu of Hong Kong shared two Chinese hymns with us. The first, "Lord God, Hear My Prayer," employs a sixth-century B.C. Confucian chant as the tune for a hymn asking for forgiveness and guidance. The second, "Praise to You, O Lord Jesus Christ," borrows the tune of a patriotic song dating from the twelfth century A.D. to accompany the text of an ordination hymn. The two hymns are among those being prepared for a new Lutheran hymnal in Hong Kong which will use more local music than earlier hymnals.

The ancient music of the first hymn is of a kind rarely heard any longer, except in a few Confucian temples in China. People can recognize it as being "ancient Chinese music" without relating it to temple worship.

The music of the second hymn, however, is a tune which is readily recognized as belonging to a poem written by Yue Fei (1103-1141), "a famous patriotic general who repelled the Jurchen invasion in order to recapture the lost 'thousand-mile land.' Because of corruption and jealousy in the imperial court, he was recalled to the capital on the eve of winning the war, and was put in jail and died there at age 39," said Professor Wu.

"He is looked upon by all Chinese not only as a hero, but as a symbol of fidelity and total loyalty to one's country. His poem and the song 'The River All Red' are well-known to all Chinese people and have an inspiring and invigorating patriotic influence on them. Singing this ordination hymn in a Chinese congregation, one cannot help but remember Yue Fei and his fidelity to his country. So the question is, is it appropriate to use this hymn with such a famous musical tune, that has such strong historical background? And is it appropriate to take the meaning of fidelity even to death from the example of Yue Fei and transform it to our Christian context, calling for faithfulness and obedience to God even until death?"

Responses

There is historical precedent for deliberately taking over a tune and putting it to a similar-but-different use. The practice, known as "contrafaction," was popular at the time of the Reformation. (For example, "*Innsbruck, ich muss dich lassen*" became "*O Welt, ich muss dich lassen.*") However, a consensus quickly developed in our discussion that in the case of the second hymn the disadvantages surely outweigh the benefits. The text and tune match up well, the hymn would obviously not be difficult for a congregation to learn, and some of the allusions are desirable. Nevertheless, it would seem that the reference to a political hero is so strong in this case as to overwhelm the intended Christian meaning.

Several questions could be asked: What is the judgment of the people to whom the original song "belongs"? Are the people of Christian congregations mature enough in faith to distinguish the hymn from its origin? How might newly converted members interpret such a hymn? Is it appropriate at an ordination to sing a hymn which might import unwanted meanings (heroism, patriotism) into the very idea of ordained ministry? Is it really the intention of the Church to detract from the patriotic hymn?

A parallel case from another context was brought out when a participant from Finland said that because of the strong patriotic associations with Sibelius' tune "Finlandia," she is unhappy to encounter this as a tune for hymns in other countries.

Because music does not have absolute meaning, it is vital to pay heed to the referenced meaning of a tune. Because it is powerfully evocative, it is necessary to be cautious in employing the music of other religions (as in the case of the first hymn). It is especially the case with new Christians: there may be a powerful desire to distance themselves from whatever is associated with the rituals of their old religion—and music may figure prominently here.

On the other hand, where the Christian text in its unity with the tune successfully transforms the song, and where the faithful are able to distinguish the theological content from the cultural form, traditional music should not be excluded from Christian worship, but welcomed.

Inculturation of worship should not mean wholesale assimilation of artifacts (e.g. songs) from the local culture.

The factor of acceptance by the congregation is important, of course. It seems that melodies are more likely to be accepted and used the more they resemble melodies that are already in the people's repertoire. It was reported that Presbyterians in Brazil are allowing congregations to have a strong hand in the creation of a new hymnody by publishing great quantities of hymns, and allowing the people to sort them out; ten years from now they expect to have a good feel for what is acceptable or useful.

With regard to associations, it needs to be asked for whom the associations are effective. If a few people associate "A Mighty Fortress" with anti-Catholicism, for example, does that mean the hymn should for that reason be avoided?

Hymnody is an area in which the issue of cultural borrowing is especially acute, perhaps because it involves each worshiper so personally. Participants shared many experiences in which their churches are facing difficult judgments in this area: Youth may prefer to sing songs from another culture entirely. An "old hymnal" may be full of hymns from other (German or Anglo-American) cultures. The correction of gender bias may cause conflict. The life of new hymns is, sadly, short—this is the influence of a consumer culture.

All of these emphasize the need to seek criteria for the borrowing and lending of music.

Case Study 6
"Giving Thanks" in Papua New Guinea—Implications for Eucharist

Marcus Felde of Papua New Guinea brought a case study in which a linguistic difficulty becomes the basis of a reflection on the meaning of the word *Eucharist*. It was suggested by what Eugene Brand has written: "The most basic sense in which Lutherans need to recover the Eucharist is the restoration of thanksgiving and joy to the celebration of this sacramental meal."[1]

Communion is not celebrated frequently in most congregations of the Lutheran Church in Papua New Guinea. The mood of the service is also not so much joyful thanksgiving as humble repentance. There are obvious historical reasons for this, since this was also the character of the service in the German, American, and Australian churches that sent the missionaries.

But the question is how to present the alternative. "Thanking" is in some ways a notion alien to cultures that are strongly tied to habits of reciprocity, or even retribution. The language of thanking is imported, not just into the Pidgin language but even into some of the seven hundred different indigenous languages. For example, in Jabêm the word is *dange*, from the German *danke*. In Duna, though, the closest expression is either "very good" or "I am happy," neither of which explicitly acknowledges the freeness of the other's giving. There is evidence that the idea of thanking is being assimilated into the idea of reciprocity, as for example when a congregation asks who is willing to go to another congregation and *bekim tenkyu bilong ol* (reciprocate the thankoffering which they had brought to our thanksgiving day last year).

Having observed this difficulty, we are driven to ask what is really meant by thanking in the cultures that have been home to the Christian Church for many centuries.

Responses

It is difficult to analyze this linguistically. However, we may be guilty of a superficial judgment when we say that thanking was not traditionally a part of a culture. We need to search for the dynamic equivalent within the society. Thanks may be given in words, but also by actions.

---

[1]   "A Lutheran Agenda for Worship after Dar-es-Salaam," in *A Lutheran Agenda for Worship* (Geneva: Lutheran World Federation, 1979), 26.

Is not thanking itself part of a reciprocal exchange? A favor is given, and thanks are returned. Thanks are how the gift is "reciprocated." In fact, it may be that a gift offered in return is the best sort of thanks, as long as the exchange is not between people who give only in order to receive.

In the Eucharist, the words "we thank" only verbalize what the action already does. In our analysis, it is useful to distinguish the cultural value (gratitude) from the cultural pattern ("Thank you"); also the words from the rite.

Are we assuming, as Lutherans, that grace precludes reciprocity? Is it not reciprocity, though of another kind, when we respond with thanksgiving to what God has done for us? This is not payment for salvation.

Is the Eucharist being experienced in Papua New Guinea only as a gift, rather than as thanksgiving, perhaps even as an overwhelming gift, which makes our response feeble and futile?

In western cultures, does saying "Thank you" make it unnecessary to reciprocate, perhaps in a more genuine way? Does not gift-giving even in such cultures in fact imply a covenant between giver and receiver? Is there not also in such cultures a tacit compliance with the norm of reciprocity?

Reference was made to C. S. Lewis, who came to appreciate the value of praise as being a way of enjoying God's gifts more profoundly. Since one cannot give back equal measure for God's gifts to me, God gives one the dignity of allowing one to return praise and thanks.

Romans 12 certainly calls for a thankful reciprocity, in the offering of ourselves as living sacrifice. Luther, with his talk of the "delightful exchange" (*fröhliche Wechsel*), alluded to a kind of commerce in our relationship with God. And the offertory aspect of Eucharist, with its ancient tradition of gathering gifts for the poor as a response to God's gifts to us, is liturgical evidence of reciprocity that is not antithetical to thanksgiving. However, there is evidence in some cultures where reciprocity is important (Japan was mentioned) that strongly reciprocal customs may become terrible burdens.

Discussion of the eucharistic prayer itself evoked various comments: In Chile, this prayer may be written by the people themselves, so that they are keenly aware that giving thanks is at the heart of the liturgy. While it was said that the eucharistic prayer helps to teach what is central, it should not be forgotten that the whole action is eucharistic, not just one prayer.

In a culture in which behavior is strongly governed by an obvious norm of reciprocity, it is the task of Christian worship not to oppose reciprocity as such, but to articulate the different-ness of Christian reciprocity, in which our whole lives are lived thankfully in response to God's good gift.

Case Study 7
Worship in the Consumer and Entertainment Context of North America

Eric Dyck of Canada presented a probing and witty commentary on the many ways in which the North American context has become inhospitable to the actions and message of Christian worship. Society has lost the sorts of connections which culture normally provides, holding body and spirit together and rooting both in a cultural memory that gives meaning to the present and future. In the place of these connections, each need that an individual feels is analyzed and then satisfied, all in a piecemeal fashion.

In place of culture, which usually integrates, society gives itself imitations of culture. Community is replaced by life-style enclaves of those who share similar needs; the natural environment is simulated; for something larger than life, there are Ninja turtles and Star Trek. Although there is an evident hunger for something transcendent that might ground this jumbled existence, even that hunger is satisfied with imitations or simulations of transcendence. In this context, where an ever-responsive and therefore ever-shifting marketplace holds sway, even the Church faces the temptation to join the act. It seems that if the Church responds quickly to felt or imagined needs, it will succeed like any other business. The worship of the Church, in such a context, unconsciously begins to compete as entertainment against other forms of entertainment.

"Christianity is subverted by consumerism and turned into an entertainment form because when it serves only to amuse, then its primary feature of being countercultural is disabled. The movement which stood in opposition to the norms of the empire and developed as an ideology yearning for a new reign of justice and righteousness undergoes conversion into an image of pious sentiment, community joy, and popularism," said Pastor Dyck.

The pastoral question then becomes "whether to oblige and make the Church marketable" or to "situate humanity in God's time, around a table which is historic, current, and proleptic, and firmly integrates itself within a tradition and a vision determined by the integrity of its own structure.... Unlike the post-modern building of mirror-glass which can only reflect the world around it, the edifice of the Christian community proclaims a reality both incarnate and transcendent. In reality, outside the shopping mall, Generation X echoes St. Augustine's prayer: 'Our hearts are restless till they rest in thee, O Lord.' "

Responses

Discussion focused first on the fact that what is highlighted here is not behavior that fits with classical or traditional notions of "culture." Nevertheless, as patterned behavior based on the values of the society, it must be regarded as culture, even if it is transitory in nature.

In response to the case study's strong criticism of this culture, it was suggested that we must always begin with respect for the culture of the people, if we mean to address it and even redeem aspects of it for our worship. The culture which is here characterized as "junk culture" has many laudable aspects, as well as deplorable elements. The question is the same here as with any other culture: With what sort of methodology do we approach our study of the culture, so that understanding it we may both make Christian worship meaningful in this context and also that we may address this very culture with God's Word? What components of this culture may be assimilated into worship? How? What role will they play? Which elements are compatible with the nature and purpose of the liturgy, and which are incompatible? Surely even in the consumer/ entertainment/marketing society there is a notion of solemnity, for example.

We should also not underestimate the extent to which many of the described elements—desire for youth and beauty, faddishness in religion, etc.—have been present in other cultures in much earlier days.

Nonetheless, the criticism of the shallowness of consumer culture seems absolutely correct. It is also true that there is a real danger of Christian worship becoming nothing more than an exercise in nostalgia or the satisfaction of personal wishes. In such a context, can any sort of liturgy totally avoid being used for these purposes? Probably not.

What characteristics of this society can properly mark our worship? Perhaps its democratic principles may be evident in the roles of the people in worship; perhaps its concern for the environment may be brought under the praise of the Creator; its concern for the well-being of people, while standing under judgment for its self-centeredness, is certainly not all wrong. North Americans are faced with a situation in which they must be careful not to allow worship to be borrowed for other purposes than its own; and yet they must find a way (to borrow from the first case study) to go faithfully and effectively about the business of bringing into being a eucharistic people.

BIBLIOGRAPHY

S. Anita Stauffer

Abercrombie, Stanley. *Architecture as Art: An Esthetic Analysis.* New York: Van Nostrand Reinhold Company, 1984.

Adey, Lionel. *Hymns and the Christian "Myth."* Vancouver: University of British Columbia Press, 1986.

African Culture and Anglican Liturgy: The Report of the Kanamai Consultation. Bramcote, Nottingham, England: Grove Books, 1993.

Al Faruqi, Lois Ibsen. "An Islamic Perspective on Symbolism in the Arts." *Art, Creativity, and the Sacred.* Ed. by Diane Apostolos-Cappadona. New York: Crossroad, 1984.

Altshuler, David and Linda. "Judaism and Art." *Art, Creativity, and the Sacred.* Ed. by Diane Apostolos-Cappadona. New York: Crossroad, 1984.

Amalorpavadass, D. S. "Theological Reflections on Inculturation." *Studia Liturgica,* Part 1—20:1 (1990), 36-54; Part 2—20:2 (1990), 116-136.

Anker, Peter. *L'Art Scandinave.* La Pierre-qui-Vire, France: Zodiaque, 1969. (English translation: *The Art of Scandinavia.* London: Paul Hamlyn, 1970.)

Arbuckle, Gerald A. "Inculturation not Adaptation: Time to Change Terminology." *Worship,* 60:6 (November 1986), 511-520.

Arnheim, Rudolf. *The Dynamics of Architectural Form.* Berkeley, California: University of California Press, 1977.

Avila, Rafael. *Apuntes sobre las implicaciones socio-politicas de la Eucaristia.* Bogota: Policrom Artes Graficas, 1977. (English translation: *Worship and Politics.* Maryknoll, New York: Orbis Books, 1981.)

Balasuriya, Tissa. *The Eucharist and Human Liberation.* Maryknoll, New York: Orbis Books, 1979.

Baldwin, David. "There's a Sweet, Sweet Spirit in This Place." *Faith and Form,* XXV (Fall 1991), 24-26.

Baumstark, Anton. *Comparative Liturgy.* London: A. R. Mowbray, 1958.

Beasley-Murray, G. R. *Baptism in the New Testament.* Grand Rapids, Michigan: William B. Eerdmans Publishing Company, 1984.

Beckwith, Roger T. *Daily and Weekly Worship: From Jewish to Christian.* Bramcote, Nottingham, England: Grove Books, 1987.

—————. "The Jewish Background to Christian Worship." *The Study of Liturgy.* Ed. by Cheslyn Jones, Geoffrey Wainwright, and Edward Yarnold. London and New York: Oxford University Press, 1978.

Benko, Stephen. *Pagan Rome and the Early Christians.* Bloomington, Indiana: Indiana University Press, 1984.

Bevans, Stephen B. *Models of Contextual Theology.* Maryknoll, New York: Orbis Books, 1992.

Biezais, Haralds, ed. *Religious Symbols and their Functions.* Stockholm: Almqvist & Wiksell, 1978.

Blankenburg, Walter. "Luther und die Musik." *Kirche und Musik: Gesammelte Augsätze zur Geschichte der gottesdienstliche Musik.* Ed. by Erich Hübner and Renate Steiger. Gottingen: Vandenhoeck und Ruprecht, 1979.

—————. "Vom unaufgebbaren Platz der Musik in der Theologie." *Kirche und Musik: Gesammelte Augsätze zur Geschichte der gottesdienstliche Musik.* Ed. by Erich Hübner and Renate Steiger. Gottingen: Vandenhoeck und Ruprecht, 1979.

Bobb, Donald. "African Church Music." *Journey of Struggle, Journey in Hope: People and Their Pilgrimage in Central Africa.* Ed. Jane Heaton. New York: Friendship Press, 1983.

Bognar, Botond. *Contemporary Japanese Architecture.* New York: Van Nostrand Reinhold Company, 1985.

Borello, Andrew. "The Contextualization of Liturgy and Especially Liturgical Texts." *Shaping English Liturgy.* Ed. by Peter Finn and James Schellman. Washington: Pastoral Press, 1990.

Bouyer, Louis. *Rite and Man: Natural Sacredness and Christian Liturgy.* Notre Dame, Indiana: University of Notre Dame Press, 1963.

Boyer, Pascal, ed. *Cognitive Aspects of Religious Symbolism.* Oxford: Oxford University Press, 1993.

Bradshaw, Paul F. *Daily Prayer in the Early Church.* New York: Oxford University Press, 1982.

——————. *The Search for the Origins of Christian Worship*. London: SPCK, 1992.

——————, and Hoffman, Lawrence A., eds. *The Making of Jewish and Christian Worship*. Notre Dame, Indiana: University of Notre Dame Press, 1991.

Brand, Eugene L. "A Lutheran Agenda for Worship after Dar-es-Salaam." *A Lutheran Agenda for Worship*. Geneva: Lutheran World Federation Department of Studies, 1979.

——————. "Ecumenism and the Liturgy." *Worship*, 58:4 (July 1984), 305-315.

——————. "Lutheran Worship in Cultural Context." *Lutheran Forum* (Reformation 1982), 14-17.

——————, ed. *Worship among Lutherans*. Geneva: Lutheran World Federation Department of Studies, 1983. (Portuguese translation by Luis Marcos Sander, *A liturgia entre os luteranos*, São Leopoldo, Brazil, 1989. Spanish translation by Carlos Lisandro Orlov, *La liturgia entre los luteranos*, Buenos Aires, 1985.)

Braukamper, Ulrich. "Aspects of Religious Syncretism in Southern Ethiopia." *Journal of Religion in Africa*, XXI:3 (August 1992), 194-207.

Brilioth, Yngve. *Eucharistic Faith and Practice: Evangelical and Catholic*. Trans. by A. G. Hebert. London: SPCK, 1965.

Brown, Peter. "Christianity and Local Culture in Late Roman Africa." *Journal of Roman Studies*, LVIII:1-2 (1968), 85-95.

Brunner, Paul. "Liturgical Adaption of Indigenous Music." *China Missionary Bulletin*, 9 (December 1957), 668-669.

——————. "The Liturgy of Baptism in the Missions." *China Missionary Bulletin*, 11 (March 1959), 237-248.

Brunner, Peter. *Zur Lehre vom Gottesdienst der in Namen Jesu versammelten Gemeinde. Leiturgia, Handbuch des evangelischen Gottesdienstes*, Volume 1. Ed. by Karl F. Müller and Walter Blankenburg. Kassel: Johannes Stauda Verlag, 1954. (English tanslation: *Worship in the Name of Jesus*. St. Louis, Missouri: Concordia Publishing House, 1958.)

Buchanan, George W. "Worship, Feasts, and Ceremonies in the Early Jewish-Christian Church." *New Testament Studies*, 26 (1980), 279-297.

Burki, Bruno. "Traditional Initiation in Africa." *Studia Liturgica*, 12:4 (1977), 201-206.

Butler, John F. *Christian Art in India*. Madras, India: Christian Literature Society, 1986.

——————. "Further Thoughts on Church Architecture in India." *The Indian Journal of Theology*, VIII:4 (October/December 1959), 135-150.

——————. "Nineteen Centuries of Christian Missionary Architecture." *Journal of the Society of Architectural Historians*, 21 (1962), 3-17.

——————. "The Theology of Church Building in India." *The Indian Journal of Theology*, V:2 (October 1956), 1-20.

Byaruhanga Akiiki, A. B. T. "The Philosophy and Theology of Time in Africa: (1) The Bantu Case." *African Ecclesial Review*, 22:6 (December 1980), 357-369.

Caldarola, Carlo. *Christianity: The Japanese Way*. Leiden: E. J. Brill, 1979.

Candy, Susan. "Art and Asian Spirituality." *Mission and Art*. Ed. by Masao Takenaka and Godwin R. Singh. Hong Kong: Christian Conference of Asia, and Asian Christian Art Association, 1994.

Carroll, Kevin. "African Textiles for Church Linen and Vestments." *Inculturation of Christianity in Africa*. Eldoret, Kenya: AMECEA Gaba Publications, 1990. 241-248.

Christensen, Thomas G. *An African Tree of Life*. Maryknoll, New York: Orbis Books, 1990.

Chung, ChangBok. "Indigenization of Worship: The Holy Dinner." *Northeast Asia Journal of Theology*, 18-19 (March/September 1977), 46-52.

Chupungco, Anscar J. "A Definition of Liturgical Inculturation." *Ecclesia Orans*, V:1 (1988), 11-23.

——————. "A Filipino Attempt at Liturgical Inculturation." *Ephemerides liturgicae*, 91:4-5 (1977), 370-376.

——————. "A Historical Survey of Liturgical Adaptation." *Notitiae*, 174 (January 1981), 28-43.

——————. *Cultural Adaptation of the Liturgy*. New York: Paulist Press, 1982.

——————. "Greco-Roman Cultural and Liturgical Adaptation." *Notitiae*, 153 (April 1979), 202-218.

——————. *Liturgical Inculturation*. Collegeville, Minnesota: Liturgical Press, 1992.

——————. *Liturgies of the Future: The Process and Methods of Inculturation*. New York: Paulist Press, 1989.

——————. *Shaping the Easter Feast*. Washington, D.C.: Pastoral Press, 1992.

——————. *Towards a Filipino Liturgy*. Quezon City, Philippines, 1976.

——————. *Tradition and Progress*. Washington, D.C.: Pastoral Press, 1994.

Clarke, Sundar. *Let the Indian Church Be Indian*. Madras, India: Christian Literature Society, 1985.

Collins, Mary. "Critical Ritual Studies: Examining an Intersection of Theology and Culture." *Essays on Religion and Culture*. Ed. by John May. Chico, California: Scholars Press, 1981.

Coomaraswamy, Ananda K. "The Origin and Use of Images in India." *Art, Creativity, and the Sacred*. Ed. by Diane Apostolos-Cappadona. New York: Crossroad, 1984.

Congregatio pro Culto Divino, Citta del Vaticano. "Le Missel Romain pour les dioceses du Zaire." *Notitiae*, 24 (1988), 454-472.

Connor, John H. "When Culture Leaves Christianity Behind." *Missiology: An International Review*, XIX:1 (January 1991), 21 29.

Cooper, J. C. *An Illustrated Encyclopaedia of Traditional Symbols*. London: Thames and Hudson, 1978.

Costen, Melva W. "African Roots of Afro-American Baptismal Practices." *Journal of the Interdenominational Theological Center*, XIV:1-2 (1986-1987), 23-42.

Cramer, Peter. *Baptism and Change in the Early Middle Ages, c.200 - c.1150*. Oxford: Oxford University Press, 1993.

Crockett, William R. "Christianity and Culture in Modern Secular Society." *Studia Liturgica*, 20:1 (1990), 28-35.

"Culture and Liturgy: II." *National Bulletin on Liturgy*, 19:105 (September-October 1986).

Curry, Terrence M. "Designing a Building for a Nigerian Church." *Faith and Form*, XXIV (Winter 1990-91), 36-39.

Dale, Kenneth J. "Some Aspects of the Cultural Context of Japan and Their Challenge to the Confessing Christian Church." *Northeast Asia Journal of Theology*, 22-23 (March/September 1979), 72-95.

Dargie, David. "Xhosa Church Music." *Concilium*, 202 (1989).

Davies, J. G. "The Introduction of the Numinous into the Liturgy: An Historical Note." *Studia Liturgica*, 8:4 (1971-1972), 216-223.

——————. *The Origin and Development of Early Christian Architecture*. New York: Philosophical Library, 1953.

Davis, Charles. "Today's Culture and the Meaning of Baptism." *Ecumenical Review*, 39:2 (April 1987), 163-172.

Debuyst, Fréderic. *L'Art chrétien contemporain*. Paris: Nouvelles Editions Mame, 1988.

Delattre, Roland. "Ritual Resourcefulness and Cultural Pluralism." *Soundings*, 61 (1978), 281-301

Denyer, S. *African Traditional Architecture*. London: Heinemann, 1978.

DeSouza, Carlito. "Christian Art in India." *China Missionary Bulletin*, 10 (September 1958), 651-657.

Dillistone, F. W. *The Power of Symbols in Religion and Culture*. New York: Crossroad, 1986.

DiSante, Carmine. Jewish Prayer: *The Origins of Christian Liturgy*. New York: Paulist Press, 1985.

Dix, Dom Gregory. *Jew and Greek: A Study in the Primitive Church*. Westminster, England: Dacre Press, 1953.

——————. *The Shape of the Liturgy*. London: A. & C. Black, 1945.

Donnelly, Marian. *Art in the Scandinavian Countries*. Boston, Massachusetts: MIT Press, 1992.

Eco, Umberto. *Art and Beauty in the Middle Ages*. New Haven, Connecticut: Yale University Press, 1986.

Eliade, Mircea. *Rites and Symbols of Initiation*. New York: Harper & Row, 1958.

——————. *Symbolism, the Sacred, and the Arts*. New York: Crossroad, 1990.

—————. *The Sacred and the Profane*. New York: Harcourt Brace Jovanovich, 1959.

Egbulem, Chris Nwaka. "An African Interpretation of Liturgical Inculturation: The Rite Zairois." *A Promise of Presence*. Ed. by Michael Downey and Richard Fragomeni, Richard. Washington: Pastoral Press, 1992.

Éla, Jean-Marc. *Ma Foi d'Africain*. Paris: Éditions Karthala, 1985. (English translation: *My Faith as an Africain*. Maryknoll, New York: Orbis Books, 1988; London: Geoffrey Chapman, 1989.)

Emminghaus, Johannes H. *The Eucharist: Essence, Form, Celebration*. Collegeville, Minnesota: Liturgical Press, 1978.

Endo, Shasuku. "Bridging the Gap between Christianity and Japanese Culture." *The Japan Christian Quarterly*, 56 (Fall 1990), 227-236.

England, John C. "Doing Theology with People's Symbols and Images — an Historical Outline of Resources." ATESEA Occasional Papers No. 8: *Doing Theology with People's Symbols and Images*. Singapore: Association for Theological Education in South East Asia, 1989.

Eusden, John D. "Chartres and Ryoan-ji: Aesthetic Connections and Affecting Presence." *Cross Currents*, 43:1 (Spring 1993), 38-46.

Feeley-Harnik, Gillian. *The Lord's Table: Eucharist and Passover in Early Christianity*. Philadelphia: University of Pennsylvania Press, 1981.

Felde, Marcus. "Local Theologies—License to Sing." *The Hymn*, 40:3 (July 1989), 15-20.

Felix, Wilfred. "Inculturation: Reflections in the Asian Context." *SEDOS Bulletin*, 21:6 (15 June 1989), 185-194.

Fête, Joseph N. "The Cultural Background of the Roman Ritual of Baptism." Unpublished S.T.M. Thesis, Yale Divinity School (New Haven, Connecticut USA), 1981.

Finn, Thomas M. *Early Christian Baptism and the Catechumenate: Italy, North Africa, and Egypt*. Collegeville, Minnesota: Liturgical Press, 1992.

—————. *Early Christian Baptism and the Catechumenate: West and East Syria*. Collegeville, Minnesota: Liturgical Press, 1992.

Finney, Paul Corby. "Early Christian Architecture: The Beginnings." *Harvard Theological Review*, 81:3 (1988), 319-339.

Fisher, Eugene J., ed. *The Jewish Roots of Christian Liturgy*. New York: Paulist Press, 1990.

Fitzpatrick, Joseph P. *One Church, Many Cultures*. Kansas City, Missouri: Sheed & Ward, 1987.

Fleming, Daniel Johnson. *Christian Symbols in a World Community*. New York: Friendship Press, 1940.

—————. *Heritage of Beauty: Pictorial Studies of Modern Christian Architecture in Asia and Africa Illustrating the Influence of Indigenous Cultures*. New York: Friendship Press, 1937.

Foley, Edward. *Foundations of Christian Music: The Music of Pre-Constantinian Christianity*. Bramcote, Nottingham, England: Grove Books, 1992.

—————. *From Age to Age: How Christians Celebrate the Eucharist*. Chicago: Liturgy Training Publications, 1991.

Francis, Mark R. "Adaptation, Liturgical." *The New Dictionary of Sacramental Worship*. Ed. by Peter Fink. Collegeville, Minnesota: Liturgical Press, 1990.

—————. *Liturgy in a Multicultural Community*. Collegeville, Minnesota: Liturgical Press, 1991.

Friesen, Albert W. D. "A Methodology in the Development of Indigenous Hymnody." *Missiology: An International Review*, X:1 (January 1982), 83-96.

Geertz, Clifford. *The Interpretation of Cultures*. New York: Basic Books, 1973.

Gilombe, Mudiji-Malamba. "African Churches." *Church Building* (Spring 1990), 8-11.

Gittins, Anthony J. *Gifts and Strangers: Meeting the Challenge of Inculturation*. New York: Paulist Press, 1989.

Glasswell, Mark E., and Fasholé-Luke, Edward W., eds. *New Testament Christianity for Africa and the World*. London: SPCK, 1974.

Goethals, Gregor T. *The Electronic Golden Calf: Images, Religion, and the Making of Meaning*. Cambridge, Massachusetts: Cowley Publications, 1990.

Gorringe, Timothy. *Love's Sign: Reflections on the Eucharist*. Madurai, India: TamilNadu Theological Seminary, 1986.

Grabar, Andre. *Christian Iconography: A Study of Its Origins*. Princeton, New Jersey: Princeton University Press, 1968.

Griffiths, Bede. "Liturgy and the Missions." *China Missionary Bulletin*, 12 (February 1960), 148-154.

Gy, Pierre-Marie. "The Inculturation of the Christian Liturgy in the West." *Studia Liturgica*, 20:1 (1990), 8-18.

Hahn, Ferdinand. *The Worship of the Early Church*. Philadelphia: Fortress Press, 1973.

Hao, Yap Kim. "Inter-Contextualization." *Asia Journal of Theology*, 4:1 (April 1990), 36-44.

Happel, Stephen. "Classicist Culture and the Nature of Worship." *Heythrop Journal*, XXI:3 (July 1980), 288-302.

Harbakk, Ernst. "The Tao Wind Mountain." *Areopagus*, 11:1-2 (Fall 1987), 12-14.

Hastings, Adrian. "Western Christianity Confronts Other Cultures." *Studia Liturgica*, 20:1 (1990), 19-27.

Hawn, C. Michael. "A Survey of Trends in Recent Protestant Hymnals: International Hymnody." *The Hymn*, 42:4 (1991), 24-32.

Hayes, Bartlett. *Tradition Becomes Innovation: Modern Religious Architecture in America*. New York: Pilgrim Press, 1983.

Healey, Joseph. "Inculturation of Liturgy and Worship in Africa." *Worship*, 60:5 (1986), 412-422.

Heldman, Marilyn E. "Architectural Symbolism, Sacred Geography and the Ethiopian Church." *Journal of Religion in Africa*, XXII:3 (August 1992), 222-241.

Hesselgrave, David, and Rommen, Edward. *Contextualization: Meanings, Methods, and Models*. Leicester, England: Apollos, 1989.

Hiebert, Paul G. "Critical Contextualization." *International Bulletin of Missionary Research*, 11:3 (July 1987), 104-112.

Ho, Koon-Ki. "Silence and the Japanization of Christianity." The *Japan Christian Quarterly*, 53 (1987), 71-76.

Hoefer, Herbert E., ed. *Christian Art in India*. Madras, India: Gurukul Lutheran Theological College and Research Institute, 1982.

Hoffman, Lawrence A. *Beyond the Text*. Bloomington, Indiana: Indiana University Press, 1982.

—————. *The Art of Public Prayer*. Washington: Pastoral Press, 1988.

Hofinger, Johannes. "Liturgical Arts in the Missions." *China Missionary Bulletin*, 10 (December 1958), 1001-1010.

Holeton, David R., ed. *Liturgical Inculturation in the Anglican Communion*. Bramcote, Nottingham, England: Grove Books, 1990.

Holleman, A. W. J. "Early Christian Liturgical Music." *Studia Liturgica*, 8:3 (1971-1972), 185-192.

Huffman, Walter, and Stauffer, S. Anita. *Where We Worship*. Minneapolis: Augsburg Fortress, 1987.

Ikenga-Metuh, E. "The Revival of African Spirituality: A Leaf from African Instituted Churches." *Encounter of Religions in African Cultures*. Geneva: Lutheran World Federation, 1991.

Ishii, Masami. "Some Problems in the Relationship Between Japanese Culture and Christianity." *Northeast Asia Journal of Theology*, 22-23 (March/September 1979), 38-61.

Jungmann, Josef A. *The Early Liturgy*. Notre Dame, Indiana: University of Notre Dame Press, 1959.

Kain, Anthony. "'My Son's Bread': About Culture, Language and Liturgy." Ed. by Michael Downey and Richard Fragomeni. *A Promise of Presence*. Washington: Pastoral Press, 1992.

Kakiuchi, Junko. "The Peace Symbols and Images of the Japanese: Theology and Japanese Thought." ATESEA Occasional Papers No. 8: *Doing Theology with People's Symbols and Images*. Singapore: Association for Theological Education in South East Asia, 1989.

Kavanagh, Aidan. "Jewish Roots of Christian Worship." *The New Dictionary of Sacramental Worship*. Collegeville, Minnesota: Liturgical Press, 1990.

—————. "Liturgical Inculturation: Looking to the Future." *Studia Liturgica*, 20:1 (1990), 95-106.

—————. *The Shape of Baptism*. New York: Pueblo Publishing Company, 1978.

Kilmartin, Edward J. *Christian Liturgy: Theology and Practice*. Volume I. Kansas City, Missouri: Sheed & Ward, 1988. Chapter 2.

—————. *Culture and the Praying Church*. Canadian Studies in Liturgy, No. 5. Ottawa: Canadian Conference of Catholic Bishops, 1990.

Kiwovele, Judah B. M. "The Indigenization of Christian Worship." *A Lutheran Agenda for Worship*. Geneva: Lutheran World Federation Department of Studies, 1979.

Klauser, Theodor. *A Short History of the Western Liturgy*. Second edition. Oxford: Oxford University Press, 1979.

Komonchak, Joseph A. "The Local Church and the Church Catholic: The Contemporary Theological Problematic." *The Jurist*, 52:1 (1992), 416-447.

Koyama, Kosuke. "The Tradition and Indigenisation." *Asia Journal of Theology*, 7:1 (April 1993), 2-11.

Krautheimer, Richard. *Early Christian and Byzantine Architecture*. Fourth edition. New York: Penguin Books, 1986.

Kretschmar, Georg. "Recent Research on Christian Initiation." *Studia Liturgica*, 12 (1977), 93-102.

Langan, Thomas. "Accommodating Cultures without Dissolving the Unity of the Faith." *Creative Inculturation and the Unity of Faith*. Rome: Pontifical Gregorian University, 1986. 41-53.

Lathrop, Gordon W. *Holy Things: A Liturgical Theology*. Minneapolis: Fortress Press, 1993.

—————. "The Prayers of Jesus and the Great Prayer of the Church." *Lutheran Quarterly*, XXVI.2 (May 1974), 158-173.

Lawson, E. Thomas. "Cognitive Categories, Cultural Forms and Ritual Structures." *Cognitive Aspects of Religious Symbolism*. Ed. by Pascal Boyer. Cambridge: Cambridge University Press, 1993.

Leaver, Robin A. "Theological Dimensions of Mission Hymnody: the Counterpoint at Cult and Culture." *African Journal of Theology*, 16:3 (1987), 242-254.

Ledogar, Robert, ed. *Katigondo: Presenting the Christian Message to Africa*. London: Geoffrey Chapman, 1965.

Lee, Archie C. C. "The 'Aniconic God' and Chinese Iconolatry." ATESEA Occasional Papers No. 4: *Doing Theology with Religions of Asia*. Singapore: Association for Theological Education in South East Asia, 1987.

"Liturgy and the Cultural Mosaic." *National Bulletin on Liturgy*, 26:133 (Summer 1993).

Loh, I-to. "Toward Contextualization of Church Music in Asia." *Asia Journal of Theology*, 4:1 (April 1990), 293-315.

Lott, Eric J., ed. *Worship in an Indian Context.* Bangalore, India: United Theological College, 1986.

Loudi, Boka di Mpasi. "Freedom of Bodily Expression in the African Liturgy." *Concilium*, 132:2 (1980).

Lumembu, L. Kasanda. "Inculturation in Action: African Rites and Liturgies." *SEDOS Bulletin*, 23:5 (15 May 1991), 133-138.

Lund, Kjell. "The Spirituality of Space: Scandinavian Culture." *Faith and Form* (Spring 1993), 13-17.

Luther, Martin. *Liturgy and Hymns.* Vol. 53 of *Luther's Works* (American Edition). Ed. by Ulrich S. Leupold. Philadelphia: Fortress Press, 1965.

Lutheran World Federation. *A Lutheran Agenda for Worship.* Geneva: LWF Department of Studies, 1979. (Portuguese translation by Getulio Bertelli, *O culto luterano*, Sao Leopoldo, 1982. Spanish translation by Robert Hoeferkamp, *Temario luterano para el culto*, Mexico City and Bogota, 1981.)

—————. *Declaracio'n de Caracas sobre liturgia* (Statement of Latin American Lutheran Consultation on Liturgy, Caracas, Venezuela, 1986). Buenos Aires: LWF Department of Studies, 1986. (English translation by Gerhard Cartford, *Caracas Statement on Liturgy*, Buenos Aires, 1986. Portuguese translation by Luis Marcos Sander, *Declaracao de Caracas sobre liturgia*, Sao Leopoldo, 1989.)

—————. *Confessing Christ in Cultural Contexts.* Two volumes. Geneva: LWF Department of Studies, 1981 and 1983.

—————. *Report on the Follow-up Church Construction Seminar for Eastern Africa.* March 1985, Nairobi, Kenya. Geneva: LWF Department of Church Cooperation, 1985.

Luzbetak, Louis J. *The Church and Cultures.* South Pasadena, California: William Carey Library, 1970.

Maldonado, Luis, and Power, David, eds. *Symbol and Art in Worship.* Concilium 132 (1980). Edinburgh: T. & T. Clark, 1980.

Malm, William. *Music Cultures of the Pacific, the Near East and Asia.* Englewood Cliffs, New Jersey: 1967.

Mananzan, Mary John. "Paschal Mystery from a Philippine Perspective." *Any Room for Christ in Asia?* Ed. by Leonardo Boff and Virgil Elizondo. *Concilium* (1993/2), 86-94.

Mannion, M. Francis. "Culture, Liturgy and." *The New Dictionary of Sacramental Worship.* Collegeville, Minnesota: Liturgical Press, 1990.

—————. "Liturgy and Culture" (Four-part series). *Liturgy 80* (April 1989, July 1989, October 1989) and *Liturgy 90* (February-March 1990).

—————. "Liturgy and the Present Crisis of Culture." *Worship*, 62:2 (March 1988), 98-123.

Maquet, Jacques. *The Aesthetic Experience: An Anthropologist Looks at the Visual Arts*. New Haven, Connecticut: Yale University Press, 1986.

Martey, Emmanuel. *African Theology: Inculturation and Liberation*. Maryknoll, New York: Orbis Books, 1993.

Martin, James Alfred Jr. *Beauty and Holiness: The Dialogue between Aesthetics and Religion*. Princeton, New Jersey: Princeton University Press, 1990.

Martin, Ralph P. *Worship in the Early Church*. Grand Rapids, Michigan: William B. Eerdmans Publishing Company, 1974.

Martinez, German. "Cult and Culture: The Structure of the Evolution of Worship." *Worship*, 64:5 (September 1990), 406-433.

Mayer, Anton L. *Die Liturgie in der europaischen Geistesgeschichte*. Darmstadt: Wissenschaftliche Buchgesellschaft, 1971.

McManus, Frederick R. "The Possibility of New Rites in the Church." *The Jurist*, 50 (1990), 435-458.

Meeks, Wayne A. *The First Urban Christians: The Social World of the Apostle Paul*. New Haven: Yale University Press, 1983.

Miles, Margaret R. *Image as Insight: Visual Understanding in Western Christianity and Secular Culture*. Boston: Beacon Press, 1985.

Minamiki, George. *The Chinese Rites Controversy*. Chicago: Loyola University Press, 1985.

Mitchell, Leonel L. "At All Times and in All Places, or Each One in His or Her Own Place: Universality and/or Cultural Particularlity in the Liturgy." *American Theological Library Association Proceedings*, 1990.

Moore, Albert C. *Iconography of Religions*. London and Philadelphia: SCM Press and Fortress Press, 1977.

Nattiez, Jean-Jacques. *Music and Discourse: Toward a Semiology of Music*. Trans. by Carolyn Abbate. Princeton, New Jersey: Princeton University Press, 1990.

Nettl, Bruno. *Excursions in World Music*. Englewood Cliffs, New Jersey: Prentice Hall, 1992.

—————. *Theory and Method in Ethnomusicology*. London: 1964.

Nida, Eugene A. *Message and Mission: The Communication of the Christian Faith*. New York: Harper & Brothers, 1960.

Niebuhr, H. Richard. *Christ and Culture*. New York: Harper and Row, 1951.

Nielsen, Ingeline. "Church Music in Asia: From Yesterday to Tomorrow." *The Hymn*, 38:3 (July 1987), 29-31.

Ning, Shu. "The Relationship between Christianity and Chinese Culture: An Analysis in the Light of Cultural Communication." *China Study Journal*, 7:2 (August 1992), 4-10. (Originally in *Nanjing Theological Review*, 14-15 [September 1991]).

Nishi, Kazuo, and Hozumi, Kazuo. *What Is Japanese Architecture?* Tokyo: Kodansha International, Ltd., 1983.

Nketia, J. H. Kwabena. "The Contribution of African Culture to Christian Worship." *International Review of Missions*, 47:187 (July 1958), 265-278.

—————. *The Music of Africa*. New York: Norton, 1974.

Ostling, Richard N. "Africa's Artistic Resurrection." *Time* (March 27, 1989), 76-79.

—————. "The Basilica in the Bush." *Time* (July 3, 1989), 38-39.

Otto, Rudolf. *The Idea of the Holy*. London: Oxford University Press, 1950.

Ozment, Steven, ed. *Religion and Culture in the Renaissance and Reformation*. Kirksville, Missouri: Sixteenth Century Journal Publishers, 1989.

Patmury, Joseph, and England, John, eds. ATESEA Occasional Papers No. 13: *Doing Theology with the Festivals and Customs of Asia*. Singapore: Association for Theological Education in South East Asia, 1994.

Pereira, T. *Towards an Indian Christian Funeral Rite*. Bangalore, India, 1980.

Pietri, Charles. "Liturgy, Culture and Society: The Examples of Rome at the End of the Ancient World (Fourth-Fifth Centuries)." *Liturgy: A Creative Tradition*. Vol. 162:2 of *Concilium*. Ed. by Mary Collins and David Power. Edinburgh: T. & T. Clark, 1983.

Pilgrim, Richard B. "Foundations for a Religio-Aesthetic Tradition in Japan." *Art, Creativity, and the Sacred*. Ed. by Diane Apostolos-Cappadona. New York: Crossroad, 1984.

——————. "The Architecture of *Ma*: Toward an Architectural Theology in Japan." *Faith and Form*, XXVI (Spring 1993), 9-12.

Piryns, Ernest D. "Japanese Theology and Inculturation." *Journal of Ecumenical Studies*, 24 (1987), 535-556.

Plenty Good Room: The Spirit and Truth of African American Catholic Worship. (Washington, D.C.: United States Catholic Conference, 1990).

Pocknee, C. *Water and the Spirit*. London: Darton, Longman & Todd, 1967.

Poerwowidagdo, Judo. "Communicating the Gospel through Indonesian Symbols and Images: Old and New." ATESEA Occasional Papers No. 8: *Doing Theology with People's Symbols and Images*. Singapore: Association for Theological Education in South East Asia, 1989.

Power, David N. *Worship: Culture and Theology*. Washington: Pastoral Press, 1990.

Puthanangady, Paul. "Cultural Elements in Liturgical Prayer." *Shaping English Liturgy*. Ed. by Peter Finn and James Schellman. Washington: Pastoral Press, 1990.

——————. "Inculturation of the Liturgy in India Since Vatican II." *Liturgy: A Creative Tradition*. Vol. 162:2 of *Concilium*. Ed. by Mary Collins and David Power. Edinburgh: T. & T. Clark, 1983.

Quasten, Johannes. *Music and Worship in Pagan and Christian Antiquity*. Washington: Pastoral Press, 1983.

Rasolondraibe, Peri. "Healing Ministry in Madagascar." *Word & World*, IX:4 (Fall 1989), 344-350.

Ray, Benjamin C. *African Religions: Symbol, Ritual, and Community*. Englewood Cliffs, New Jersey: Prentice-Hall, Inc., 1976.

Reeder, Rachel, ed. *Liturgy: The Church and Culture*. Washington: Liturgical Conference, 1986.

Reif, Stefan C. *Judaism and Hebrew Prayer: New Perspectives on Jewish Liturgical History*. Oxford: Oxford University Press, 1993.

Richard, Lucien. "Christology and the Needs for Limits: The Contextualization of Theology." *One Faith, Many Cultures: Inculturation, Indigenization, and Contextualization*. Ed. by Ruy Costa. Maryknoll, New York: Orbis Books, 1988.

Robinson, Gnana, ed. *Influence of Hinduism on Christianity*. Madurai, India: Tamilnadu Theological Seminary, 1980.

Rordorf, Willy. *Sunday*. London: SCM Press, 1968.

Ruhnau, Bernhardt. "Celebrating Easter among the Turkana Nomads." *African Ecclesial Review*, 22:6 (December 1980), 386-392, 398.

Ryan, John Barry. "Preparing a Global Perspective in Liturgical Studies." *Worship*, 60:4 (July 1986), 291-304.

Saether, Arne. *Kirken Bygg og Bilde: Rom og liturgi mot et tusenårsskifte*. Asker, Norway: Utgitt På Eget Forlag, 1990.

Sahi, Jyoti. "Popular Spirituality in India." *SEDOS Bulletin*, 21:5 (15 May 1989), 146-154.

Sanon, Anselme. "Cultural Rooting of the Liturgy in Africa Since Vatican II." *Liturgy: A Creative Tradition*. Vol. 162:2 of *Concilium*. Ed. by Mary Collins and David Power. Edinburgh: T. & T. Clark, 1983.

Santoja, Jakub. "On-the-floor Leisure Sitting ('Lesehan'): as a Secular and Religious Symbol." ATESEA Occasional Papers No. 8: *Doing Theology with People's Symbols and Images*. Singapore: Association for Theological Education in South East Asia, 1989.

Scheer, Anthonius. "The Influence of Culture on the Liturgy as Shown in the History of the Christian Initiation Rite." *Structures of Initiation in Crisis*. Ed. by Luis Maldonado and David Power. New York: Seabury Press, 1979.

Schineller, Peter. *A Handbook on Inculturation*. New York: Paulist Press, 1990.

————. "Inculturation of the Liturgy." *The New Dictionary of Sacramental Worship*. Ed. by Peter Fink. Collegeville, Minnesota: Liturgical Press, 1990.

Schmidt, Herman, and Power, David, eds. *Liturgy and Cultural Religious Traditions*. Vol. 2 of *Concilium*. New York: Seabury Press, 1977.

Schnijder, A. C. J. M. "Cosmopolitization of Mankind and Adaptation of the Liturgy." *Studia Liturgica*, 8:3 (1971-1972), 169-184.

Schreiter, Robert J. *Constructing Local Theologies*. Maryknoll, New York: Orbis Books, 1985.

Searle, Mark. "Culture." *Liturgy: Active Participation in the Divine Life.* Ed. by James Moroney. Collegeville, Minnesota: Liturgical Press, 1990.

Seasoltz, R. Kevin. "Cultural Pluralism and the Churches' Prayer." *Liturgy*, 3:2 (1983), 43-49.

Sendoro, Elinaza. "From the Point of View of Worship." *The Concept of the Church in an African Setting.* Report of Lutheran World Federation Regional Consultation in Eastern Africa, September 1973, Arusha, Tanzania.

Senn, Frank C. *Christian Worship and its Cultural Setting.* Philadelphia: Fortress Press, 1983.

——————. "Lutheran Liturgy in a Pluralistic and Ecumenical Age." *Dialog*, 26:4 (1987), 286-291.

——————. "The Lord's Supper, Not the Passover Seder." *Worship*, 60:4 (July 1986), 362-368.

Shiina, Rinzo. "The Japanese People and Indigenous Christianity." *Japanese Religions*, 1 (1959), 18-21.

Shorter, Aylward. *African Christian Spirituality.* Maryknoll, New York: Orbis Books, 1980.

——————. *African Culture and the Christian Church.* Maryknoll, New York: Orbis Books, 1974.

——————. "Prayer in African Cultural Tradition." *Inculturation of Christianity in Africa.* Eldoret, Kenya: AMECEA Gaba Publications, 1990. 251-259.

——————. *Toward a Theology of Inculturation.* London: Geoffrey Chapman, 1988.

Sigal, Phillip. "Early Christian and Rabbinic Liturgical Affinities: Exploring Liturgical Acculturation." *New Testament Studies*, 30 (1984), 63-90.

Singh, Nikky-Guinder Kaur. "Symbol as Universal Construction: Toward a Deconstruction of Syncretism." *Journal of Ecumenical Studies*, 28:2 (Spring 1991), 299-323.

Smits, Kenneth. "Liturgical Reform in Cultural Perspective." *Worship*, 50:2 (March 1976), 98-110.

Stauffer, S. Anita. "Inculturation and Church Architecture." *Studia Liturgica*, 20:1 (1990), 70-80.

──────. *On Baptismal Fonts*. Bramcote, Nottingham, England: Grove Books, 1994.

Stommel, Eduard. "Christliche Taufriten und antike Badesitten." *Jahrbuch fur Antike und Christentum*, 2 (1959), 5-14.

Stott, John, and Robert T. Coote, eds. *Down to Earth: Studies in Christianity and Culture* (Papers of the Lausanne Consultation on Gospel and Culture). London: Hodder and Stoughton, 1981.

Takenaka, Masao. *Christian Art in Asia*. Tokyo: Kyo Bun Kwan, and Christian Conference of Asia, 1975

──────. *Cross and Circle*. Hong Kong: Christian Conference of Asia, 1990. Section 5: Cultural Expression.

──────, and O'Grady, Ron. *The Bible through Asian Eyes*. Auckland, New Zealand: Pace Publishing, and Kyoto, Japan: Asian Christian Art Association, 1991.

Talley, Thomas J. *The Origins of the Liturgical Year*. New York: Pueblo Publishing Company, 1986.

Terrin, A. *Leitourgia*. Brescia, Italy, 1988.

Thangaraj, M. Thomas. "Towards a Singable Theology." *Venturing into Life: The Story of the Tamilnadu Theological Seminary*. Ed. by Samuel Amirtham and C. R. W. David. Madurai, India: Tamilnadu Theological Seminary, 1990.

Thiel, J. F., and Helf, H. *Christliche Kunst in Afrika*. Berlin: Dietrich Reimer, 1984.

Tovey, Phillip. *Inculturation: The Eucharist in Africa*. Bramcote, Nottingham, England: Grove Books, 1988.

Turner, Harold W. *From Temple to Meeting House: The Phenomenology and Theology of Places of Worship*. The Hague: Mouton Publishers, 1979.

Uzukwu, E. Elochukwu. *Liturgy: Truly Christian, Truly African*. Eldoret, Kenya: Gaba Publications, 1982.

Vatican Congregation for Divine Worship and the Discipline of the Sacraments. *The Roman Liturgy and Inculturation: Fourth Instruction for the Right Application of the Conciliar Constitution on the Liturgy*. (Rome, 29 March 1994). Appears in English in *Origins*, 23:43 (14 April 1994), 745-756.

Van Thiel, Paul. "African Music and Dance in Christian Liturgy." *Inculturation of Christianity in Africa*. Eldoret, Kenya: AMECEA Gaba Publications, 1990. 189-196.

—————. "African Religious Music: Text, Tone, and Tune," I and II. *Inculturation of Christianity in Africa*. Eldoret, Kenya: AMECEA Gaba Publications, 1990. 169-188.

Von Bruck, Michael. "Religionswissenschaft und interkulturelle Theologie." *Evangelische Theologie* (3/92), 245-261.

Wainwright, Geoffrey. "Christian Worship and Western Culture." *Studia Liturgica*, 12:1 (1977), 20-33.

—————. *Doxology*. London and New York: Oxford University Press, 1980. Chapter XI.

—————. "The Localization of Worship." *Studia Liturgica*, 8:1 (1971), 26-41.

Walter, E. V. "The Places of Experience." *Philosophical Forum*, XII:2 (Winter 1980-1981), 159-181.

Walton, Janet R. *Art and Worship*. Wilmington, Delaware: Michael Glazier, Inc., 1988.

Walton, Rikvah. "Beyond Sentimentality: The Consciousful Design of Ceremonial Objects." *Cross Currents*, 43:1 (Spring 1993), 82-91.

Warren, Michael. *Faith, Culture, and the Worshiping Community*. Revised edition. New York: Paulist Press, 1993.

Wegman, Herman. *Christian Worship in East and West*. Trans. by Gordon Lathrop. New York: Pueblo Publishing Company, 1976.

Wemen, Henry. *African Music and the Church in Africa*. Uppsala, Sweden: 1960.

Werner, Eric. *The Sacred Bridge: Liturgical Parallels in Synagogue and Early Church*. New York: Schocken Books, 1970.

—————. *The Sacred Bridge: The Interdependence of Liturgy and Music in the Synagogue and Church during the First Millenium*. New York: KTAV Publishing House, 1984.

Westerhoff, John H. III. "Celebrating and Living the Eucharist: A Cultural Analysis." *The Eucharist*. Vol. 3 of *Alternative Futures for Worship*. Ed. by Bernard J. Lee. Collegeville, Minnesota: Liturgical Press, 1987.

Whelan, Thomas. "African Ethnomusicology and Christian Liturgy." *Inculturation of Christianity in Africa*. Eldoret, Kenya: AMECEA Gaba Publications, 1990. 201-210.

White, James F. "Worship and Culture: Mirror or Beacon?" *Theological Studies*, 35:2 (June 1974), 288-301.

White, L. Michael. *Building God's House in the Roman World: Architectural Adaptation among Pagans, Jews, and Christians*. Baltimore and London: Johns Hopkins University Press, 1990.

Wicker, B. *Culture and Liturgy*. London: Sheed & Ward, 1963.

Wilfred, Felix. "Christian Inculturation and World Religions." *SEDOS Bulletin*, 21:1 (15 January 1989), 37-44.

Williams, Peter. *The Organ in Western Culture*. Oxford: Oxford University Press, 1993.

Yarnold, Edward. "Baptism and the Pagan Mysteries in the Fourth Century." *Heythrop Journal*, 13 (1972), 247-267.

LIST OF PARTICIPANTS

Study Team on Worship and Culture

The Rev. Prof. Adiss Arnold
Gurukul Lutheran Theological College, Madras, India

The Rev. Dr. Mark P. Bangert
Lutheran School of Theology, Chicago, Illinois, U.S.A.

The Rev. Eric Dyck
Montreal, Quebec, Canada

The Rev. Prof. Marcus P. B. Felde
Martin Luther Seminary, Lae, Papua New Guinea

The Rev. Dr. Julius Filo
Evangelical Theological Faculty of the Commenius University,
Bratislava, Slovak Republic

Ms. Anne Lisbeth Gjøvikli
Church of Norway National Council, Oslo, Norway

The Rt. Rev. William Gorski
Evangelical Lutheran Church in Chile, Santiago, Chile

The Rev. Jens Hauschild (Cartigny only)
Buckeburg, Germany

The Rev. Dr. Nelson Kirst
Escola Superior de Teología, São Leopoldo, Brazil

OKR Hans Krech
Evangelical Lutheran Church in Germany, Hannover, Germany

The Rev. Dr. Gordon W. Lathrop
Lutheran Theological Seminary, Philadelphia, U.S.A.

The Rev. Dr. Pirkko Lehtiö (Hong Kong only)
Lutheran Theological Seminary, Hong Kong

The Rev. Prof. Mark Luttio
Japan Lutheran Theological Seminary, Tokyo, Japan

Ms. Helena Tallius Myhrman
Stockholm, Sweden

The Rev. Melkamu Negeri
Addis Ababa, Ethiopia

The Rev. Dr. Nils-Henrik Nilsson
Church of Sweden, Commission on Congregational Life, Stockholm,
Sweden

The Rev. C. Lisandro Orlov
Buenos Aires, Argentina

The Rev. Prof. Markus Roser
Ecole de Théologie de Baboua, Bangui, Central African Republic

The Rev. Louis Sibiya
Pietermaritzburg, Republic of South Africa

The Rev. Frank Stoldt (Cartigny only)
Minneapolis, Minnesota, U.S.A.

The Rev. Karen Ward
Evangelical Lutheran Church in America,
Division for Congregational Life, Chicago, Illinois, U.S.A.

Prof. Mabel Wu
Lutheran Theological Seminary, Hong Kong

Ecumenical Participants

The Rev. Dr. Anscar J. Chupungco, O.S.B. (Roman Catholic)
Paul VI Institute of Liturgy, Bukidnon, The Philippines

The Rev. Terry MacArthur
(World Council of Churches; Cartigny only)
Geneva, Switzerland

The Rev. Prof. Tomas Maddela (Anglican; Hong Kong only)
Asian Institute for Liturgy and Music, Manila, The Philippines

Archdeacon Themba Vundla (Anglican; Cartigny only)
Umlazi, Natal, Republic of South Africa

Dr. Karen Westerfield Tucker (Methodist; Hong Kong only)
Duke University Divinity School, Durham, North Carolina, U.S.A.

LWF Staff

The Rev. S. Anita Stauffer
Study Secretary for Worship and Congregational Life
Department for Theology and Studies

Ms. Regula Dominguez, Secretary